ETHICS IN
CONGRESS

ETHICS IN CONGRESS

From Individual to Institutional Corruption

Dennis F. Thompson

THE BROOKINGS INSTITUTION
Washington, D.C.

Library of Congress Cataloging-in-Publication data

Thompson, Dennis F. (Dennis Frank), 1940–
    Ethics in Congress : from individual to institutional corruption /
Dennis F. Thompson.
        p. cm.
    Includes bibliographical references and index.
    ISBN 0-8157-8424-4 (cl : alk. paper). — ISBN 0-8157-8423-6
(pa : alk. paper)
        1. United States. Congress—Ethics. 2.Political corruption—
United States. I. Title.
JK1140.T48   1995
364.1'323'0973—dc20   95-14604
                                                            CIP

9 8 7 6 5 4 3 2 1

The paper used in this publication meets the minimum requirements of
the American National Standard for Information Sciences—Permanence
of Paper for Printed Library Materials, ANSI Z39.48-1984.

Typeset in New Century Schoolbook

Composition by Harlowe Typography Inc.,
Cottage City, Maryland

Printed by R. R. Donnelley and Sons Co.
Harrisonburg, Virginia

Foreword

Criticism of the ethics of Congress has never been more persistent. Yet as most informed observers maintain, the integrity of individual members has never been so generally creditable. Members are understandably wary of more ethics regulation, but the press and the public are reasonably suspicious of the current process in which members judge each other. In the confusing cycle of charges and countercharges that ensues, Congress is increasingly distracted from its legislative business, and public confidence in its capacity to govern is eroded.

In this systematic study of ethics in the contemporary Congress, Dennis Thompson argues that problems of ethics call for new ways of thinking about legislative misconduct and new procedures for dealing with it. He urges the press, the public, and Congress to pay less attention to individual corruption and more to institutional corruption—conduct that is closely connected with the responsibilities of office, such as raising campaign contributions and helping constituents resolve problems with government. He counsels us to move the discussion beyond a focus on bribery, extortion, and simple personal gain and explore the world of implicit understandings, ambiguous favors, and political advantage.

The author comes to the subject of congressional ethics as a political philosopher known for his contributions to democratic theory and political ethics. In this book he combines that theoretical approach with a practical understanding of the role of the representative in the modern Congress. Many of the major ethics cases of recent years—those of David Durenberger, the Keating Five, and Speaker James Wright—structure his consideration of the forms that corruption takes in the legislature. His analyses of the concept of corruption and the principles of legislative ethics turn out to have important practical implications. Thompson shows why neither elections nor courts can resolve questions of ethics, and why stronger ethics committees and a new quasi-independent body are needed to formulate and enforce congressional standards of conduct. He also recommends changes in the procedures and practices of congressional ethics. Much of his analysis and many of his recommendations could also serve as guides for ethics reform in other branches and other levels of government.

Thompson wrote most of this book while he was a visiting fellow in the Governmental Studies program at Brookings in 1993–94. He was on leave from Harvard University, where he is Alfred North Whitehead Professor of Political Philosophy and founding director of the university's program in Ethics and the Professions. The writing and research for this project was supported by Brookings and Harvard.

The views expressed here are those of the author and should not be ascribed to the institutions that supported this work, or to the trustees, officers, or staff members of the Brookings Institution.

Bruce K. MacLaury
President

May 1995
Washington, D.C.

Contents

Preface

The reputation of Congress is not high, and anyone who writes about its ethics runs the risk of either encouraging the bashers or joining the apologists. I intend this book to give comfort to neither. Despite its stern subtitle and serious criticism, it is not another sweeping attack branding the institution as corrupt to its core. It was written in a spirit of respect for Congress and with an attitude of admiration for most of those who serve as members. Because of the conflicting demands that representatives confront, theirs may be the most challenging job in our democratic society, not only politically but ethically. They deserve our understanding and support as they try to meet those challenges. But they also deserve our criticism when they fail.

For reasons I present in the pages that follow, I do not believe that members of Congress individually or collectively have in recent years adequately met the important challenge of establishing and maintaining institutional standards of ethics. The criticisms I offer are intended to be constructive and nonpartisan. They are directed not only to members and their staffs but also to the academy, the press, and the public. We all share responsibility for the state of congressional ethics, and we should all take responsibility for trying to improve it.

If the perspective of a sympathetic critic that this book adopts is uncommon, its method is no less so. I have paid less attention than is customary to boundaries between disciplines and divisions within political science. By education and temperament I am a political theorist. As I made my way around Capitol Hill, I was sometimes asked in one form or another, "What is a political theorist like you doing in a place like this?" I was in fact not quite so out of place as I might have seemed. I had long been fascinated by the problems that representatives face in modern democracies and had devoted major portions of three books and several articles to them. I had testified many times on congressional ethics, the first time fifteen years ago. During the investigation and hearings on the Keating Five in 1990–91, I served as a consultant to Robert Bennett, special counsel to the Senate ethics committee. Still, I had never spent any sustained time in the natural habitat of members, and when Brookings invited me to spend a year studying Congress at closer range, I could not resist. The result is this somewhat unorthodox blend of theoretical analysis, empirical inquiry, and institutional analysis. I hope readers will find it an approach that should be more widely adopted in political science.

During 1993–94 I conducted some thirty-five interviews, about half with members or former members of Congress who had served on ethics committees or had been the subject of the committees' inquiries. The other half were with staff and former staff of the committees, attorneys who had appeared before the committees, ethics officials in the executive branch, lobbyists, and journalists. Given the sensitivity that most members and staff display on the subject of ethics, I believed that I would gain more and better information if I conducted the interviews on a confidential basis. The interviews, nearly all remarkably candid and thoughtful, helped me to better understand how members and their critics view problems of ethics and corruption, what issues they regard as most important, what reforms they think desirable and feasible, and what public sources of information they consider most accurate and reliable. However, except in a few instances I have not used the interviews as evidence for any claim in this book. In general, I have relied only on documents, data, and information available in the public record so that readers can judge for themselves the validity of my interpretations and arguments. In any case, the purpose of this book is not to provide a historical account or empirical explanation of the events to which it refers. Those events serve as means to the larger normative ends of the book.

As the title *Ethics in Congress* implies, the book says little explicitly about the various causes of congressional corruption *outside* the institution, most notably campaign finance. Those causes have been much more thoroughly studied than the inside ones. The number of books on campaign finance alone could fill a bookshelf; those on ethics in Congress can be counted on one hand. By concentrating on the internal sources of the problem, I do not mean to suggest that the external ones are less important. On the contrary, I am inclined to believe that the system of campaign finance is the single most important cause of legislative corruption. But the faults of that system have received so much attention that they have become an excuse for ignoring the deficiencies of Congress's own practices. Much could still be done to improve institutional ethics in Congress under the present system of campaign finance, and if by some political miracle that system were radically reformed, many of the problems of institutional ethics I discuss would remain. Furthermore, because the approach to legislative ethics developed here applies to corruption in many different kinds of institutions, it can also help in understanding the deficiencies of campaign finance and other practices that lie outside Congress.

The scope of the book is both narrower and broader than its title might suggest. It is narrower because it does not cover all congresses. Although the appendix presents a catalog of cases from 1789 to 1992, most of the cases I discuss date from the past two decades. The scope of the book is broader in at least three respects. First, its general arguments as well as some of its specific proposals should be useful to those interested in ethics in other branches and levels of government as well as in professional ethics more generally. Second, students of political corruption will, I hope, find value in the conception of institutional corruption developed here. Among other advantages, the conception offers a way to link the structural approach characteristic of traditional political theory with the individualist approach typical of modern social science. Finally, and perhaps most important, throughout the book I have tried to show how the study of legislative ethics can illuminate the general theory and practice of representation in contemporary democracy. Ethics holds a mirror up to the best and the worst in our representatives and the institutions in which they serve.

In writing this book, I have greatly benefited from the assistance of friends and colleagues. Roger Davidson, John Kingdon, David Wilkins, and Ken Winston gave me constructive criticisms on nearly every part of the book. Mildred Amer, Gary Jacobson, Charles Herz, Thomas Mann, Douglas Price, Alan Rosenthal, and Andrew Stark offered valuable suggestions on several sections. For comments on earlier versions of the work, I am grateful to Arthur Applbaum, Charles Beitz, Robert Bennett, Morris Fiorina, Charles Fried, Amy Gutmann, Benjamin Klubes, Sanford Levinson, Thomas Scanlon, Judith Shklar, and Alan Wertheimer. During my year in Washington, I learned much from the stimulating group of scholars, graduate students, and former public officials whom Thomas Mann had gathered in the Governmental Studies program at Brookings. I am also indebted to the members of Congress, their staffs, and the many others who granted interviews.

An invitation to deliver the James A. Moffett Lecture at Princeton University in 1992 gave me the first opportunity to try out some of the arguments of this book in public. I am grateful to the university's Program in Ethics and Public Affairs and the Center for Human Values for providing that opportunity. In a substantially revised form, the lecture became an article in *American Political Science Review*, vol. 87 (June 1993). Many critics, friendly and otherwise, have helped me see better both the truth and error in my earlier writings on ethics and representation; some of those writings I draw on here (where indicated in the notes). I also make occasional use of testimony I have given to congressional and other governmental bodies, specifically before the Senate Select Committee on Ethics (1980–81), the House Bipartisan Task Force on Ethics (1989), the Connecticut Legislators' Ethics Conference (1993), the Joint Senate-House Committee on the Organization of Congress (1993), and the Senate Ethics Study Commission (1993).

No author could ask for more dedicated research assistants than those who worked on this project. Mary Ann Noyer, then at Brookings, created the database of cases with which we worked and prepared the catalog of cases. Ted Aaberg at Harvard located many of the legal and other scholarly sources used here. Simone Sandy provided additional assistance at critical points in the project. At Brookings, James Schneider edited the manuscript, Laurel Imig verified its factual accuracy, and Julia Petrakis prepared the index. Judy Chaney and Susan Stewart provided efficient administrative support. At Harvard, Helen Hawkins and Jean McVeigh contributed in many important ways to the project, not the least of which was keeping the rest of my professional life from collapsing into chaos.

Introduction

More members of Congress have been investigated and subjected to sanctions for ethical misconduct in the past decade and a half than in the entire previous history of the institution.[1] In recent seasons, both the House and the Senate have been producing "bumper crops" of ethics cases. Among the fruits of the harvest are the first expulsion of a member of Congress for corruption, formal disciplinary measures against four senators and eleven representatives, and some forty admonishments, electoral defeats, or resignations.[2] The period also yielded the longest running and most publicized hearing on charges of violating ethical standards: the case of the so-called Keating Five.

Some see in the proliferation of cases the signs of pervasive corruption. Half of all Americans say they believe that most members of Congress are corrupt. Half also agree with the statement that "Congress as an institution is corrupt." This attitude persisted even after the control of Congress changed hands in 1995. Nearly 70 percent of citizens believed that the 104th Congress would be no less corrupt than its predecessor.[3] One of its current leaders once declared, "the present-day Congress has become the most corrupt of the modern era."[4]

However corrupt Congress may be today, few of its members engage in the flagrant behavior that used to be common in the institution. Conduct generally accepted in earlier eras would now be grounds for expulsion. In the nineteenth century, respected members openly accepted money for personal use from companies directly affected by the legislation the members supported. Daniel Webster, for example, was on retainer from the Bank of the United States. While serving as the bank's leading defender in Congress, he not-so-subtly reminded its president, "If it be wished that my relation to the Bank be continued, it may be well to send me the usual retainers."[5] Bribing members did not even become illegal until 1853.[6] It took the blatant bribery of the Crédit Mobilier scandal in the 1870s to move Congress to act against corrupt members. Even then, it censured but declined to expel them as the investigating committees had recommended.[7]

Throughout the nineteenth and the first part of the twentieth century, Congress was more willing to sanction its members for political crimes (disloyalty and sedition) and rhetorical excesses (describing another member as "the champion . . . of fraud," among other insults) than for corruption.[8] In the first half of the twentieth century there were no censure proceedings in the House for individual corruption, and none of the four corruption cases considered by the Senate resulted in congressional sanctions.[9] During the 1950s some members regularly appeared drunk in committee and on the floor, and others put mistresses on the payroll. Neither their colleagues nor the press thought it appropriate to publicize let alone punish such conduct.[10] A study of House members' attitudes toward standards of conduct in the late 1960s found that although practices of "dubious propriety" were thought to be widespread, most respondents were "unwilling to impose further regulations."[11]

The change in ethical climate came suddenly, too suddenly to be attributed to a transformation in the moral character of the members. In 1976 the House "shouted down" an attempt to expel Andrew J. Hinshaw, a California Republican who had been convicted of accepting a bribe. Scarcely four years later it voted unanimously to expel Michael J. "Ozzie" Myers, a Pennsylvania Democrat who had been caught taking bribes in the ABSCAM investigation.[12] Myers no doubt deserved his punishment, but his offense was no worse than Hinshaw's or that of many other members who had gone unpunished in the past. Nor do any of the cases after Myers's seem much worse than his or others in previous years. (Myers even had an excuse that some of his colleagues found plausible: he would not have committed the crime if an FBI sting operation had not tempted him.)

There is no evidence that the character of members in recent Congresses is worse than that of their predecessors. On the contrary, most informed observers of the institution believe that the legislators' integrity and competence are greater than in the past.[13] One historian commented in the late 1970s that the intellectual level of Congress was "as high as at any time in our history, except the first generation of the Founding Fathers, and [then] we really were ruled by an aristocracy."[14] While acknowledging that no one can be certain about such general estimates, Senator Paul Simon also noted an improvement in the quality of members. He added, "What is certain is that the outright corrupt . . . are a small minority."[15]

If the character of members is not worse, and indeed may be better, why has the number of ethics cases increased so dramatically? Two causes are probably most significant. First, violations of ethics rules are now more likely to be discovered and investigated. Congress itself is more open to public scrutiny than ever before and so are the personal and political lives of its members.[16] The press is more vigilant, more eager to expose corruption wherever it can be found (and some would say, even where it cannot).[17] More charges are brought against members.[18] The ethics committees have larger staffs and greater resources to investigate charges.[19] Given these factors, one should expect to see more ethics cases of all kinds, even if corruption were decreasing.

A second cause affects the kinds of cases as much as the number. There are more offenders because there are more offenses. The codes adopted in 1977 and given legal force by the Ethics in Government Act in 1978 not only tightened existing rules on financial disclosure and other practices that were already regulated, but also prohibited practices (such as use of office accounts for campaign purposes) that had been unregulated.[20] Members and challengers must disclose more about their finances and have less discretion in managing them. There are more rules than there used to be, and more rules than in any other political system. A comparative study of twenty-five countries with the most developed ethics rules for national legislators found that regulations in the United States are "clearly the most restrictive."[21]

What is behind this escalating concern about ethics? Some critics see ethics regulation as part of a modern Puritanism, a product of overly zealous reformers who believe corruption is rampant and that the only way to stop it is by enacting more rules and bringing more charges. The reformers have succeeded in imposing an unprecedented number of regulations on public officials in all branches of government. They have been joined by prosecutors who reap political advantage in bringing charges against corrupt and not-so-corrupt public officials. The problem, the critics say, is not political corruption but those who seek to eliminate it. The "ethics police," a new breed of activists who devote their careers to fighting corruption, have produced a "culture of mistrust" that has made the difficult job of governing that much harder.[22]

No doubt much of the public concern about ethics in Congress is generated by ethics reformers themselves, while some of it is simply "politics by other means."[23] But the demand for ethics regulation in Congress has grown beyond anything the ethics police could have instigated on their own. It is a manifestation of a public mood that has affected not only all government but much of society. Since the early 1970s governments at both federal and state level have eagerly responded to public demands for new rules to limit campaign contributions, require disclosure of financial interests, restrict the gifts officials may accept, and regulate the types of jobs they may take after they leave office.[24] New investigative bodies such as public integrity agencies or special prosecutors have been established. Federal prosecutions of public officials have multiplied dramatically.[25] At least twenty-two state legislatures now have independent ethics commissions, many of which effectively regulate the conduct of legislators as well as campaign practices and lobbyists.[26] In its first year the federal Office of Government Ethics had fewer than twenty employees and contact with only a small network of officials working part-time on matters of ethics in other agencies. By 1993 the office had tripled in size and was coordinating some 8,000 officials who devote at least part time to ethics work in federal agencies.[27]

The revival of concern about ethics has spread well beyond government. Few institutions or professions have escaped scandal in recent years, and most have responded by strengthening both their ethics procedures and their ethics training. In 1982 only 1 percent of American hospitals had ethics committees; today more than 60 percent of large hospitals have them. After years of ignoring the problem, the American Medical Association has begun to address the conflicts of interest that physicians frequently face. In most large scientific laboratories that receive federal support, scientists are now expected to undergo ethics training.[28] Large corporations are hiring ethics consultants, promulgating codes of ethics, and providing ethics workshops for their employees.[29] The legal profession is under increasing criticism for ethical failings of various kinds and is now considering new approaches to professional discipline.[30] Accountants, architects, clergy, computer programmers, engineers, social workers, veterinarians, among others, have turned their attention to formulating or strengthening the standards of conduct in their professions.[31]

So Congress is not alone. Although the public has even less confidence in politicians than in those who follow other vocations, both the distrust and the efforts to deal with it are part of the same widespread trend.[32] Whatever its many causes, the distrust has given rise to a growing demand for accountability, an insistence that those who exercise power over us or in our name answer to us. As voters, patients, clients, customers, we increasingly find our lives affected by decisions made by others—whether politicians, doctors, lawyers, or managers. These decisions and the conditions under which they are reached are becoming increasingly complex and often raise issues that the public finds unfamiliar. The ethical problems we face are not only more complex, but the people we face them with are more diverse, as more and more people from different backgrounds influence the actions that public and private institutions take. In these circumstances it should not be surprising that citizens question traditional forms of accountability and begin to look for new and often more demanding forms. Citizens cannot make most decisions themselves, but they can control the conditions under which they are made to try to ensure that those who make them act in the interest of those whom they are supposed to serve.

Along with the general demands for accountability, members of Congress face formidable challenges, specific to the institution, that make their ethical life more difficult. The role of representatives in the contemporary Congress has become more complex. Constituents are asking for more help with individual problems with government, and asking more forcefully. Political campaigns have become vastly more expensive and funds more difficult to raise. The legislative process is increasingly specialized. Legislative life is less collegial.[33] Under these conditions, traditional norms and customs provide less guidance, and members and the public have less confidence about what legislative duties require. It is therefore not surprising that the conduct of members raises more questions and produces more controversy. In this uncertain and unsupportive environment, members are more likely to violate an ethical standard. Even when they have not done wrong, an increasingly distrustful public is more likely to believe that they have.

In light of these growing tensions in the role of representatives, we should not accept either of the extreme interpretations of the ethics movement in government. The increase in ethics regulation is not necessarily a sign that Congress or society faces a "crisis of public corruption."[34] But neither should we conclude that more ethics reform is unnecessary or counterproductive. Although the extensive regulations of recent years have not solved the problem of corruption, that does not necessarily mean that more changes would not be beneficial.

This study steers a course between these extremes. It regards the growth of interest in ethics as a legitimate response to the growing demand for accountability in an increasingly complicated political environment. More complex forms of corruption are more common, and the traditional codes of conduct have become inadequate. Thus the task of ethics reform is far from finished, but it should shift its focus from individual corruption to what is here called institutional corruption.[35] The chief aim of the chapters that follow is to clarify the nature of institutional corruption and the place it should have in the theory and practice of congressional ethics.

Giving increased attention to institutional corruption supports a more constructive response to demands for greater accountability. Instead of simply generating more rules and mounting more investigations to prevent the familiar forms of individual corruption, we should put more effort into identifying the less familiar institutional forms and devising remedies appropriate to them. Instead of declaring a crisis of corruption or bemoaning the culture of mistrust, we should try to distinguish carefully the kinds of corruption likely to thrive in the current political environment and try to tailor our responses to their distinctive dangers.

In this spirit this study moves from the stark land of bribery, extortion, and simple personal gain to the shadowy world of implicit understandings, ambiguous favors, and political advantage. Moving beyond the individual corruption that has preoccupied social scientists, political reformers, and ethics committees, the study focuses on the institutional corruption they have neglected.

Like all forms of corruption, the institutional kind involves the improper use of public office for private purposes.[36] But unlike individual corruption, it encompasses conduct that under certain conditions is a necessary or even desirable part of institutional duties. The "use of public office" is institutional in this sense. What makes the conduct improper is also institutional in the sense that it violates principles that promote the distinctive purposes of the institution.[37] It is still individuals who are the agents of institutional corruption and individuals who should be held accountable for it, but their actions implicate the institution in a way that the actions of the agents of individual corruption do not.

Legislative corruption is *institutional* insofar as the *gain* a member receives is political rather than personal, the *service* the member provides is procedurally improper, and the *connection* between the gain and the service has a tendency to damage the legislature or the democratic process. When a member takes a bribe in return for a political favor, the personal gain is not part of the salary and the service provided is not part of the job description. The exchange serves no legitimate institutional purpose. This is straightforward individual corruption. But when a member accepts a campaign contribution, even while doing a favor for the contributor, the political gain may or may not be corrupt. It is not if the practice promotes political competition or other desirable goals of the institution. But it is corrupt if it undermines institutional purposes or damages the democratic process. When several senators repeatedly and improperly intervene in regulatory proceedings on behalf of an important campaign contributor, they may not be individually corrupt but their actions constitute institutional corruption.

Recognizing institutional corruption is not always easy because it is so closely related to conduct that is a perfectly acceptable part of political life. The individual member's contribution to the corruption is filtered through institutional practices that are otherwise legitimate and may even be duties of office. Members are required to solicit campaign contributions, for instance, and they are expected to help constituents with their problems with government. Even when members engage in these practices in a corrupt way, colleagues may not recognize that they have done anything wrong or that any serious harm has been done.

Yet the harm that institutional corruption causes to the legislature and the democratic process is often greater than that caused by individual corruption. Intertwined with the duties of office, institutional corruption by its nature strikes at the core of the institution, threatening its central purposes. It is also more systematic and more pervasive than individual corruption, which typically consists of isolated acts of misconduct with effects limited in time and scope. Cases of institutional corruption in Congress are increasing. In the past fifteen years, nearly a third of the cases in which the ethics committees took official action could be considered cases of institutional corruption. Of all the corruption cases before 1978, only a quarter qualify as institutional.[38]

Ethics in Congress deserves attention not because members are more corrupt (they are not), not because citizens are more distrustful (they are), but because the institution itself continually poses new ethical challenges. The complexity of the institutional environment in which members of Congress work invites more calls for accountability and creates new occasions for corruption. As the role of a representative in the modern Congress changes, so too must the informal norms and formal rules of conduct in the institution.

The purposes of these rules—the rationale for legislative ethics—is the subject of the first chapter of this book. Because these purposes are often misunderstood, the importance of ethics regulation is often underestimated. The chapter defends this importance and lays the groundwork for later chapters by presenting the principles of legislative ethics that help identify the damage that institutional corruption does and the measures that could prevent the damage.

Chapter 2 introduces the three major ethics cases that serve as leitmotifs in the rest of the book. They help develop the contrast between individual and institutional corruption and illustrate the tendency of Congress and the public to convert one into the other, a tendency that contributes to the neglect of institutional corruption. This chapter also presents an analytic comparison of the two types, showing how they differ with respect to each of the three elements that characterize any kind of corruption (the *gain* received, the *service* provided, and the *connection* between them).

These elements set the agenda for the three subsequent chapters. Chapter 3 argues that neither personal nor political gain in public office is as unconditionally improper as is often assumed. By offering a more precise account of what makes each wrong, the chapter develops the difference between them and describes some measures that could control each. Chapter 4 focuses on the virtues and vices of constituent service and proposes standards to guide members' interventions in the proceedings of executive agencies. Chapter 5 shows why the close connection between gain and service that defines individual corruption is a deficient criterion in legislative ethics. Emphasizing the significance of mixed motives in legislative behavior, the chapter argues for standards that relate individual conduct to the legislative process. Chapter 6 turns to the process of enforcement: the tribunals of ethics. It shows why neither the electoral process nor the judicial process is a sufficient mechanism and argues for stronger ethics committees and the creation of a new, quasi-independent body that would take over some of the responsibility for enforcing standards of conduct.

Although the subject of this book is congressional ethics, its conclusions have broader implications for the theory and practice of representative democracy. The study of legislative ethics can reveal much about the changing role of the representative in contemporary American democracy. Through the lens of ethics we can see the extremes of the role: the disgrace into which representatives can fall and the ideals to which they should aspire. With a concept of institutional corruption, we can better understand the connections between individual conduct and structural conditions in the American democratic system. Each of the elements of institutional corruption connects acts of individual officials to attributes of democratic government. Legislative ethics is not just about how members of Congress should behave, but also about how a democratic process should function.

Purposes of
Legislative Ethics

No one learns his ethics in Congress. . . . No one needs to be
told by his colleagues what is right, fair, and honorable.

In his testimony before a House
Task Force on Ethics, former Representative Otis Pike cited the
best-selling book *All I Really Need to Know I Learned in Kindergarten* to drive home his point that members learn their ethics very
early in life.[1] Some critics might be tempted to respond that too
many members have indeed learned all their ethics in kindergarten—and in an especially unruly classroom. They need to go back
to school to learn the basic moral lessons they have forgotten. Challenging Pike and his colleagues on grounds of the weak moral character of members, however, misses the more important problem with
his view: his conception of legislative ethics. Along with many others, he assumes that ethics in Congress requires only that members
act on basic principles of personal ethics. The good legislator is morally equivalent to the good person.

This is a common but mistaken view of legislative ethics—and
of political and professional ethics in general. Certainly, any kind of
ethics requires some basic moral dispositions and presupposes some
fundamental moral principles like those Pike had in mind. But personal ethics and legislative ethics are quite different creatures, and
confusing them does neither any good. The first step in discovering
what kind of ethical standards are needed to deal with institutional
corruption is to understand the differences between personal and

legislative ethics. After describing those differences, this chapter analyzes the basic purposes of legislative ethics and presents the principles that should guide efforts to realize those purposes.

Personal Ethics and Legislative Ethics

Legislative ethics is a species of political ethics, which prescribes principles for action in public institutions. Like political ethics, legislative ethics differs from personal ethics in origin, function, and content. Personal ethics originates in face-to-face relations among individuals. It is a response to the social need for principles to guide actions toward other individuals across the whole range of personal relations. Legislative ethics originates in institutional circumstances. It arises from the need to set standards for impersonal relations among people who may never meet and who must judge each other at a distance.

The function of personal ethics is to make people morally better, or, more modestly, to make the relations among people morally tolerable. Legislative ethics serves to guide the actions of individuals, but only in their institutional roles and only insofar as necessary for the good of the institution. Legislative ethics uses personal ethics only as a means—not even the most important means—to the end of institutional integrity.

In their most general form, the contents of the ethical principles of public and private life have a common foundation. Certainly, one wishes both friends and legislators to respect the rights of others, to fulfill their obligations to their communities, to act fairly and speak truthfully. But in this form the principles are too general to guide conduct in the complex circumstances of legislative life. Once the principles are translated into the particular standards suitable for public institutions, they often recommend conduct that is distinct from, sometimes even contrary to, the conduct appropriate for private life. As a result, the content of legislative ethics differs from that of personal ethics.

For example, some conduct that may be wrong in private life is properly ignored by legislative ethics. The public may think less of politicians who enjoy hard-core pornography or commit adultery, but as long as they keep these activities private and do not let them affect their public responsibilities, legislative ethics does not proscribe them. Indeed, it may protect some of them. It should protect conduct that if disclosed could distract public discussion from more important matters of public policy. Prominent public officials may need some special legal protection for their right of privacy.

Conversely, some conduct that is permissible or even praiseworthy in personal ethics may violate the principles of legislative ethics. Returning a favor or giving preference to a friend is often admirable in private life, but though useful in public life, such an act is more often ethically questionable and sometimes even criminal. Furthermore, many of the problems of legislative ethics, such as restrictions on types of employment that legislators can follow after the end of their legislative career, do not arise at all in private life. Others such as conflict of interest do not arise in the same form or to the same extent.

The contrast between the ethical demands of public and private life has never been more plainly put than it was by an anonymous supporter of Grover Cleveland in the presidential campaign of 1884. Cleveland's opponent, James G. Blaine, had corruptly profited from public office but lived an impeccable private life. Cleveland had a reputation for public integrity but had been forced to acknowledge fathering an illegitimate child. "I gather that Mr. Cleveland has shown high character and great capacity in public office," said Cleveland's supporter, "but that in private life his conduct has been open to question, while, on the other hand, Mr. Blaine, in public life has been weak and dishonest, while he seems to have been an admirable husband and father. The conclusion that I draw from these facts is that we should elect Mr. Cleveland to the public office which he is so admirably qualified to fill and remand Mr. Blaine to the private life which he is so eminently fitted to adorn."[2]

The separation between private and public life is not, of course, quite so sharp as these observations imply. Some kinds of otherwise private immorality may affect an official's capacity to do a job. As citizens we may not care if the chair of the House Administration Committee has an affair, but we may legitimately object if he gives his mistress a job on the committee staff, especially if she says, "I can't type. I can't file. I can't even answer the phone." Even if the member does not misuse the powers of his office, his private life may become so scandalous that it casts doubt on his judgment and undermines his effectiveness on the job. Perhaps the chair of the Ways and Means Committee should feel free to date an Argentine strip-tease dancer, but when he appears on a Boston burlesque stage to praise her performance, citizens properly take notice.[3]

Even when private conduct bears some relation to the duties of public office, public discussions of the ethics of politicians have an unfortunate tendency to dwell on private conduct to the neglect of conduct more relevant to the office. Senator John Tower's drinking problem may have deserved some discussion during the hearings on his nomination to be secretary of defense, but it surely deserved less than his activities as a consultant for defense contractors.[4] Yet because of the public preoccupation with private immorality, citizens heard little about these financial dealings, which probably would have revealed much more about his record as a senator and his capacity to head the Department of Defense.

This tendency to dwell on personal ethics also means that some conduct clearly of legitimate public concern is viewed almost entirely from the perspective of personal ethics. This doubly distorts the problem. First, it gives the transgression of personal ethical standards more prominence than it deserves compared to other problems. The overdrafts by members in the House Bank that caused such a public outcry in 1991 is a case in point. Because the scandal seemed to fit easily into the category of a violation of personal ethics, it generated more outrage than more serious problems, such as the failures in the regulation of the savings and loan industry, where individual villains in government were less easy to find. The perspective of personal ethics also distorted the House Bank scandal by emphasizing individual greed and arrogance more than institutional negligence and incompetence. It was the institutional faults, the management practices and appointment procedures, that needed attention and represented the more enduring and potentially far-reaching problem. Individuals were to blame for these faults, and individuals could be held accountable for correcting them. The faults also revealed an ethical failure, but it was not the kind usually found in a catalog of personal vices.

Another effort to dissolve the differences between personal and legislative ethics comes from the critics of Congress who object to the professionalization of the role of the legislator. They seek to restore the ideal of the citizen-legislator by limiting terms of office, making the job part-time, and reducing salaries. "Cut Their Pay and Send Them Home" is the slogan of a prominent proponent of this approach. Congress could then repeal the ethics rules that keep members from "holding real jobs and leading normal lives."[5] The implication is that there is no need for any special standards of ethics for legislators.

This longing for the return of the citizen-legislator to the modern Congress is misguided. Like the activities of all major institutions in American society, the business of legislation has grown more specialized and complex. A member of Congress now faces formidable challenges in campaigning for reelection, mastering the substance of legislation, serving constituents, and collaborating with colleagues. If members do not develop the expertise and experience necessary to cope with these challenges, others (staff, lobbyists, bureaucrats) will, and they will come to dominate the legislative process.

Nor is it clear that professionalism has the harmful effects on legislative ethics that some of its critics imply. According to one, "professionalism disconnects and distances the professional . . . from those whom he or she intends to serve," whereas representative government should be "characterized by the close connection . . . between the representative and represented."[6] The more legislators adopt the practices of professionals (including any distinctive ethical standards), the less, it would seem, they can fulfill their duties as representatives.

This contrast between professionalism and representation is misleading on both sides. On the one side it distorts professional ethics, which does not presume that distance between professionals and those they serve is generally desirable. The kind of distance traditionally assumed to be appropriate, for example, between doctors and their patients or lawyers and their clients is now widely criticized as paternalistic.[7] On the other side the contrast exaggerates the closeness that effective representative government requires between legislators and constituents. At the least, there is no reason to assume that legislators are currently too distant from their constituents. Indeed, some critics of professionalism (who also favor term limits) argue that legislators are now too responsive. These critics embrace term limits as a way to put more distance between legislators and constituents so as to give legislators greater latitude to deliberate about the common good.[8]

To defend the need for legislative ethics, it is not necessary to resolve this dispute among the critics of professionalism or to decide whether term limits or any of the other antiprofessional reforms are desirable. Even the claim that legislators should maintain a closer connection to their constituents itself takes a position on the proper role of a legislator and is therefore a view *within* legislative ethics, not a denial of the need for it. We cannot escape the need for some ethical standards to define the role of the legislator, no matter what position we take on the question of the proper role between legislators and constituents. That question is one that simply does not arise in personal ethics.

The critics of professionalism might still argue that the right answer to this question would give legislators as much ethical discretion as ordinary citizens enjoy. Legislative ethics, they might insist, should not place any more constraints on legislators than personal ethics imposes on ordinary citizens. The point presumably would be to permit legislators to continue to live as much as possible like ordinary citizens so that they could better represent the experiences of their constituents.

But this argument underestimates both the range of experiences that modern legislators are expected to represent and the implications of the trust that they are obligated to uphold. It is no longer possible, if it ever was, for legislators, individually or collectively, to have personal knowledge of the vast range of experiences relevant to making policy in a pluralist society. Legislators must represent some citizens whose experiences they will never share and therefore must sometimes distance themselves from their own experience. No matter how "normal" the lives legislators lead, they still have to act on behalf of citizens whose lives differ from theirs and assure citizens that they are acting effectively. Personal experience and the personal ethics that guides it are not sufficient to fulfill these purposes.

No matter how limited their terms, or how short their hours, legislators hold a position of public trust.[9] While in office and on the job, they exercise power over other citizens and are accountable to them in ways that citizens are not ordinarily accountable to each other. In this respect even part-time legislators are professionals and may be held to the more stringent ethical standards that professional ethics presupposes.[10] For example, to avoid conflicts of interest, which could prejudice their judgment and undermine their constituents' confidence, legislators have to accept restrictions on the kinds of outside work they do while in office and the jobs they take after they leave.

The failure to appreciate the special ethical demands of public life may partly explain why so many new (and some old) public officials find the requirements so exasperating. Many who come to Washington to serve in government regard the ethics rules they find there at best meddlesome and at worst insulting. They did not have to follow such rules in their personal affairs and their business dealings in private life, and yet they were (often rightly) regarded as having high moral character by citizens in their own communities. They experience a sort of reverse spin on *Mr. Smith Goes to Washington*. Instead of finding lower standards of conduct in government, they are shocked to find higher standards, or what from their standpoint are simply more restrictive ones. Being respectable in their own communities and corporations, they find it hard to understand why they should take these more restrictive standards seriously. This is all the more true for those who do not have as much respect for government as they do for institutions in the private sector.[11] As a result of this way of thinking, some develop such contempt for the ethics rules of government that they ignore them and then find themselves in serious trouble. In this way the confusion of personal and political ethics can turn private virtue into public vice.

The Priority of Legislative Ethics

Another reason that some public officials do not take legislative ethics seriously is that they believe its importance has been exaggerated. Some version of a common complaint has been voiced frequently and in many different ways in recent years: "I'd like to see people, instead of spending so much time on ethical problems, get at the problems that really affect the people of this country."[12] There is an important truth in the contention that issues of public policy are more important than any problem of legislative ethics (or government ethics more generally). This truth may be underscored by conducting a simple thought experiment: Would you rather have a morally corrupt legislature that solved such major social problems as inadequately distributed health care and pervasive crime, or a morally pure legislature that failed to solve any of them? Given only those alternatives, you would not be alone if you chose to sacrifice moral purity.

Ethics is not a primary goal of government in the way that national defense, economic prosperity, or public welfare are. These and other goals of public policy are part of the reason citizens establish and maintain government. Standards of ethics are supposed to facilitate the making of good public policy; they are in this respect a means to an end. But from this truth it does not follow that ethical matters are less important than other matters. First, ethics is not only a means. Honest government is a good in itself, valuable independently of any good policies the government may make. How officials treat citizens and how officials treat each other often shapes, for better or worse, the moral character of the democratic process as much as the policies officials and citizens choose. Second, even insofar as ethics is only a means, it is not an ordinary sort of means. It is a necessary means to good government. In the many ways this book explores, legislative ethics provides the preconditions for the making of good public policy. In this respect, it is *more* important than any single policy because all other policies depend on it.

The saga of the Keating Five, which figures prominently in later chapters, illustrates one important consequence of the failure to recognize the priority of ethics. The five senators accused of improperly assisting a major campaign contributor were otherwise respectable members who had enjoyed distinguished public careers. Yet their failure to take care to avoid questionable conduct caused them to spend the better part of two years defending themselves to the Senate ethics committee and the public and probably permanently damaged their effectiveness in the legislature. In addition, the case became almost a full-time concern for the six senators on the committee and their staffs, and cost taxpayers more than a million dollars in legal fees. A lot of legislative business did not get done because of this case. Whatever one thinks of the five senators, the point stands. If legislators do not first pay attention to ethics, they are likely to find that they will not later be able to give enough attention to other substantive legislative issues.

When ethics are in disorder, or when citizens believe they are, disputes about ethics drive out discussion about public policies. We need to pay attention to ethics so that ethical controversy does not distract us from matters that would otherwise be more important. Ethics makes democracy safe for debate on the substance of public policy.

The Scope of Legislative Ethics

Like political ethics, legislative ethics begins with the problem of moral disagreement. In a pluralist society citizens do not always agree on what is good or just legislation. Members of the legislature seek agreement while expecting that disagreement will persist. The challenge for legislative ethics is to devise rules that will help legislators make good and just policy even while they continue to disagree about what it is. Under these circumstances the best hope is to encourage a process that is justifiable from as many moral perspectives as possible. If the process is reasonable, fair, and open, it is presumably more likely to produce just laws or at least laws that citizens can reasonably accept. The aim is to make the legislative means moral even while legislators dispute the ends. The province of legislative ethics is therefore the integrity of the legislative process.

The principles of legislative ethics occupy the territory between general conceptions of good and theories of justice on the one side and particular rules of political procedure (rules of order, due process, administrative regulations) on the other. Legislative ethics deals in matters less sublime than the ideals of human virtue and social justice, but its aims are more lofty than procedural propriety. The principles of legislative ethics are not mere rules of the road, and they represent more than a modus vivendi among adversaries. They themselves have moral content. Following the principles is a moral good; it promotes an ethical process independent of the ethics of the outcome. Acting on relevant reasons, doing one's fair share, giving others an account of one's activities—all are actions that constitute ethical conduct at the same time that they promote the other ethical ends: moral deliberation and just legislation.

The purpose of legislative ethics is therefore more positive than might be assumed from reading the rules enacted in its name. Many take the form of negative commandments, as in "No member . . . shall knowingly accept . . . any gift from any other person."[13] This negative mode is perfectly understandable and indeed justifiable. Actions that people want to prevent can usually be stated with more precision and less disagreement than can those they wish to promote. The prohibition against taking bribes is like a perfect duty, a rule against a specific kind of action that can be specified in advance. An exhortation in favor of voting on the merits is more like an imperfect duty, an obligation that might reasonably be satisfied by any one of a whole range of actions. What the standard requires in specific cases is often contestable. Also, preventing corruption is usually more urgent than promoting integrity. Measures that would do something about corruption are more feasible and the consequences of doing nothing are more immediate, or at least more obvious.

But if most of the standards of legislative ethics legitimately seek to prevent corruption, their ultimate aim is to promote the integrity of legislators and the legislative process. There would be little point in punishing the malefactors if there were no hope of encouraging benefactors. Citizens rightly expect more than minimally honest politics, more than a legislature where members do not lie, cheat, or steal (though they may be thankful if they get only that). The positive aspect of legislative ethics is important not only as an ultimate goal, but also as an indirect influence on the way the negative rules are interpreted and enforced.

Principles of Legislative Ethics

The primary purpose of legislative ethics is to sustain institutional conditions in the legislature that promote the integrity of the democratic process. In its general form the purpose is expressed by the ideal of deliberation, proclaimed by the Founders and venerated throughout American history.[14] As James Madison declared, Congress must "deliberate; for deliberation is implied in legislation."[15]

More often defiled than fulfilled, the ideal nonetheless captures the distinctive virtue of a democratic legislature in our constitutional system. In a deliberative process, members consider policies on their merits, treat citizens and colleagues fairly, and publicly account for their actions.[16]

These characteristics express the three basic principles of legislative ethics, which guide this inquiry into the practice of ethics in Congress. The principles prescribe standards that increase the likelihood that members will act deliberatively in these ways in the legislative process broadly understood, including constituency service, administrative oversight, and campaigns. As part of political ethics the principles naturally embody many of the same general values, and even imply some of the same specific prescriptions, as principles of executive and judicial ethics. But legislators face some special problems resulting from their role as representatives and their collegial interdependence that give legislative ethics a distinctive content. For example, the proscription of conflicts of interest poses a different problem for legislators than it does for executives. In general, institutional ethics proceeds best by focusing on the virtues and vices of one institution at a time.

Independence: Deciding on the Merits

The first principle, expressing the value of independence, holds that a member should act on reasons relevant to the merits of public policies or reasons relevant to advancing a process that encourages acting on such reasons. The value in its pure form suggests a legislator beholden to no power but the commands of reason. Yet the pure form should not be even an ethical ideal.[17] Members have obligations to their constituents, their parties, and their colleagues and should not try to remain completely independent, even if it were politically possible. Instead, what the principle seeks is independence from influences that are clearly irrelevant to any process of deliberation. Personal pecuniary considerations are a prime candidate for irrelevant influences. Many ethics rules are therefore designed to decrease the likelihood that members will make decisions on the basis of factors such as personal gain that have no relation to the merits of policies or processes that would promote the public good.

The point is not to prevent personal gain as such. Despite the strong condemnations of personal gain in most codes of government ethics, there is nothing *in itself* wrong with personally benefiting from holding public office.[18] There is no reason in principle to single out financial from the other rewards of holding office. Earned income per se should not be suspect. The House and (more hesitantly) the Senate were right to ban all honoraria. But the reason they were right is not that members should never receive pay for outside activity. It is rather that the ban was the only practicable way to end the widespread abuse of what would have otherwise been acceptable practice. Honoraria had become more than merely personal gain; they had become the core of a system of income enhancement that interfered with institutional duties.

What is wrong with personal gain is that it distorts deliberation. It distracts a member from public duties, taking time and attention from what should be the principal concerns of office and overpowering the already unsteady inclination to pursue the public good. The aim of rules against personal gain, then, should be to keep members' minds concentrated as far as possible on the substance of issues and standards of fairness rather than on benefits that they, their friends, or their favorite causes might receive.

That we should object not to personal gain as such but to its effect on legislative judgment and fairness has implications for the kinds of standards legislative ethics should emphasize. General prohibitions on personal gain should be retained if they are the most effective way to discourage the undesirable effects of that gain. But less attention should be given to isolated or random conflicts of interest and more to *patterns* of potential influence. Ethics rules might, for example, treat conflicts arising from members' large, diversified financial holdings less seriously than conflicts arising from smaller holdings concentrated in specific industries. The rules could also set different standards for different roles in the legislature: they might, for example, grant the chair and perhaps members of the committee on banking less latitude in their current holdings and postemployment dealings in the financial sector of the economy. Similarly, restrictions on dealings with persons who have a direct interest in legislation could take more account of the role that a member actually has in influencing the type of legislation in question.

Giving more attention to potential influence would also highlight conduct that adversely affects the legislative process as a whole. Some widespread practices, such as accepting travel from groups interested in specific legislation, might become more serious violations of ethical standards than accepting improper gifts. That a practice is widespread makes it worse. Rather than being an excuse, the plea that everyone is doing it should strengthen the case against an individual member charged with improper conduct.

Fairness: Playing by the Rules

The second principle of legislative ethics, grounded on the value of fairness, prescribes that members of Congress should fulfill their obligations to colleagues, staff, challengers, other officials, and the institution as a whole. Fairness speaks first to the rights of members: protecting their legitimate claims is in the interest of the institution as well. But it is less often appreciated that fairness also implies that members have obligations. "There is never any discussion in this place of the obligation of a member to the institution," one House member commented, "and if people talk about it, they are embarrassed."[19] These are obligations of fair play, and they include such duties as doing one's share of the legislative chores (such as serving on the ethics committee), using perquisites (the frank, office staff) only for official business, accepting responsibility for the reputation of the institution, and respecting the legitimate interests of the executive and judicial branches.

The obligations of fair play are difficult to codify and are therefore the least developed part of legislative ethics. But they are not the least important. Members who neglect their institutional responsibilities, who fail to carry their share of the burden of common chores, who malign the institution and its members without taking responsibility for improving it, who abuse the privileges of office even in petty ways may cause as much damage to the legislative process as financial conflicts and violations of postemployment rules. As Representative Lee Hamilton has testified, "members have to recognize that many seemingly small routine acts can undermine the basic perception of Americans in the integrity of their government just as much as the front page scandals do."[20]

Although it may not be possible to discipline members for most of these failures of institutional responsibility, legislative ethics must find ways to condemn them and ultimately to diminish their frequency. (Chapters 3 and 6 will indicate how some of the institutional strategies that social scientists have proposed to deal with the problem of free riders in other contexts may also be useful in the legislature.)

Accountability: Sustaining Public Confidence

The third principle of legislative ethics, based on the value of accountability, holds that members should act so as to create and maintain public confidence in their own actions and in the legislative process.[21] Even if members fully satisfied the first two principles, even if they were to act independently and fairly, citizens could still harbor reasonable doubts. There is a gap between acting for the right reasons and being perceived as acting for the right reasons. Politicians are inclined to blame the press for that gap, and the press no doubt makes it larger than it would otherwise be, sometimes in ways that are misleading and unfair. But the gap is inherent in public life, one of the characteristics that distinguishes legislative ethics from personal ethics. Citizens judge the ethics of members at a distance. They do not have the usual cues of personal relations, and they cannot be confident of the motives or the influences that move members to act.

Perhaps citizens are too cynical and too grudging in granting their trust to politicians. But politicians themselves have a responsibility not only to act for the right reasons but also to provide reasonable assurance that they are doing so. This is a responsibility that in legislative ethics finds its expression in rules prohibiting conflicts of interest, restrictions on the types of jobs that can be taken after a legislative career, and most notably injunctions to avoid the appearance of impropriety. These provisions regulate the circumstances under which members act rather than directly prohibiting bribery, extortion, and other manifest instances of improper influence.

During the hearings in the case of the Keating Five, Senator Alan Cranston objected to the suggestion that his conduct should be judged by how it appeared. He insisted that only he could judge his own motives. "You were not there. *I* was there. And *I* know that what I knew at the time . . . convinced me that my [actions] were appropriate."[22] Cranston expressed precisely the antithesis of the principle of accountability.

Most members do not openly repudiate the principle as Cranston did, but some act in ways that implicitly disregard its demands. Senator Max Baucus of Montana did not violate any rules when he led a filibuster against the Clinton administration's attempt to increase the grazing fees on federal land.[23] But given his personal interest in the policy, he might have considered taking a less active role in the debate. He is part owner of a large ranch that benefits from this subsidy (and may be one of the largest of a relatively small number of beneficiaries). His opposition to the increase may very well have been based on its merits, because he may honestly believe that it harms many of his constituents more than it benefits other taxpayers. But the citizens, including some of his own constituents, who question his conduct are justified. They legitimately wonder whether he is allowing himself to be unduly influenced by his own interests. Under the circumstances, they cannot be faulted for talking more about his motives than about the merits of his position.

The confidence that ethics regulation is supposed to give citizens is not just some general good feeling about the legislature and its members. By demonstrating that they are prepared to follow and to enforce the principles of legislative ethics, members offer greater assurance that they are making decisions on the merits and with due regard for fairness. If citizens have this assurance, they are themselves more likely to concentrate on the merits and fairness of decisions and less likely to raise questions about the motives of members.

Legislative Ethics and Institutional Corruption

Each of the three principles seeks to protect and promote a different aspect of the integrity of the legislative process: the reasons on which members act, the terms on which they cooperate, and the methods by which they are held accountable. Together the principles prescribe conduct that would make the process more deliberative and therefore more fully in accord with the ideals of the American democratic tradition. But in the harsh realities of politics, protection inevitably receives more attention than promotion. The ultimate end may be the pursuit of integrity, but the immediate means is the prevention of corruption. Legislative ethics therefore aims first to prevent the corruption of legislative judgment, cooperation, and accountability.

Legislative ethics deals with both individual and institutional corruption. The standards it affirms would prohibit personal gain (a form of individual corruption) as well as improper political gain (a form of institutional corruption). But because the principles of legislative ethics are rooted firmly in the purposes of the institution, the principles are especially appropriate for understanding institutional corruption and formulating standards to prevent it.

With their institutional accent, the principles of legislative ethics should remind us that individual offenses—bribery, extortion, and other improper forms of personal gain—are not the only or even the primary kind of corruption threatening democratic government. The principles caution us to stay on the alert for a more ambiguous but often more corrosive kind of corruption that takes place within the heart of the institution. Members who act not for personal gain but out of mixed, even noble, motives may still be the agents of a most serious corruption. It is corruption under the cover of public duty. To confront it, citizens and legislators must turn their attention from individual to institutional corruption.

Dynamics of Legislative Corruption

Everybody is talkin' these days about . . . graft, but nobody thinks of drawin' the distinction between honest graft and dishonest graft. There's all the difference in the world between the two.

According to George Washington Plunkitt, the Tammany Hall leader who dominated New York City politics in the early part of the twentieth century, dishonest graft consists in the "blackmailin' [of] gamblers, saloonkeepers, disorderly people." Plunkitt did not approve of this and other familiar forms of extortion and bribery; no one makes big fortunes that way. Honest graft is another matter, however. Plunkitt saw nothing wrong with using inside information to make a personal profit on a sale of land to the city. "I might sum up the whole thing by sayin': 'I seen my opportunities and took 'em.'"[1]

An authoritative political dictionary assures us that honest graft is "no longer considered permissible."[2] Certainly the conduct that Plunkitt commended would be illegal at any level of government today. But the essential distinction between honest graft and dishonest graft, redefined for modern sensibilities, is alive and well. It survives as a distinction between legal and illegal corruption, embodied in the difference between a campaign contribution and an outright bribe. Taking money from wealthy contributors who expect a legislator to use his power for their benefit looks a lot like accepting a bribe, and may have much the same effect. That is why many critics of the American system of campaign finance regard it as a form of corruption.[3] But unlike bribery, the practice of accepting

26

contributions and doing favors is an accepted, even cherished, part of the American political system. Politicians and their supporters see their opportunities and take them.

In this way the customs of campaign finance and constituent service become prime candidates for turning into institutional corruption. They are part of the job description of a politician in the American political system, yet under certain conditions they constitute corruption. Although the customs may be morally no better—and are often worse—than forms of individual corruption, they so closely resemble practices that are an integral part of legitimate political life that we are reluctant to criticize politicians who follow them. The honest graft of Plunkitt's day has become the institutional corruption of ours.

The significance of institutional corruption can be understood only if it is clearly distinguished from individual corruption. This chapter develops the distinction by examining three paradigms of ethics violations by members of Congress (one of each type and one that includes both). In each case there is a dynamic at work, a process of corruption conversion, that moves each kind of corruption toward the other. In this process two tendencies lead to overlooking or obscuring the significance of institutional corruption. The first is the tendency to individualize misconduct, the inclination of those who bring or judge charges—notably ethics committees—to construe cases of institutional corruption as cases of individual corruption. To the extent that the accusers or judges succeed, the wrongdoing is contained and the institution and other members are exonerated. In the Keating Five case, the Senate ethics committee reserved its most severe sanction for Senator Alan Cranston, whose conduct could be most easily made to fit the pattern of individual corruption.

The second tendency, to institutionalize misconduct, might seem to be the opposite of individualizing it, but this tendency also has the effect of discounting the importance of institutional corruption. Only its agents are different: accused members and their defenders are the ones typically disposed to emphasize the institutional aspects of alleged misconduct. Either they try to excuse the conduct as an institutional fault (it is not so bad because other members do it) or they try to justify the conduct as an institutional privilege (it is not wrong at all because other members accept it). Cranston's plea that other senators did what he had done is an instance of the former. David Durenberger's claim that his book deals were methods that any member could use to supplement income is an example of the latter. To the extent that the accused members are successful in evading sanctions, they manage to show not only that their own conduct but also the institutional practices in question are less corrupt than they seemed at first. Both these tendencies of conversion reinforce the belief that institutional corruption is not as serious a wrong as individual corruption and thus encourage the neglect of institutional corruption.

The Elements of Corruption

In the tradition of political theory, corruption is a disease of the body politic. Like a virus invading the physical body, hostile forces spread through the political body, enfeebling the spirit of the laws and undermining the principles of the regime.[4] The form the virus takes depends on the form of government it attacks. In regimes of a more popular cast, such as republics and democracies, the virus shows itself as private interests. Its agents are greedy individuals, contentious factions, and mass movements that seek to control collective authority for their own purposes. The essence of corruption in this conception is the pollution of the public by the private.

The modern conception of corruption, which includes both the individual and institutional kind, preserves this essence. Private interests contaminate public purposes in a democracy when they influence the government without the warrant of the democratic process. That warrant is necessary but not sufficient to legitimate the interests as public purposes. If private interests bypass the democratic process to enlist public authority in furthering their purposes, they become agents of corruption. But if they subject themselves to the rigors of the democratic process, they may earn a legitimate place on the public agenda; they may be transformed into public purposes.[5]

The democratic process is the modern surrogate for the consensus on the public good that traditional theorists hoped citizens could recognize but that still eludes contemporary pluralist societies. In the absence of a common conception of the common good, citizens find common ground in the process by which they agree on particular policies. But, of course, they may reasonably disagree about the democratic process itself: the ideals it implies, the forms it should take, the procedures it requires. The appeal to process does not by any means avoid the problem of disagreement, but it does shift the disagreement to more open ground where the representatives of many more diverse views are more likely to find a place to stand.

A complete conception of corruption for our time would require a full-blown theory of democracy. But even in the absence of such a theory, some progress can be achieved in analyzing corruption in particular institutions, such as Congress, if basic principles of legislative ethics, such as those presented in chapter 1, are accepted. The principles, of course, presuppose certain democratic values, but the principles are likely to be compatible with a wide range of views about both the process and substance of contemporary politics. The idea that corruption involves bypassing the democratic process is not partial toward any particular view about democracy.

More progress is likely if we follow the modern conception of corruption, which is more limited in scope than the traditional conception. First, it focuses on government rather than society. Its primary subject is the improper use of public office, even though it does not ignore the social and economic forces that influence such use. The pursuit of private purposes remains an essential element in the conception. Second, the modern conception characteristically involves an exchange or pattern of exchanges. In the simplest instance a private citizen bribes a public official; in more complex cases citizens and officials interact in a system of incentives that encourage such exchanges. This kind of relationship has three elements: a gain by a public official, service to a private citizen, and an improper connection between the gain and the service. These three elements are the basis on which individual and institutional corruption may be distinguished.

Gain by Officials

When a public official accepts a bribe, it is not compensation for doing the job. Neither are gifts, foreign trips, sexual favors, or employment for the official's family members. Whether proper or not, these are all instances of personal gain. *Personal gain* refers to goods

that are useable in pursuit of one's own interest (including that of
one's family) but are not necessary for performing one's political role,
or are not essential by-products of performing the duties of that role.
Some personal gain is of course perfectly acceptable: that which falls
within the limits of conventional standards of compensation, which
is approximately equal for all officials in similar circumstances. Officials who go beyond those limits, who use public office to enrich
themselves or their families, raise suspicions and invite accusations
of ethical if not criminal transgression. A member's "obligations to
the public should not be subordinated to his personal financial interests."[6] Improper personal gain typically signals the presence of
individual corruption.

Contrast this kind of gain with the political kind that characterizes institutional corruption. Political gain involves goods that are
useable primarily in the political process and are necessary for doing
a job or are essential by-products of doing it.[7] When members accept
a campaign contribution, even if they do a favor for the contributor,
the political gain may or may not be corrupt. Whether it is corrupt
depends in part on whether it undermines or promotes the legislative process or the democratic process more generally. Unlike personal gain, the more (fairly gained) political gain the better. As
citizens, we not only tolerate legitimate political gain; we encourage it.

The distinction is significant because in the American political
system (and any democracy based on elections) the pursuit of political profit is a necessary element in the structure of incentives in a
way that the pursuit of personal profit is not. The system depends
on politicians' seeking political advantage: we count on their want-
ing to be elected or reelected. Among the political advantages they
must seek are campaign contributions (other advantages include
endorsements, organizational support, leadership positions, and legislative victories). As long as they acquire those advantages in ways
that promote the purposes of the democratic process and in particular those of the legislature, they are simply doing their job. But
when the pursuit of political gain undermines those purposes, politicians not only fail to do their job, they disgrace it. They betray
their public trust in a more insidious way than when they use their
office for personal gain, which is incidental to their role. Political

gain is essential to their role, a duty of office: those who seek it improperly therefore betray their duty while doing it.

Service to Citizens

The main difference between individual and institutional corruption with respect to service turns on what makes the service improper: its *merit* or its *manner*. In individual corruption the citizen does not deserve the service the member provides.[8] For cases of institutional corruption the question is not whether the service is deserved but how it is provided. Unlike the justice of a citizen's claims, this question depends on the norms of the particular institution and the procedures that promote its purposes. It is institutional in this sense.[9]

When a member brings the grievance of a constituent to the attention of an administrative agency, the member is not only serving this citizen but also democracy. At least, the member is serving the form of a democracy that assigns legislators the duties of ombudsman. But because the service is so closely related to the institutional duties of the member, the way the member performs the service is as important as the justice of the constituent's cause. If the member threatens an administrator with an unwarranted cut in funding of the administrator's agency, he or she may be guilty of institutional corruption even if the constituent's cause is just.

The Connection between Gain and Service

In individual corruption in the legislature, the link between the gain and the service is an *individual motive* in the mind of the legislator. To establish the corruption, we have to show that a legislator knew or should have known that the gain was provided in exchange for the service or that the legislator solicited the gain in exchange for the service. In institutional corruption the link is an *institutional tendency*. We have to show only that a legislator accepted the gain and provided the service under institutional conditions that tend to cause such services to be provided in exchange for gains. When members routinely combine fundraising and constituent service (for example, using the same staff members to perform both), they create the conditions of institutional corruption. More generally, as chapter 5 shows, any action performed under conditions that tend to violate one of the principles of legislative ethics constitutes institutional corruption.

In both individual and institutional corruption, the connection between the gain and service may take the form of improper influence; and in both, certain institutional conditions may be relevant to showing that the influence is improper. But in the case of institutional corruption, the fact that a legislator acts under institutional conditions that tend to create improper influence is sufficient to establish corruption, whatever the legislator's motive. A legislator who solicits contributions in his or her office from a lobbyist while discussing legislation in which the lobbyist is interested is engaging in institutional corruption. Action under these conditions is not merely evidence of corruption, it constitutes the corruption.

Furthermore, a member who does favors for contributors without regard to the reasonable reactions of the public engages in institutional corruption, whether or not the member has succumbed to improper influence. In the circumstances of modern government, citizens must judge their representative at a distance, and they are justified in believing that contributors are improperly influencing a representative who acts without due attention to public sensitivities. The belief itself is likely to lessen confidence in government and may encourage further individual and institutional corruption. Thus the circumstances to which institutional corruption refers include those conditions under which citizens judge (assessing officials at a distance, for example), as well as those under which officials act (combining fundraising with service).

This way of understanding the connection between gains and service has a consequence that might at first seem puzzling. The consequence is that in some situations there is no significant difference in the type of connection that exists between personal gain and service and the type that exists between political gain and service. It does not make any difference, as far as the *connection* is concerned, whether a member receives a valuable gift for personal use or a large contribution for a political campaign if they both come from groups for whom the member routinely does big favors. The same kind of institutional conditions justifies a finding of improper influence in either case. Thus there are instances in which the gain is personal but the connection is institutional. In such cases, is the corruption individual or institutional? The answer is that it is both. The element of gain is a characteristic of individual corruption, but the institutional tendency is part of institutional corruption.

That a single act can simultaneously exhibit elements of both individual and institutional corruption does not undermine the importance of the distinction between them. On the contrary, it makes the distinction all the more useful. Because corruption consists of more than one element, any adequate distinction between kinds of corruption should allow for impure cases. A purely individual instance occurs when the gain is personal, the service undeserved, and the connection based on an individual motive. In purely institutional corruption the gain is political, the service procedurally improper, and the connection based on institutional tendencies. Impure examples combine elements of both kinds of corruption. A case is impure when, for example, the gain is political and the service procedurally improper but the connection is based on an individual motive. Even in such a situation, however, the transgression is more institutional than individual because two of its three elements are institutional.

The three-element distinction between types of corruption thus accommodates the more complex patterns of corruption that are likely to occur in actual political life and supports more nuanced responses that can be tailored to the particularities of those patterns. Furthermore, the distinction enables us better to resist the tendency to turn institutional corruption into individual corruption, especially because most cases are impure. We are more likely to see that just because an official has a corrupt motive, the corruption need not be only individual. Or just because we cannot find a corrupt motive, the corruption is not therefore completely institutional.

Three cases can illustrate the importance of the distinction between types of corruption. None is completely pure, but each can serve as a paradigm for one (or both) of the types. The first, the case of David Durenberger, comes close to an instance of pure individual corruption. The second, that of the Keating Five, exemplifies institutional corruption. The third, that of House Speaker James Wright, includes both types, each in a relatively pure form.[10]

The Individual Corruption of David Durenberger

In response to a complaint from the Minnesota Bar in 1988, the Senate ethics committee began an inquiry into arrangements that Senator David Durenberger had made with Piranha Press, which had published two of his books. These arrangements, the committee eventually found, were "simply a mechanism to evade the statutory limitations on honoraria."[11] Durenberger improperly used his office for personal gain because he solicited the gain from groups with an interest in legislation who might expect service in return.

For many years members of Congress supplemented their income by collecting honoraria for giving speeches, usually to corporations and groups with an interest in legislation. Recognizing the conflict of interest in this practice, both chambers began placing limits on honoraria in 1974 but did not completely ban them until 1991. During a two-year period beginning in 1985, Durenberger made 113 appearances, supposedly to promote his books. Piranha Press paid him $100,000 for the appearances, an amount almost double the amount the rules at the time permitted him to receive from honoraria. It collected fees from the organizations that sponsored the events and passed them along to Durenberger, who ignored the honoraria limits and also violated other rules.[12]

The events for which Durenberger received fees seemed more like speaking engagements for which members traditionally received honoraria than like book promotions. None of the groups he appeared before invited him to speak about his books. Several complained when they were asked to pay the fee, some even suggesting that the request was unethical. The president of the Group Health Association of America said he believed his organization "was being 'hustled' by Piranha Press."[13] At many of the events no copies of the books were available, and the senator rarely mentioned them in his speeches. When he did, he disparaged them ("what this really is, is 44 speeches").[14] Indeed, Piranha Press did not seem like a book publisher at all. Durenberger's efforts for Piranha from 1985 to 1987 generated sixteen times more in speaking fees than in book sales. Piranha had published only one other book—a how-to manual on wrestling holds.

Durenberger asserted that he was "justified in thinking that a good speech or appearance before an audience promoted his publisher and his books, even if neither was mentioned."[15] He also pointed out that he had never attempted to conceal this arrangement with Piranha. He had reported the income on his financial disclosure forms and even recommended the scheme to several other senators as a way to earn income beyond the honoraria limits. Furthermore, he had secured an advisory opinion from the Federal Election Commission stating that the income from the speaking engagements would be considered "stipends" rather than honoraria (although he neglected to tell the commission that the fees would go first to Piranha Press).

Durenberger's defense was an attempt to institutionalize his conduct. He implied that any member of Congress could legitimately engage in the practice. If his scheme could be used by any member, then it could be seen not as individual corruption but as institutional privilege. He also tried to summon the authority of another agency, the FEC, to lend official sanction to the practice.

One difficulty with Durenberger's defense was that other senators had appeared with him on many of these occasions, and all of them had reported the fees they received as honoraria.[16] His colleagues had not considered the additional fees legitimate personal gain. More important, if his colleagues had accepted his argument and adopted his practice, they would have done more than merely expand the privileges of office. They would have also multiplied the occasions for individual corruption, thereby turning a single case into a system of individual corruption. Rather than legitimating the practice, Durenberger's argument would spread its harm even further.

The ethics committee, rightly, declined to accept Durenberger's argument. They evidently agreed with Special Counsel Robert Bennett, who concluded, "This very hungry fish, Piranha Press, was allowed to engage in a feeding frenzy on responsible organizations who thought they were sponsoring traditional honorarium events . . . the evidence shows that Senator Durenberger . . . allowed himself and the stature of his office to be used as the bait, and he got $100,000 for his trouble."[17]

A year after the committee had begun its inquiry into the book promotions, the news media raised a new charge. The senator had been reimbursed for rent he paid on a condominium in which he stayed in Minneapolis when he returned to the state for official business. Members properly receive reimbursement for living expenses in the conduct of their duties. The trouble was that Durenberger owned the condominium: he was paying himself rent. It might seem that such obvious double-dipping would be easily detected. But the terms of the ownership, arranged by several lawyers, and at various points including a complicated partnership, a blind trust, and backdated documents, left some of the partners, and perhaps Durenberger himself, confused. It also left a legacy of criminal charges against the senator and two of his partners that produced a series of court decisions on the question of whether the investigation violated congressional immunity.[18]

The ethics committee concluded that Durenberger's partnership was a mechanism for "effectively transferring to the United States Senate and the American taxpayer the cost of maintaining what was essentially his personal Minneapolis residence."[19] This second finding illustrates a form of individual corruption that differs from the kind displayed in the book promotion. In the book promotion the personal gain and the expected service went to different parties. The corruption is in the *connection*, the presumption of improper influence of those who pay on the member who receives. This represented individual corruption in the mode of traditional influence peddling. The gain is reciprocal because it involves an exchange, actual or possible. In the condominium scam the gain and the service went to the same person: the member himself. This was simple personal gain, individual corruption in the form of simple theft from the public till. It was, even from a Plunkittian perspective, dishonest graft.

Yet Durenberger was no Plunkitt. He was "right out of the best-and-brightest tradition of Minnesota politics evident in both parties, the tradition of Humphrey and Mondale."[20] He had led Republican efforts on health care reform, helped write major environmental legislation, and worked for more openness in the intelligence agencies.[21] He was admired on both sides of the aisle. He had even served on the ethics committee. His personal life was marked by misfortune: his first wife died of cancer, leaving him with four sons to raise, his second marriage collapsed in 1985, and his financial problems worsened. The ethics committee took note of the "severe emotional and traumatic events" in the senator's personal life, but nevertheless recommended unanimously that the full Senate take action against him. On July 25, 1990, as Durenberger asked for forgiveness, the Senate voted 96–0 to "denounce" him. In September 1993, facing a federal indictment over the condominium deal, he announced his retirement.

Individual corruption, this case makes clear, does not require a sinister villain. In the modern Congress the hapless rather than the avaricious member is the more likely perpetrator of such corruption. There are more lucrative and less risky ways to amass personal wealth illicitly than by exploiting a public office. Durenberger fell on hard times, and it is understandable that his colleagues would feel sympathy for him, as most people would. But one can also agree with the committee, which had no doubt that he should be held responsible for his misdeeds.

It is significant that the committee felt it necessary to show that his conduct was deliberate, that he knowingly "brought the Senate into dishonor and disrepute."[22] As the special counsel pointed out, the Senate does not have to find that a member actually intended to violate a rule or law in order to impose disciplinary action. Criminal law requires specific intent, but people who hold a public trust should be held to a higher standard.[23] Yet both the special counsel and the committee evidently considered it important to argue that Durenberger did have the guilty mind that criminal law requires. They acted as if they believed that the case would be stronger, indeed might be convincing, only if they could establish a corrupt motive. The closer the case came to the paradigm of individual corruption, the better for conviction. In this they rode the dynamics of corruption, reflecting the tendency of those who judge to keep corruption as individual as possible.

The Institutional Corruption of the Keating Five

The senators who are remembered together as the "Keating Five" included Democrats Dennis DeConcini (Arizona), Alan Cranston (California), John Glenn (Ohio), and Donald Riegle (Michigan) and Republican John McCain (Arizona).[24] They were first brought together by Charles Keating, Jr., a successful real estate financier and developer with business interests in several states. As head of a home construction company in Phoenix, Keating bought Lincoln

Savings and Loan in California in 1984. Exploiting the newly relaxed regulations for thrift institutions, he shifted Lincoln's assets
from home loans to high-risk real estate projects and other speculative investments. He lived lavishly at the company's expense and
engaged in questionable foreign trading and stock manipulation,
counting on his political connections to keep the federal and state
regulators at bay. For more than five years he and his army of
lawyers battled state regulators who believed that Lincoln and its
parent company were violating a variety of rules governing accounting and investment practices and financial disclosure. In 1989 Lincoln collapsed, wiping out the savings of 23,000 (mostly elderly)
uninsured depositors and costing federal taxpayers more than
$2 billion. It was the biggest failure in what came to be the most
costly financial scandal in American history. Lincoln came to sym-
bolize the Savings and Loan crisis. Keating himself was eventually
convicted on charges of fraud and racketeering and went to prison.

But to many in the financial community during the years before
the collapse, Keating was a model of the kind of financial entrepre-
neur that the Republican administration wished to encourage
through its policy of deregulation. Many saw him as a freewheeling
businessman, perhaps a little too interested in high living and a
little too willing to play fast and loose with the rules, but basically
an honest financier whose willingness to take risks had made lots
of money for himself and those who worked for him, and provided
jobs and investment opportunities for many people in the region.

Keating's most visible political lobbying was directed against a
new rule prohibiting direct investment by S&Ls, which many legitimate financial institutions and members of Congress also opposed.
Keating's most prominent and persistent target was Edwin Gray,
the head of the three-member Federal Home Loan Bank Board that
regulated the industry and a supporter of the rule. Gray was himself
a controversial figure. He had been appointed by the Reagan administration, but some high officials in the administration were trying
to remove him. The press reported that he was waging a vendetta
against Keating. Even an impartial observer at the time could have
seen Gray as an inflexible bureaucrat, well intentioned, perhaps,
but unimaginative and hostile toward newcomers to the industry.

The fateful meeting that would forever link the Keating Five
took place on April 2, 1987, in the early evening in DeConcini's office.

Gray has said he was told to bring no aides. Only he and the four senators showed up (Riegle, who evidently helped arrange the meeting, was expected to attend but did not). Still, four senators at a meeting in one office impressed Gray as unusual. The senators asked why the investigation of Lincoln and their "friend" Keating was taking so long, and they cited a letter from a managing partner of the respected accounting firm Arthur Young that concluded that federal regulators were harassing Lincoln. (The author of the letter, Jack Atchison, went to work for Keating a year later.)

Gray claimed that the senators proposed a deal: if he would abolish the direct investment rule, Keating would move Lincoln back into traditional home loans. Gray, who was desperately seeking more funds from Congress to take over troubled S&Ls, said he was intimidated by this show of force. The senators all deny that any deal was proposed. Gray told them that he did not know much about the Lincoln case and suggested that they talk directly to the regulators in San Francisco.

And so they did, a week later, in what was to become the most scrutinized meeting in the hearings. Present in DeConcini's office were four regulators from the San Francisco office (one of whom took notes that read like a transcript), and all five senators (though Cranston appeared only briefly during the two-and-a-half-hour meeting to express his support). The senators indicated they believed that the government was harassing a constituent whose companies made important economic contributions in their regions. Several, particularly DeConcini, pressed Keating's case vigorously, but as the regulators revealed more and more unfavorable information about Lincoln, the tone of the meeting began to change. The revelation that the examiners were about to make a criminal referral against Lincoln appeared to be the turning point in the meeting.

After the meeting none of the five had any more contact with Ed Gray or the San Francisco regulators. McCain and Riegle had no further dealings with Keating. McCain had already broken off relations with Keating, who had called him a wimp for refusing to put pressure on the Bank Board. Glenn arranged a brief lunch the following January, but the ethics committee concluded that, although this showed "poor judgment," Glenn's actions were not "improper."[25]

Cranston and DeConcini continued to act on Keating's behalf. During a two-month period in early 1989 Cranston approached regulators at least six times (once in an early morning phone call to a Bank Board member at home) to express his interest in the proposed sale of Lincoln. (To satisfy regulators, Keating had agreed to sell Lincoln, but the buyers turned out to be his business associates.) DeConcini, who had lobbied for Keating's causes in earlier years, also called state and federal regulators repeatedly about the sale of Lincoln.

The Keating Five, especially DeConcini and Cranston, certainly provided this constituent with good service. Because corruption typically involves an exchange of some kind, one should ask, what did the senators get in return? The answer is $1.3 million. But this figure, handy for headline writers, obscures some important details, in particular the timing and uses of the funds, that should affect any assessment of corruption. Cranston received the bulk of the contributions (almost $1 million), most of it in 1987 and 1988 while he was actively intervening for Keating. But the money primarily went to voter registration groups, the largest portion to the felicitously named Center for Participation in Democracy, headed by Cranston's son.

McCain and Glenn received the largest totals in campaign and political action committee funds, but all well before (in McCain's case five years before) Keating enlisted their help with his problems at Lincoln. Riegle and DeConcini solicited contributions while intervening for Keating. Riegle received $78,250 and DeConcini $48,000 in direct contributions to their 1988 campaigns. Keating had also given contributions to DeConcini earlier and had committed himself to raise larger amounts in the future. In addition, Keating often acted as a broker for others, and sometimes as a "bundler," taking "the separate individual contributions and bundling them together . . . claiming credit for the harvest."[26] All the contributions were technically within legal limits.

In February 1991, slightly more than a month after its hearings ended, the ethics committee rebuked four of the senators. DeConcini and Riegle received a more severe scolding than McCain and Glenn and announced their retirement two and one-half years later (in the same month that Durenberger disclosed he was leaving). Cranston's conduct was more serious, the committee said, and it warranted further action. (Ironically, it was Cranston who had been one of the earliest and strongest advocates of campaign finance reform in congressional elections.) In November, after much behind-the-scenes negotiation, the committee reported to the full Senate that Cranston had "violated established norms of behavior in the Senate." To avoid a stronger resolution by the committee (which would have required a Senate vote), Cranston formally accepted the reprimand. In a dramatic speech on the floor he also claimed that he had done nothing worse than most of his Senate colleagues had done.

Cranston's defense exemplifies in a cynical form the dynamics of corruption conversion. The accused member seeks to sanitize his own conduct by showing that it is a legitimate institutional practice. He represents his conduct as part of a normal competitive process in which all politicians are encouraged by the political system to solicit support and bestow favors in order to win elections. What he is doing is not only not individually corrupt, but institutionally required.

If permitted to run its course, this dynamic results in either exonerating the member completely—he did only what had to be done to get reelected—or condemning the entire institution as corrupt—he is just one of "the Keating 535."[27] To counter this tendency, those who accuse the member, and those who investigate and judge the charges, try to individualize his conduct. They try to make the conduct look as much like individual corruption as possible.

Committee members could agree to sanction Cranston more severely than the others because his conduct seemed more like individual corruption. The connection between the gain he received and the service he provided was relatively tight, close enough to establish something like a corrupt motive. Cranston made the connection explicit in a memorable line delivered at a dinner at the Belair Hotel, where he "came up and patted Mr. Keating on the back and said, 'Ah, the mutual aid society.'"[28]

But the counterdynamic of the accusers creates its own problems. Forcing a case into the mold of individual corruption obscures some of its most disturbing aspects, specifically those of institutional corruption. First, with respect to the question of official gain, none of the Keating Five fits the portrait of the politician out to enrich himself from public office. None even tried, as Durenberger did, to supplement his salary. Only one, McCain, ever received anything from Keating for his personal use, and the gifts were never an important issue in the hearings.[29] The problem in this case, then, is not personal but political gain. The more one thinks of the gain in personal terms, the less likely one is to confront the difficult task of distinguishing proper from improper political gain.

The strain toward individual corruption also distorts the second element of corruption in any case of this kind. The five senators claimed there was nothing improper about the help they gave Keating. The benefits he received were all provided in the name of constituent service, a normal practice in a district-based political system in which representatives have to compete for the support of voters and campaign contributors. The senators also claimed that they gave Keating no special favors, that they would do the same for any constituent who had a similar problem with the government. During the hearings much of the controversy centered on whether this claim was true. Favoritism is indeed the critical question about constituent service if the concern is individual corruption.

But the methods the Keating Five used in this case point up another question at least as important. Instead of asking whether a member would provide this service equally for any constituent, we should ask whether the service should be provided in this way at all. We should consider the possibility that what the Keating Five did for Keating no member should do for any constituent. Some ways of providing constituent service, even if provided without favoritism and in a just cause, may still violate principles of legislative ethics. They may be improper because they damage the legislative process in a democracy (for example, by interfering with quasi-adjudicatory processes or taking place in secret). That at least is the possibility that a search for institutional corruption takes seriously. (It is a possibility that chapter 5 explores in detail.)

A preoccupation with individual corruption can also distort the third element of corruption, the connection between the gain and service. Looking for a corrupt motive, the committee did not seem to be very disturbed when they found only an appearance of impropriety. Such an appearance connects the gain and service through institutional tendencies and public confidence rather than individual motive and private judgment. DeConcini and Riegle, whose actions created such an appearance, showed only "insensitivity and poor judgment."[30] Yet these actions may have caused as much damage to the legislative process and public confidence as did Cranston's more blatant conduct. Even if DeConcini and Riegle were not in any way influenced by Keating's contributions, citizens could reasonably believe there was a connection. If so, the senators neglected their responsibility (affirmed by the principle of accountability) to consider the effects of their actions on the reasonable reactions of citizens.

The so-called appearance standard that expresses this responsibility was the subject of much criticism during the hearings. The special counsel favored it, the Keating Five and their attorneys attacked it, and most of the committee mistrusted it. But some such standard has long been part of the code of both chambers, and (as chapter 5 argues) should have an important role in congressional ethics. We are more likely to see its advantages if we are on the alert for institutional corruption than if we are fixated on individual corruption.

The Diverse Corruptions of James C. Wright, Jr.

"Let me give you back this job you gave to me as a propitiation for all of this season of bad will that has grown up among us. . . . I will resign as Speaker of the House."[31] With these words, James Wright brought his thirty-four-year career in the House to a dramatic end and became the first Speaker in history to be forced from office. The season of bad will—the unusually bitter partisanship in the chamber, the tensions between the leader and other members, and the battles within each of the parties—no doubt contributed to his downfall. So did his aggressive style of leadership, his lack of close personal ties to members, and revelations about the criminal past of one of his top aides. But the immediate cause was the unanimous vote by the House ethics committee to begin an adjudicatory proceeding on five alleged violations of the House rules. After a seven-month investigation overseen by Special Counsel Richard J. Phelan, the committee concluded in April 1989 that "there is reason to believe such violations occurred."[32]

The charges against Wright combine in the same case the individual and institutional corruption found, respectively, in the cases of Durenberger and the Keating Five. One of the charges against Wright, that income he received from his book violated the House limits on honoraria and outside income, resembles the charge against Durenberger. Another charge, that he used undue influence with the Federal Home Loan Bank Board when intervening on behalf of four fellow Texans, paralleled the accusation against the Keating Five. The principal official at the Bank Board whom Wright tried to influence was even the same Edwin Gray.

The presence of both kinds of corruption in the same case offers an opportunity for a direct comparison. Confronted with a case of both kinds of corruption, the House ethics committee took seriously only the allegations of individual corruption, even though they were arguably less serious than those of institutional corruption.

The charge that Wright used his book, *Reflections of a Public Man*, to supplement his income beyond allowable limits was the most serious of the many complaints of individual corruption that the special counsel and the committee considered. The committee found only two others worth further investigation: accepting gifts from a longtime friend, George Mallick, who supposedly had a direct interest in legislation, and profiting from an oil well deal that benefited his blind trust in questionable ways.[33] The committee turned these three matters into sixty-nine counts against Wright.[34]

Most of the copies of Wright's book were sold in bulk to lobbyists and supporters and to groups that invited him to speak. Wright said that the $55,000 he received from the sale of the books should be considered royalties, which are not subject to the stringent limits of honoraria. But the committee concluded that these transactions amounted to "an overall scheme to evade the outside earned income limitations" of the House.[35] The unusual arrangements with the publisher (a royalty rate of 55 percent), the context of the sales (the sponsoring groups treated their purchases as compensation for a speech), and perhaps the content of the book itself (a collection of anecdotes and stories many of which were lifted from others) led the committee to doubt that Wright's proceeds from the book were bona fide royalties.[36]

Wright said that he simply wanted "to get the widest possible distribution of the book."[37] This begins to sound like a justification that would make the marketing scheme part of his job. By writing and distributing his book, he was fulfilling the responsibility of a representative to communicate his ideas to his constituents. But then his constituents and the rest of us might well ask why he should receive extra compensation for doing his job. This or any similar effort to turn the sales into an institutional duty was bound to boomerang.

Another line of defense, implicitly suggested by Wright and explicitly developed by sympathetic commentators, acknowledged that the sales might have been a personal gain and ideally should be prohibited, but that they are implicitly sanctioned by the institution. As one commentator suggested, "Wright had found a loophole. . . . Perhaps he had seen it as a gray area. If one could accept honoraria from lobbyists, which was profiting from one's office, what was wrong with selling them large numbers of books? The principle— taking money from lobbyists—was the same, wasn't it?"[38]

The trouble was that accepting honoraria from lobbyists in the amounts and under the circumstances of these book sales was not permitted under any plausible interpretation of the rules. Moreover, even if he and his lawyers could have succeeded in showing that he had exploited a loophole, Wright's conduct did not meet the higher standards to which he himself had once said the members and especially the Speaker should be held. True, the amounts of money were small, the personal gain was petty, but "it was the very pettiness . . . that damaged him the most. It demeaned him, made him seem a small man, a conniver."[39] To try to implicate the institution in this kind of conduct could not ultimately win him support, ethical or political.

On the major charge of institutional corruption, the special counsel concluded that Wright had improperly intervened with officials of the Bank Board on four occasions in violation of the House guidelines on relations with executive or independent agencies.[40] The special counsel devoted some ninety-three pages of discussion to evidence and analysis of the charge of improper intervention.[41] On one occasion Wright tried to get a regulator dismissed because of his homosexual associations. Yet when the committee turned to the charge toward the end of their report, they dismissed it with only four short paragraphs of comment.[42] Wright may have been "intemperate" in dealing with officials of the Bank Board, but any criticism of a legislator for intervening under these circumstances "jeopardizes the ability of Members effectively to represent persons and organizations having concern with the activities of executive agencies." Intervention is part of the job, and there is "a constant tension between the legislative and executive branches . . . in carrying out their respective responsibilities."[43]

In dismissing this charge, the committee was conforming to the dynamic observed in the other cases: its members were more prepared to find a violation the more they could construe the conduct as individual corruption, and they were more reluctant to criticize conduct the more they saw it as being part of the job of a legislator. In this way they join the accused member in trying to convert what could be institutional corruption into institutional duty.

In one respect the committee did recognize an institutional dimension to the corruption: they found that the "apparent gifts" Wright received from George Mallick indicated that he "failed in his duty to exercise reasonable care to avoid even the appearance of impropriety."[44] Furthermore, the committee held that a corrupt motive would not be necessary to establish a violation. It appealed to the precedent of the Korean influence case ("Koreagate") in the mid-1970s, in which several members accepted gifts and campaign contributions from a South Korean businessman who was seeking to influence congressional positions on foreign policy.[45] If the *circumstances* of a donation or gift suggested impropriety, the House ethics committee at that time held, the member could be sanctioned for not taking due care to avoid that impression.[46]

But in the Wright case the gesture toward accepting the concept that institutional corruption is improper conduct was compromised because the charge to which the committee applied these institutional standards was itself weak. It could be reasonably questioned whether most of the $145,000 that Wright received from Mallick over a ten-year period—use of a car and a condominium and salary for his wife—should qualify as "apparent gifts" under the rules.[47] Also, Mallick's interest in legislation does not seem very direct. The committee said it was "distinct from [that of] the public at large by virtue of his extensive real estate and oil and gas investments."[48] But on this standard, his interest in legislation seems no more direct than that of many prominent businessmen.

It could be argued that the usual understanding of "direct" in previous cases had been too permissive, but Mallick's interest did not easily fit the rule as it had been understood in the past. On the

standard criteria for individual corruption, then, the charge is difficult to sustain. It almost appears as if, in the absence of a strong
case for showing individual corruption, the committee was forced to
look for other kinds of wrong. They seemed to turn to institutional
corruption as a last resort. This is also what the dynamic of corruption would lead one to expect. Individual corruption is still the preferred charge, to be supplemented by a finding of institutional corruption only if necessary to make the case.

Others were not so hesitant about raising the charges against
Wright to the level of institutional corruption. Newt Gingrich, who
as a relatively junior member initiated and pursued the ethics campaign against Wright, saw him as a prime exhibit in the case for his
complaint that recent Congresses are "the most . . . corrupt of the
modern era."[49] He also evidently thought that the Speaker's growing
power posed a serious threat to the future of the Republicans in the
House. Gingrich's relentless crusade caused many observers to conclude that the attack on Wright was entirely politically motivated.
Even some Republicans who closely followed the case against Wright
believed that "if Gingrich hadn't manipulated the press and got all
those stories, there wouldn't have been an investigation."[50] (The
charges the committee later found valid were not those that Gingrich brought; his were never sustained.) Other observers said that
Special Counsel Phelan, though a longtime Democrat, had sought
the job in order to serve his own political ambitions, and that the
Democrats on the ethics committee relied too much on his conclusions.[51] But the fact remains that at least some of the charges
against Wright were serious and deserved serious investigation.
Gingrich, the special counsel, and finally the committee—whatever
their motives—did not bring down a public official who was completely innocent.

Nevertheless, the charge of institutional corruption as pressed
by Gingrich and his followers itself did institutional damage by politicizing the ethics process even more than was normal in legislative
politics. This had two effects. First, it was unfair to Wright. He was
in effect found guilty and forced from office simply on the basis of a
finding equivalent to an indictment by a grand jury. The committee
had found only that there was reason to believe he committed the
violations. Wright had not even had a chance to defend himself fully

before the committee. Partly as a result of this case, the House has modified its procedures, but (as will be suggested in chapter 6) some further changes may be required to ensure fairness to members.

The other, more general, effect of politicizing the ethics process is to reinforce what may be called the cycle of accusation. Ethics charges on one side are countered by charges on the other, and a new round begins. Making charges develops its own momentum, independent of their substance. That is why the "season of bad will" did not end on that last day of May in 1989 when Wright announced his resignation. Tony Coelho, the House whip and Wright's expected successor, resigned a few days before Wright's announcement amid charges of underpaying his taxes, conflict of interest, and questionable fundraising practices. Gingrich found himself charged with using his staff for campaign work (and earlier for a book deal that seemed at first like Durenberger's). Even the chair of the ethics committee, Representative Julian Dixon, came under suspicion for the business activities of his wife.

When ethics charges become yet another political weapon, they lose their moral authority. They not only fail to control individual or institutional corruption but may even contribute to it. They undermine confidence in the process and Congress's ability to take charges seriously. Perhaps the ultimate lesson of the Wright case is that the institution needs to protect itself from the unethical use of ethics charges. This is so even if Wright was rightly accused. Congress must ensure that the process by which members are accused and punished is fair. That is no less a value of legislative ethics than enforcing the standards of conduct in the first place.

A case such as Wright's that includes both kinds of corruption is particularly fertile ground for nourishing a cycle of accusation. In the presence of such a rich variety of kinds of corruption, the opportunities for making charges and countercharges are multiplied. Accusations of individual corruption are met with defenses of institutional corruption, and complaints of institutional corruption are answered with allegations of individual corruption. In the ensuing ethical turmoil it is difficult to separate the serious from the trivial, the legitimate from the spurious. Both individuals and the institutions suffer. That is another reason why we need to distinguish more clearly between the two kinds of corruption and to formulate distinct standards for each.

Gains of Office

Members . . . should not seek private gain from public office.

The commandment against seeking private gain from public office, prominently proclaimed on the first page of the *House Ethics Manual*, expresses one of the oldest principles of the ethics of public office.[1] At least since Cicero, it has been "beyond debate that officials of the government are relied upon to act for the public interest not their own enrichment."[2] But what exactly the principle prohibits is not so clear, and its ambiguities are the source of many of the problems in implementing legislative ethics in our time. Some kinds of gain from holding office are worse than others, and some are not improper at all. In particular, the pursuit of political gain is a necessary and desirable part of the American political system. Legislative ethics needs to attend to these differences because different kinds of gain call for different kinds of standards and procedures.

The Legitimacy of Personal Gain

Nearly three-quarters of the charges of violating ethical standards that Congress has officially considered qualify as cases of individual corruption, all of which have involved some kind of personal gain.[3] The gain most commonly comes in the form of financial benefit, but sexual gratification, jobs for family and friends, and perks of office play their part. All these goods are perfectly legitimate objects of human desire.[4] Why do they become improper because they are gains of office? The answer is not so obvious as is usually assumed.

Just before Louisiana Governor Richard Leche went to jail for corruption in the 1930s, he remarked: "When I took the oath of Governor, I didn't take any vows of poverty."[5] Instead, the governor took a vow of enrichment, turning his $7,500 salary into an annual income of more than $280,000. His rationalization was so blatant that it is usually taken as an amusing piece of cynicism. But the humor plays off a background norm in American culture: politicians are not expected completely to give up the pursuit of material gain. The governor was right in assuming public office is not like entering a monastery. His mistake was in acting as if it were like joining a criminal conspiracy.

Politicians should be able to reap the rewards of good work, just as do doctors, clergy, police officers, and others who follow socially valuable callings. Having an independent source of income should not be a qualification for holding public office. The Founders acknowledged this principle by rejecting the aristocratic tradition of regarding public office as voluntary service. In the Constitutional Convention, delegates voted down a proposal to have senators serve without compensation.[6] During the debate on the clause giving Congress power to set its own salaries, some delegates did raise the obvious worry that members might pay themselves too much. But others objected that they "will fix their wages so low, that only the rich can fill the offices of senators and representatives."[7] Nor did the Founders think that once a reasonable salary is set, members should enjoy no other advantages from their public service. They should not be denied, for example, the chance to hold other offices in government after they leave Congress. To impose such a ban would be to "prevent those who had served their country with the greatest fidelity and ability from being on a par with their fellow-citizens."[8]

Members today face many more restrictions on outside income while in office and on employment after they leave office, but none of the restrictions implies a general taboo on profiting from holding public office.[9] If we thought that officials should never financially benefit from their positions, we would prohibit them from keeping royalties from books, teaching for pay, and earning any outside income at all (instead of only limiting it to 15 percent of their salary, as in the House). Book royalties, genuinely earned, should be acceptable if the writing does not interfere with official duties, and the nature or source of the income does not create a conflict of interest. Unusually large advances or royalties may be grounds for reasonable suspicion.[10] Senator David Durenberger and House Speaker James Wright were condemned not because of the money they made on their books, but because of the way they made it. Instead of selling the books in the usual manner, they asked lobbyists and interest groups to buy them, often in bulk and in connection with a speaking engagement. Part of the strength of the case against Durenberger was that he did *not* try to market his book as a profit-seeking author would.

Furthermore, if we believed that officials should be prohibited from profiting from their experience in government after they leave office, we would impose high taxes on their royalties from memoirs and their fees from speaking engagements. If profiteering were the evil to be prevented, the postemployment rules should prohibit only paid lobbying, yet they also restrict some unpaid lobbying.[11] Even when members become highly paid lobbyists, it is not the salary that most of their critics condemn. When Glenn English, chair of the House subcommittee that oversees the Rural Electrification Administration, resigned from Congress in 1994, he became general manager of the National Rural Electric Cooperative Association (NREC), the most important lobbying organization on rural development.[12] English's action did not violate any ethics rules. Although there was some comment about the "hefty raise" he received, it was not his but NREC's gain that prompted the serious criticism. Critics thought that NREC's gain was not only Congress's but also the public's loss. "Talk about the revolving door," one observer remarked: "this one came unhinged." Some wondered if English's anticipation of this or a similar job could have influenced his judgment during his last years in Congress. Others thought that his inside knowledge and connections would give the special interests of rural developers an unfair advantage in the political process.

As these criticisms suggest, the problem is not all kinds of personal gain from office but only personal gain that is thought to damage the legislative process. Some general prohibitions of personal gain may be necessary to capture the kinds that cause this damage, but as Congress formulates ethics rules, it should concentrate on preventing this damage, not the gain itself. The rules against personal gain should be targeted on specific wrongs, actual or potential violations of the principles of legislative ethics. The principles typically at issue in cases of personal gain are those of independence and fairness.[13] The aim should be to prevent personal gain from interfering with a member's independent judgment and from impeding the fair functioning of the legislative process. Personal gain that does not have such effects does not fall within the province of legislative ethics and should not come within the jurisdiction of the legislature and its committees.

What kinds of personal gain violate the principles of legislative ethics? A member who accepts a gift in exchange for doing a favor does not act independently or fairly. Less explicit exchanges, such as the book deals of Durenberger and Wright, raise similar concerns. The impropriety in all such cases is to be found in the *connection* between the gain to the public official and the potential service to the private citizen. This kind of personal gain is best analyzed when the links between gain and service are considered in chapter 5. But personal gain can also be improper by itself, unconnected to any favor or service. Durenberger's condominium arrangement is an example. The connection between the gain and the favor is not at issue because the public official and the private citizen who gain are the same person. Three different forms of this simple personal gain need to be distinguished.

General Offenses

Personal gain that would be wrong both in private life and in public life should be regarded as a general offense and should be presumed to fall within the province of the ordinary legal process. Examples of such offenses include improper reimbursement of expenses, sexual misconduct involving employees, use of staff for personal services, use of illegal drugs on the job, use of campaign or office funds for personal expenses, perjury, fraud, embezzlement, and tax evasion in office.[14]

These offenses, it is true, are not exactly the same as the corresponding offenses by ordinary citizens. Many could be regarded as involving the improper use of public office for private gain, and some even refer to activities (such as campaigns) that are features only of public office. But what makes all the activities improper is not distinctive to public office. Misappropriation of funds or sexual harassment are defined in the same way and are wrong for the same reasons whether the offender is a public official or private citizen. When personal gain takes the form of one of these general offenses, it is never legitimate. Unlike financial gain that creates a conflict of interest, this kind of gain cannot be consistent with public office. Unlike perquisites of the office, it cannot be considered part of the job.

The congressional ethics committees now have jurisdiction over general offenses and have at one time or another taken action in cases that involved all the offenses just listed. Some activities are specific violations of current rules, and all could also qualify as violations of the general rule that members should not bring discredit on Congress.[15] Ethics committees should certainly retain the power to decide whether to take action on general offenses. They should be able to decide in some cases that there are compelling reasons to pursue a charge that is also under criminal investigation, and they should be able to proceed even against a member who has been found not guilty in a criminal trial. The Constitution gives Congress the responsibility for disciplining its own members (although as chapter 6 argues, this does not preclude letting other authorities do part of the job). Also, the standard of proof for a criminal conviction—"beyond a reasonable doubt"—is too stringent for a proceeding that determines whether a person is fit to hold public office. Another reason that Congress needs to keep final control over these cases is that the criminal justice system may take too long and may be subject to deliberate delay. Furthermore, some cases need to be pursued because, although the violations are equivalent to a serious crime, they escape the reach of the criminal law. Representatives Gerry Studds and Daniel Crane were found to have had sexual relationships with teenage pages, but since the legal age of consent in the District of Columbia is age sixteen, neither could be charged with a crime.[16] The only recourse was congressional discipline.

But usually there are good reasons for Congress to leave general offenses that are ordinary crimes to criminal prosecution. First, a legislature has no special expertise in such cases. They do not often turn on any facts or understandings specific to the role of legislators or the environment in which they work. Second, such cases often require extensive investigation, tracking complex financial dealings, interviewing potential witnesses, following numerous leads, and carrying out other elaborate detective work. It is not practical for Congress to maintain a permanent investigative capacity of this kind. Hiring outside firms on a temporary basis is time-consuming and open to abuse. Third, even if Congress does take action on such offenses, legal authorities usually are obliged to do so as well. The member is thus subjected to two separate processes, technically not double jeopardy but still potentially unfair. Moreover, the double process usually takes longer, and while either is in progress, the member remains under a cloud, and legislative business may be impeded. These cases also constitute a considerable burden on the ethics committees. More than half of all the cases on which they took action during the past fifteen years were also pursued by federal or state prosecutors.[17] Finally, the supposed advantage of ethics investigations in permitting a lesser standard of proof ("clear and convincing," for example, or "substantial credible evidence") does not go far in cases of this type. The more the charges look like ordinary crimes, the greater the pressure to judge them by the standards of ordinary criminal procedure, whatever the forum of judgment.

Given the increase in proceedings involving institutional corruption, the most important reason for purging the ethics process of at least some cases involving general offenses is their effect on how the committees handle institutional offenses. The more the committees deal with offenses that are equivalent to crimes, the more their standards become like the criminal law and their proceedings like a criminal trial. The committees already face considerable pressure to emulate the legal process. The dynamic of legislative corruption exaggerates the importance of the individualist elements in offenses (such as corrupt motive), which are also the most prominent elements in criminal law. The demands for uniformity in cases, the power of precedent, and the inertia of organizational routine combine to make what is standard for general offenses standard for all offenses. In a process dominated by this individualist thinking, it is difficult to give institutional offenses their due.

Conflicts of Interest

The second kind of personal gain that can violate legislative ethics is one that is perfectly legitimate in itself but tends to subvert a member's independent judgment. This is the realm of conflict of interest, a central concept in the regulation of ethics in all professions.

A conflict of interest may be described as a set of conditions in which professional judgment of a *primary interest*, such as making decisions on the merits of legislation, tends to be unduly influenced by a *secondary interest*, such as personal financial gain.[18] The primary interest is determined by the duties of role as specified by the principles of legislative ethics. Although what these duties are may sometimes be controversial (and the duties themselves may conflict), whatever they are they should be the primary consideration in any official decision a legislator makes.

The secondary interest is not illegitimate in itself, but its relative weight in a legislative decision is problematic. The aim of rules regulating conflict of interest is not to eliminate or necessarily reduce financial gain or the other secondary interests (such as preference for family and friends or desire for prestige and power). It is rather to prevent these secondary factors from dominating, or appearing to dominate, the relevant primary interest when legislators make decisions. The rules seek to minimize the influence of secondary interests that should be irrelevant to merits of decisions about such primary interests as the welfare of a member's district or the public good.

Rules on conflict of interest usually focus on financial gain, not because it is more pernicious than other secondary interests but because its benefits are more fungible and its value more objective. Money is useful for more purposes and easier to regulate by impartial rules. It is therefore a mistake to object to the constraints on financial gain by complaining that there are other kinds of influence that can have equally bad or worse effects on a legislator's judgment. A preoccupation with financial interests should not distract us from looking for new ways to control these other kinds of influence, but just because we have not been able to do more about the other interests, it does not follow that we should do less about financial gain.

The very idea of a conflict of interest in legislative ethics appears paradoxical. To avoid a conflict of interest, it might seem, legislators must not do anything in their official role that would further their own financial interests. But as James Madison emphasized, legislators should share a "communion of interests" with their constituents. This is an important difference between legislative and executive ethics. Legislators cannot adequately represent the interests of constituents without also representing some of their own. As Senator Robert S. Kerr once said, "I represent the farmers of Oklahoma, although I have large farm interests. I represent the oil business in Oklahoma . . . and I am in the oil business. . . . They don't want to send a man here who has no community of interest with them, because he wouldn't be worth a nickel to them."[19]

The traditional way of dealing with this apparent paradox has been to particularize the financial interest in the conflict. The assumption is that the more the secondary interest is specifically tied to an individual member, the more ethically dubious the conflict is. The effect of this assumption is to limit sharply the scope of conflicts. A conflict of interest exists only when a member would personally benefit from some piece of legislation in a way or to an extent that other people would not. Speaker of the House James Blaine enunciated this principle in 1874, and it has become the standard interpretation of House rule VIII and Senate rule 12.[20] Virtually the only conduct that these rules exclude is a member's voting on a controversy about his or her own seat in the House or Senate.[21] As recently as the ninetieth Congress, most House members disapproved of any regulation of conflicts of interest (beyond some modest requirements for disclosure).[22]

Responding to criticism from the public and some of their own members, both chambers have now enacted standards that cover a broader range of conflicts of interest.[23] The practice of law (or any vocation that involves a fiduciary relationship), contracts with the government, representation of foreign governments, membership on boards, and even teaching are now either prohibited or strictly regulated. Any "outside business or professional activity for compensation" is regarded as a potential problem. The House also limits the amount of outside income that members can earn to 15 percent of their salaries.

Expanding the scope of conflict of interest marks an improvement over the narrower interpretation that limited it to voting. But the expansion and the new rules still stand too much under the influence of the individualist approach. They broaden the circumstances of conflicts by bringing more secondary interests under the control of the rules, but they still assess the seriousness of conflicts almost entirely according to whether an individual member is likely to have been improperly influenced. What this neglects are patterns of conflicts, those that create or reinforce undesirable structures of influence.[24]

Structural conflicts still implicate individuals, but they refer to institutional roles rather than individual actions. Instead of trying to define a conflict by making the secondary interest more specific, we should try to make the primary interest more specific. On a structural approach to the institution, we would pay more attention to the specific nature of a member's role in the institution. If Senator Kerr chaired a subcommittee dealing with the oil depreciation allowance, the conflict would be more serious than if he had no special institutional responsibility for legislation affecting the oil industry. His obligations as committee chair are different from his obligations as a representative of his constituents (even if as a representative he also has obligations to the public interest).

The implication of this understanding of conflict of interest is that the standards should vary more than they do now according to the actual role that a member fills in the legislature. Although potentially any member may be able to exercise influence on almost any legislative issue, some hold positions in which they can more readily and more systematically affect certain issues more than others. The more closely a member's primary interests (as committee chair, for example) relate to secondary interests (personal financial interest in activities over which the committee has jurisdiction), the more stringent the restrictions should be. In some cases, members could be required to divest themselves of any substantial holdings that may be affected by actions of the committee. (Some high-level staff members are already subject to a similar requirement.)[25] The chair and members of the banking committees, for example, should be prohibited from maintaining substantial holdings in the banking industry and similar enterprises, or at least be required to place any such holdings in a blind trust and not take any action affecting an asset placed in a blind trust until advised that the asset has been divested. Also, insofar as congressional leaders have more influence over a wider range of legislation than other members do, they should be subject to stricter standards than other members. In general, ethics committees should take into account a member's actual role in the legislature instead of assuming that all members are equal, as the House ethics committee and the special counsel seemed to do in the Wright case when they went out of their way to minimize the fact that Wright was the Speaker.

An approach that is more role-specific is particularly appropriate in a Congress that is more specialized than it once was. Although recently committee recommendations have been losing more often on the floor, committees and subcommittees still dominate the legislative process, and their members are generally more influential than others on the specific legislation that falls under their jurisdiction. The picture of a legislature in which each member is equally interested in all legislation was never very accurate. It is now seriously misleading as a guide to framing standards of ethics. As far as conflict of interest rules are concerned, this specialization moves the role of a legislator somewhat closer to that of an executive and therefore justifies adopting standards somewhat more like those of the executive branch.

Another sphere in which conflict of interest rules should focus more clearly on institutional considerations is life after Congress, the world of postemployment restrictions. One aim of these restrictions is to protect legislators' independent judgment. The special influence that a former member may have on former colleagues is one source of potential corruption here. Less recognized is the potential effect of postlegislative plans on a member's judgment while still in Congress: anticipating a job as a lobbyist, the member may begin to think like a lobbyist.[26] These dangers can be serious in individual cases, but they are even more troublesome as part of patterns of influence. It is the culture of coziness, the network of close relationships linking lobbyists and legislators, that should be of chief concern. In this culture, expectations of influence multiply independently of any actual acts of individual influence.

Lobbyists make important contributions to the political process, but their contributions are more likely to be helpful than harmful if legislators do not view lobbyists as future colleagues. In the current system, many members and even more staffers find their future in lobbying. A 1994 survey found that 138 former members were lobbying Congress—1 for every 4 members serving. About half the staff directors of the most powerful committees in the Senate and the House who have left since 1988 have become lobbyists.[27] To the extent that the career path from legislator to lobbyist comes to seem easy and attractive, the healthy division of labor between the two erodes. Stringent postemployment restrictions put obstacles in that career path and help keep the roles distinct. Some evidence from the executive branch suggests that, in their last year in government, officials are more likely to favor the industry they regulate if they take a job in that industry.[28] There is no reason to assume that legislators are any freer of such temptations.

The longer that retiring members have to wait before they can lobby without limit, the greater the difference that they (and all citizens) are likely to recognize between the duties of legislators and lobbyists. How long is long enough? Because the aim should be to affect expectations as much as behavior, the length of time is hard to determine in advance. But surely the current limit of one year is too brief to create a significant break between legislating and lobbying. Restricted for only a year, former members do not have to take up another line of work; they can think of themselves as marking time—legislative lobbyists in waiting. They do not even have to wait at all, provided that they confine themselves to lobbying the executive branch and state governments. They also remain free to advise their new colleagues about how to lobby their former colleagues.

The surest way to sustain a sharp division between legislating and lobbying would be to prohibit former members from ever engaging in lobbying. A precedent would be the lifetime ban for executive branch officials, although that ban is limited to specific matters in which the former official participated "personally and substantially."[29] Certainly, more stringent limits are warranted. It is not unreasonable to ask public officials, as part of their public service, to give up some opportunities that other citizens enjoy. They should not expect to become private citizens immediately and completely at the moment they leave public office. They should carry with them some of the responsibilities of public office as they enter private life. Even citizen-legislators should not expect to become citizens immediately upon ceasing to be legislators.

But a lifetime ban goes further than is warranted. Without having tried shorter periods first, Congress could not justify such a drastic limit on the career opportunities of legislators. It would not only be unfair to legislators but undesirable for the legislature because it might discourage some talented citizens from running for Congress. The effect on legislative recruitment may not be so damaging as is often claimed, but setting the limit should be a matter of finding the right balance between the need to control the culture of coziness and the need to encourage new talent in the legislature.[30] Congress could begin by imposing a ban on lobbying in any branch for one year and extending to two years the ban on lobbying in the legislative branch.[31] After five years Congress could review the effects of this change on lobbying and recruitment.

Some have urged that if the ideal of citizen-legislator were taken more seriously, the problem of conflict of interest would not be so serious.[32] On this view, because legislators would serve for only limited terms, any conflicts of interest they have would be much like those of at least some of the people they represent. They would disclose their interests, and voters could decide whether any conflicts were disqualifying. But disclosure is not an adequate tool for ethics enforcement (see chapter 6), and term limits themselves are likely to make the problem of postemployment conflicts worse. Under a regime of limited terms, lobbyists and the corporations and groups they represent would find members much more interested in advice about political careers beyond Congress. Many citizen-legislators would no doubt find the life of a citizen-lobbyist more attractive than that of just plain citizen.[33] If term limits were enacted, even more severe restrictions on postemployment activities than have so far been proposed would probably become necessary.

Perquisites of Office

The third type of personal gain, the perquisites that members receive, is the most closely related to institutional duties. If the gain can be shown to be a necessary part of doing the job, it is no longer merely or mainly personal gain. But if the gain is not necessary to the job, it is not only personal but also likely to be unfair because a member would have an advantage compared with other members or citizens more generally. When Senator Durenberger used a campaign contribution for his personal expenses and reserved rooms in the Capitol to promote his book, he violated rules against using public office for personal gain.[34]

But the line between what is and is not necessary for the job is not often as clear as it was in Durenberger's case. The disputes about that line, even when seemingly trivial amounts of money are involved, raise significant issues about the nature of public office in a democracy. A healthy strain of populism in American democratic culture makes citizens suspicious of any privileges their representatives grant themselves. Citizens are ready—sometimes too ready—to denounce any special advantages members receive. Because the misunderstandings that result can cause substantial damage to the institution, the regulation of perquisites is more important than the value of the personal gain they provide would suggest.

The controversy over the House Bank is the most recent and most dramatic case in point. For nearly a century the sergeant-at-arms, in charge of disbursing salaries to members, had also provided a checking service for them. At least since the early 1950s the House Bank had been in the habit of honoring overdrafts by members. In annual audit reports of the bank, the General Accounting Office had repeatedly criticized the practice, but it ceased doing so in 1977 when the reports began to be available to the public. In the late 1980s the leaders in the House took some steps to improve the bank's procedures but never followed through on the major reforms the GAO and others had recommended.

In September 1991 the GAO reported that members had written more than 8,000 bad checks on the House Bank during a one-year period beginning in July 1989. The report "generated an immediate and critical response" from the press and the public.[35] The Speaker announced that the bank would close by the end of the year and asked the ethics committee to investigate. Because some members of the committee (including the chair) had written bad checks, the committee appointed a special subcommittee to decide whether a formal investigation should be conducted.

The subcommittee found that 355 current and former members had written bad checks and that 19 current and 5 former members had overdrawn their accounts by more than a month's salary. The leadership at first tried to keep secret the names of all but the most egregious offenders but finally deferred to the demand for disclosure. The ethics committee decided that no further action was required: "For . . . those who run for elective office . . . a finding of ethical violations would be no more serious in practical terms . . . than public disclosure of their banking practices."[36] The attorney general appointed a special counsel, former judge Malcolm Wilkey, who concluded an eight-month investigation without bringing criminal indictments against any of the returning members.[37]

The verdict of public opinion was less forgiving. Nearly 85 percent of people surveyed in 1992 believed that members had committed a "very serious" or "somewhat serious" ethical violation.[38] Asked which of several recent scandals bothered them most, nearly a quarter chose the House Bank case, more than named the Iran-contra affair, Pentagon overpayment of defense contractors, or the confirmation hearings of Clarence Thomas.[39] Nearly 83 percent said that members wrote the checks because they thought they could get away with it rather than because they just made a mistake.[40] More than 60 percent said that they had a less favorable opinion of Congress as a result of the reports about check bouncing (and most respondents already held highly unfavorable opinions).[41] More than three dozen members tainted by the scandal resigned or were defeated in the next election.[42]

The public reaction was far more critical than was justified by the facts. Most people seemed to assume that the House Bank was like their own bank, which would not tolerate overdrawn accounts, and that the overdrafts at the House Bank put taxpayers at risk.[43] But the House Bank was not an ordinary bank. It did not pay interest or offer any general financial services. The deposits were not public funds, and if there had been any losses, they would have been covered entirely from the funds of other members and their guaranteed salaries.[44] Most members named in the special counsel's report had not even been aware that they did not have sufficient funds to cover the checks they wrote because the bank did not typically notify depositors when their accounts were overdrawn. As measured by the size of the personal gain or the risk to the public purse, the

House Bank problem must rank as one of the least serious scandals in congressional history.

Should one conclude then that the public outrage was the result of a massive misunderstanding fueled by distortions in the press and the simmering anti-Congress sentiment in the public? Certainly the main criticisms that people put forward were simply mistaken. But at a deeper level the criticisms reflected a legitimate concern about the failure of members to attend carefully to whether the perquisites they receive are appropriate and fair. The basis of the concern can be seen in the public response to a survey question that asked respondents which of two hypothetical candidates they would be more likely to vote for.

> Congressman Smith admitted that he bounced about 30 checks at the House Bank. He says he is sorry, but you really can't blame him for bouncing a few checks. After all, the bank was poorly run, Congressmen weren't notified when their checks bounced, and their deposits weren't even recorded on time. . . . Mr. Jones says that blaming the bank is a poor excuse. After all, it was the Congress's bank, and they made up the rules and hired the people who ran it.[45]

Nearly 80 percent of the respondents said they would be more likely to vote for Jones (only 4 percent saw no difference between the two). Jones evidently appealed to the respondents because he recognized that members have a responsibility for the collective decisions of the institution. He seemed to believe that even members who had not overdrawn their accounts should have paid more attention to how the bank was managed.

To the extent that public reaction was directed against this failure of institutional responsibility, the criticism was warranted. Not only had members (especially the leaders) neglected the problems of the bank, they also failed to monitor the growth of other perks over the years. Neither chamber had undertaken a systematic review of the whole range of privileges that members enjoy, the rationale for them, or the mode of their administration. Some members may have considered some perks substitutes for the higher salary that they (rightly) thought they deserved. Many thought of the perks as if they were privileges given to members of a club or equivalent to the benefits that mid-level corporate executives receive.[46] As a result, they were vulnerable to a general attack on privileges. Perks that could be justified as necessary to doing a good job, such as the frank, were joined with perks that had little justification, such as the bank or subsidized haircuts.

To answer legitimate charges and protect against unfair criticism, Congress should establish an advisory commission to monitor and regularly review the special privileges members enjoy. The criterion for maintaining the privilege or exemption would be simply whether it is necessary or desirable for performing the duties of office, although whether a particular perk satisfies this criterion would likely be a matter of judgment and could often be controversial. On matters that affect the personal benefits of members, a commission whose participants would not be current members would have more credibility than a committee of Congress. The commission could make recommendations to the administration committees of both chambers and serve as a quasi-board of trustees for the administration of the various services.

Such a commission would not only restrain members from granting themselves perks they do not need, but also (which is even more important in the current climate) enable them to maintain perks that they do need to do their jobs well and to receive fair compensation. Congressional pensions, for example, are much higher than those of corporate executives at the same salary levels, but the higher pensions arguably may be justified as compensating for the relatively low salaries and limitations on outside income that members face. The commission could also help ensure that the administrative operations of Congress are managed by professionals and conducted fairly. Legislative ethics is a matter of responsible management as much as individual propriety.

The significance of privileges and exemptions is greater than the debates about haircuts, restaurant bills, parking, and exercise facilities might suggest.[47] Many perks—paid foreign travel, allowances for official expenses, clerk-hire accounts, funds for staffing offices in the Capitol and in home districts—affect basic legislative tasks. Others such as the franking privilege and the rules for personal use of campaign contributions have significant effects on elections.[48] Still others have effects on the operation of other branches of government—for example, the influence that members can exercise in the appointment of friends and family to positions in executive agencies.

After many years of resistance, Congress finally acted in January 1995 to end one of its most important privileges—exemptions from many of the laws it passes regulating employment.[49] Congress is now subject to the Equal Opportunity Act, National Labor Relations Act, Equal Pay Act, Age Discrimination in Employment Act, Occupational Safety and Health Act, and several other employment-related laws. The Office of Compliance, which is to oversee the application of such laws to Congress and its staff, goes some distance toward providing the kind of semi-independent body recommended earlier for administering any congressional privileges. Such a body can more credibly take into account the special difficulties that the legislative branch faces—notably the demands of electoral politics and the burdens of public scrutiny.

Duncan Hunter, Republican House member from San Diego, acknowledged that he overdrew his account at least 160 times, but he claimed that he was in "moral balance on the issue" because he contributed monthly to a scholarship fund for needy students in his home district.[50] If legislative ethics were like personal ethics, Hunter would have a point. But in the House Bank affair as in many of the disputes about personal gain, it is the moral balance of the institution that is at risk. More generally, the principle of fairness requires, and prudence suggests, that the line between personal gain and official perks be clear and justifiable. As that line blurs, criticism—fair or not—grows, and confidence in the institution deteriorates.

The Imperatives of Political Gain

Not personal but political profit was the element of gain in the corruption with which the Keating Five were charged. The Senate ethics committee found Alan Cranston to be the most flagrant offender, and the Senate reprimanded only him. Yet Cranston received nothing for his personal use from Keating: no gifts, no honoraria, no investment opportunities, not even the vacation trips to Keating's Bahamas home that John McCain and his family enjoyed. Keating gave Cranston only political contributions, most of which went to voter registration groups instead of to his own campaign. The groups were supposed to be nonpartisan.

However, like many such groups they directed their campaigns to citizens who would be likely to vote for the party that sponsored them. A former worker for Cranston's Center for Participation in Democracy commented: "We didn't even do any registration in neighborhoods where you might find Republicans. . . . You were penalized if you had [too] many Republicans."[51] Cranston therefore benefited politically from Keating's contributions, or at least believed he would benefit.[52] Why not count this political advantage as the element of personal gain necessary to show individual corruption?

This is a tempting move, and one that is commonly made. But it should be avoided. It is a mistake to try to force political contributions into the category of personal gain. Doing so obscures the important distinction introduced in chapter 2 between personal and political gain. Because political gain is a necessary part of the legislator's job in our democratic system, it should be treated differently from personal gain in at least two respects.

First, we not only tolerate but, within limits, admire the pursuit of political gain, including campaign contributions. This remains so even if we believe that a different system of campaign finance would call forth healthier forms of political ambition than those that the current system encourages. Second, political gain that exceeds the limits should be criticized on grounds different from those used to criticize a comparable excess of personal gain. Because the pursuit of political gain is so closely connected to their official role, legislators who violate the standards governing the limits of the pursuit corrupt their office directly. A legislator who accepts an illegal campaign contribution fails, by that very act, to fulfill a duty that defines the role of a representative in a democratic system, specifically a duty to compete for office fairly. A legislator who accepts a proscribed gift does not thereby violate a defining duty in that direct way; personal gain corrupts the office only if it is connected to some further official action.

That political gain is part of the job is often forgotten in the rush of making ethics charges and proposing ethics reforms. Politicians are criticized because they are ambitious, eager to win political power for themselves. They are condemned for caring so much about campaign contributions instead of concentrating on legislative business. Certainly, we are warranted in criticizing some of the ways in which politicians pursue political gains, including the ways they seek campaign contributions. But the criticism should not be based on the assumption that the pursuit of political gain, even if it is regarded as self-interested, is wrong in itself. That is not part of what makes it corrupt, if it is corrupt. Political gain in this respect is quite different from the personal gain found in individual corruption.

Some political scientists would offer a more sophisticated rationale for treating political gain as just another form of personal gain. They begin with the methodological assumption that politicians act only on self-interest, seeking to maximize their chances of reelection or in other ways to advance their careers. They would then argue that political contributions, to the extent that they help achieve these goals, constitute personal gain no less than other goods that further the self-interest of politicians. But the trouble with this expansive concept of personal gain is that it does not help identify which contributions should be permitted and which should not. As far as personal gain is concerned, all contributions are created equal: they are all either proper or they are all corrupt. If self-interest is viewed favorably, the expansive concept would not require that any contributions be prohibited, even those involving what would normally be considered bribery or extortion. If self-interest is viewed unfavorably, the expansive concept implies that no contributions should be permitted, even those serving what would normally be regarded as the public interest. In either case the self-interest assumption does not itself supply any way to distinguish legitimate from illegitimate pursuit of political gain.

A more refined model based on principal-agent theory, which is sometimes used to analyze corruption, provides no greater help with this difficulty.[53] In this model the politician acts as an agent for constituents, the principals. Because of the costs of monitoring and other factors, the principals cannot reliably control the agent's actions. In the absence of other constraints the resulting slack allows the agents to act on their own interests contrary to the interests of the principals. The model could thus show that corruption may be partly the result of the structure of incentives in the system. Agent-principal slack creates moral hazards that permit corruption. But the model is neutral between proper and improper behavior. It is no less applicable to corrupt principals and agents than to honest ones. It would treat the Keating Five as agents of Keating who carry out his corrupt purposes. It does not explain why there should be a system that allows some kinds of incentives (contributions) and not other kinds (bribes). It might be argued that taking bribes has more socially harmful consequences than accepting campaign contributions. But if this is the claim, what is wrong is no longer the personal or political gain, but a certain kind of personal gain, and it is wrong not because it is a personal gain at all, but because of its effects on the political process.

If the presence of personal gain is not necessary to make a contribution corrupt, neither is its absence sufficient to make a contribution correct. Consider this hypothetical example. Suppose that after meeting with Mother Theresa (which the real Charles Keating in fact did), a hypothetical Keating, in a fit of saintly fervor, makes this decision: he will quietly allocate a portion of his campaign contributions and those of others he solicits for the Keating Five to begin a project to support new programs to help the poor. Suppose further that the Keating Five, respecting this act of charity by a constituent, work together behind the scenes to help establish a government-sponsored foundation, the Mother Theresa Fund, to carry out Keating's project. (To add a further touch of irony, let the fund be administered at Keating's request by Edwin Gray.) None of the senators would have gained personally, and a good cause would have been served.[54] Would there be any grounds for concern about corruption?

There surely would be some. Keating would have managed to promote a private project with the aid of public officials but without the warrant of the democratic process. The cause, however noble, was not one that citizens or their representatives had chosen through legitimate procedures. Acting on principle for higher causes can be no less corrupting than private corruption and may be even more dangerous because the perpetrators can more easily enlist the help of others in their plans. Lieutenant Colonel Oliver North would not have been able to mobilize so many supporters in the Iran-contra affair had he been acting mainly for personal gain.

Corruption in the name of the public interest has a long tradition. Perhaps its most ironic exponent was Charles T. Yerkes, the Chicago magnate who led the building of the Chicago elevated railway line and later the London underground. It is said that Yerkes bribed Illinois legislators in order to pass *anti*corruption laws.[55] In supporting these laws Yerkes did not act for personal gain (or if he did, his personal goals coincided with the public interest). Yet his conduct still constituted a kind of corruption. Neither the absence of personal gain nor its coincidence with respectable political gain makes an official's action proper.

Legislative ethics, then, should not look with suspicion on political gain itself and should set with care the limits on its proper pursuit. The same principles of independence and fairness that define standards for personal gain also help determine the limits of proper political gain. But the implications of the principles for political gain differ in important respects from those for personal gain. In the case of political gain, more of the task of protecting legislative independence from the excesses of political ambition can be left to the discipline of the political process. Another difference is that the unfair effects of excessive political gain fall more on colleagues and challengers while the costs of personal gain are borne more generally by citizens in their capacity as taxpayers. The significance of these differences can be seen by examining more closely the limits that independence and fairness impose on the pursuit of political gain.[56]

Ambition and Independence

Like most virtues, the pursuit of political gain can turn vicious when pressed too hard. Seeking reelection, members serve the interests of their district, sometimes at the expense of the interest of the nation. This is the classic tension in representative government, and it manifests itself in many ways in the contemporary Congress. The dual nature of Congress—as an assembly of local representatives and as a lawmaking institution—is the theme of a standard text on Congress.[57] It is at the root of many of the problems that have occupied the attention of political scientists in recent years, such as the divergence between constituents' views of their own representatives and their views of the institution, or the tendency of individual bargaining to produce suboptimal collective outcomes.

It is not surprising, then, that many friends of legislative ethics should wish to establish a standard that calls on members to consider the public interest, not simply their own electoral interest. The most comprehensive model code for the Senate, developed by independent consultants in the early 1980s, declares that a senator "shall strive to promote the public interest and the common good . . . [and] shall not subordinate the public interest to particular interests of any individual, party, region, class, or group."[58] Similar standards could be formulated to condemn other excesses of political gain. Without in any way insisting that all politics be moderate and centrist, one could still criticize the zealous pursuit of the agenda of single-issue groups, fanatical advocacy of extremist ideologies, and a completely unrestrained partisanship. Conduct of this kind can distort legislative judgment, and thereby contribute to institutional corruption, no less than the actions of members who accept personal gifts or campaign contributions. Such conduct therefore falls within the domain of legislative ethics.

Standards to restrain excesses of political ambition could stand as reminders of the ideals of the legislative calling, and they might justify some educational programs for members and staff that would explore ways to make the electoral and legislative process more conducive to public-spirited action. They would function as aspirational principles, like the ethical considerations in the model code of the American Bar Association. However, they should not, and probably cannot, be enforced in the way the rules that the ethics committees now administer are enforced. Principles of this sort should not be used to do more than provide general guidance because their key terms such as the "public interest" are better left to be defined by the political process than by ethics committees in the legislature.

The obligations that are appropriately imposed by the principle of independence depend in two respects on the political process. First, the ideal legislator in a representative system does not pursue the public interest exclusively (whatever it may be). Such a legislator also has an ethical obligation to constituents that must be weighed against the obligation to a broader public. To find the balance between these obligations, even to decide whether they conflict, the legislator must consider the particular political circumstances at the time. Whether, for example, single-issue representation should be condemned depends on what the cause is, how many legislators are promoting it, and what its effect is on the conduct of legislative business. Ethical obligations of these kinds are contingent on what is going on in the legislative process as a whole and may differ for different members and vary over time for all members.

Second, whether the demands of constituents actually conflict with the obligations of independence also depends on what is happening in the rest of the political process. Deciding a question on its merits may actually serve the interests of constituents. If it does and they see that it does, there is no conflict between ambition and independence. Members and constituents have a mutual interest in doing what legislative ethics requires. Voting for a trade agreement, for example, may serve one's constituents, one's career, and the public interest. The difficulty arises only when a decision on the merits would go against the interests of constituents, as when the Defense Department recommends for good reason closing a military base in a member's district. Only in such cases do the ambitious representative and his constituents have a mutual interest in ignoring what legislative ethics requires. Ambition sometimes supports and sometimes undermines independence, depending on the context (what the issue is, how it is viewed after discussion, how the interests are distributed in the district and nationally). There would be no justification therefore in trying to limit ambition in general to protect the value of independence.

The case is different with the principle of fairness. The forces of ambition run more regularly against it. Representatives and constituents more consistently have a mutual interest in exploiting legislative procedures to gain political advantage. A member can use the advantages of a committee chairmanship to advance his career at the same time that he promotes the interests of his district over those of other members. Instead of providing a partial check on the harmful effects of ambition, the electoral process reinforces the temptations to seek unfair advantages. The main check on these temptations are the other members of the legislature acting collectively; in the case of electoral fairness even that is not adequate. That is why the realization of the principle of fairness should not be left to the vagaries of the electoral process. Legislative ethics needs standards, more specific and enforceable than aspirational principles, that would protect the institutional value of fairness against the hazards of ambition.

Fairness to Colleagues, Challengers, and Congress

Representative Lee Hamilton has been among the most forceful
advocates of extending the scope of ethics beyond questions of financial propriety to issues of institutional responsibility. He has urged
us to

> try to broaden our concept of public morality and what the
> standards are for a Member of this institution. We have to
> understand that you undermine the ethical integrity of this
> Congress if you greatly distort your opponent's record, if you
> use deceptive political advertising, if you mislead your con-
> stituents with regard to your involvement in getting legisla-
> tion passed or a case resolved or a project launched, or if you
> are talking about the dirty world of politics that the rest of
> the people in Washington engage in.[59]

The examples of misconduct Hamilton cites are violations of the
principle of fairness, failing to play by the rules or failing to do one's
part for their institution. His plea for a broad conception of legislative ethics is thus very much in the spirit of the turn to institutional
ethics followed here. But his list throws together two different kinds
of abuses. The first kind, illustrated by distorting an opponent's
record, are those that directly harm members or challengers. The
second kind, distorting one's role in Congress (the "dirty world of
politics"), harms the institution, not necessarily any particular
member.

The first kind of abuse is unfair to a specific identifiable person.
Although such abuses have institutional effects, the standards for
assessing them and the procedures for controlling them can be expressed in individualist terms. For those that involve unfair criticism of colleagues or challengers, some guidelines set by the ethics
committees could help. But the normal processes of political debate—criticism by opponents, commentary by the press, statements
by constituents—probably have to be relied on, as imperfect as they
are, to keep these abuses within tolerable bounds. For abuses that
involve unfair use of office in campaigns, more formal and more
stringent rules are necessary.

Abuse of the franking privilege is perhaps the best known and most criticized unfair advantage that members have over electoral challengers. The use of the frank has increased greatly in recent years, most notably in election years.[60] The volume of mail peaks just before the sixtieth day before an election (the deadline for the final preelection mailing set in the rules). Although this privilege is no doubt abused by some members, the current rules are generally adequate, and more stringent limits could impair the franking privilege's legitimate function as an aid to communication with constituents.[61]

Less often criticized but more of a problem than the frank is the use of office staff and resources for campaign work. In the Congressional Management Foundation's *Guide* (based on extensive discussions with members and staff), "balancing congressional work with campaign or political work" is listed as the second of the "top four areas of ethical risk."[62] This balance is difficult to strike. In a session organized by the foundation in 1994, more than a hundred administrative assistants in the House discussed hypothetical cases that posed problems of managing ethics in a campaign year.[63] May a member use office staff to draft a speech that is about legislative activity but that is given during the campaign? Assuming that the district office staff can work on the campaign during their free time, what should count as free time in an office where staff routinely work overtime? Is it permissible to give a member's campaign operation a mailing list of press contacts that he or she would make available to constituents if they asked? The administrative assistants who manage members' offices and usually know the ethics rules better than members themselves found it difficult during the two-hour discussion to agree on answers to these and similar questions.

The difficulty lies partly in the ambiguity of the representative's role. Much of what members do as legislators is inseparable from what they talk about in the campaign. Running for reelection is part of the job. As some courts have argued, "it simply is impossible to draw and enforce a perfect line between the official and political business of Members of Congress."[64] New York state's highest court has held that a leader of the state Senate could use public funds to hire aides whose principal duties consisted of working on the reelection campaigns of several of his colleagues.[65] It is furthermore desirable for the campaign staff to have some appreciation of what legislative work demands and for the office staff to have some understanding of what the campaign requires.

Another reason that it is difficult to agree on where the line between political and legislative work should be drawn is that the rationale for the rules is often misunderstood. The rationale most commonly given treats the abuse more like a case of improper personal gain. The *House Ethics Manual*, for example, suggests that the rules derive in large part from the provision in the criminal code that requires that "official funds are to be used only for the purposes for which appropriated."[66] In the New York case the charge against the state Senate minority leader was theft of state property.[67] During the Congressional Management Foundation session, all the arguments against using official resources in campaigns took a similar form: taxpayers should not have to pay for a member's campaign, and using one's staff for one's campaign is like stealing from the government. Surprisingly, no one raised what should be the fundamental objection to this practice: that it gives incumbents an unfair advantage in the electoral process. This unfairness surely is at least as important a reason for not appropriating public funds for electoral expenses as the standard rationale of personal gain.[68]

If mixing official and campaign resources is understood as a violation of fairness to challengers, one can appreciate why the electoral process does not provide an adequate check on the practice. It is true that the press will usually expose such abuses when it finds them, and challengers can use the exposés in their campaigns against incumbents. But these abuses are difficult to discover: reporters or challengers would have to gain more than casual access to information about the internal operations of a members' office and campaign organization. Furthermore, because all members potentially gain from flexible interpretations of the rule, they have little incentive to criticize each other or to favor more stringent standards. The ethics committees have investigated only six violations of this rule since 1970, and imposed sanctions on no member (though one, Andrew Hinshaw, was convicted on criminal charges in 1976).[69] Because all members and their staffs have to make judgment calls on the use of official resources during every campaign, the number of actual violations is probably much higher.

The fairness principle would be better served if rules on mixing official and campaign resources were more stringent and enforcement more independent. Because of the very difficulty of distinguishing the legislative from the electoral duties of a member, the separation between the staff and operations of each should be strict. For example, Congress should consider prohibiting any office staff from working in their member's campaign, even if "on leave." Rules similar to postemployment regulations could discourage former staff from joining the campaign or former campaign workers from joining the staff. Official information such as mailing lists should not be provided to the campaign operation unless it is actually provided to the public at the same time. Additional regulations may also be necessary to ensure that the management of the campaign is appropriately accountable. Rules on these matters should be enforced by the Federal Elections Commission or another independent body.

The second kind of unfairness, that directed against the institution rather than individual colleagues or challengers, is still more difficult to identify and control. It is especially insidious because it has no obvious victim. There is no one who can stand up and complain, no one to whose defense citizens can come. The abuse is well illustrated by members who "run for Congress by running against Congress." As one political scientist observed: "The beauty of the strategy" is that "everybody can use it . . . and nobody will be called to account by those under attack. . . . In the short run everybody plays and nearly everybody wins. . . . Yet the institution bleeds from 435 separate cuts. In the long run, therefore, somebody may lose."[70]

The standards and procedures for dealing with this kind of abuse must be institutional in nature. Because individuals cannot be relied on to come forward to defend the institution as they might defend themselves, standards must be established and incentives provided to discourage conduct that is unfair to Congress. It is probably not possible to formulate rules or establish penalties that would directly prohibit much of this kind of behavior. Any attempt to do so runs the risk of suppressing worthy criticism of the institutions, inhibiting political debate, and even infringing the right of free speech.

Nevertheless, two kinds of measures could help discourage Congress bashing. First, the leaders in both chambers and party caucuses could be more aggressive in defending the institution against such charges. They, or perhaps even the ethics committees, could single out for public recognition members (in either party) who consistently defend the institution under difficult political conditions or in other ways support the institution in face of pressure to abuse it. The leaders could let it be known that such institutional loyalty is likely to affect discretionary committee assignments.

Procedural reforms could also eliminate some conduct unfair to the institution. The Senate could, for example, restrict the use of "holds," an informal practice (sometimes called a "silent filibuster") that permits an individual member to block legislative action on some amendment or bill without taking personal responsibility for the outcome.[71] Using holds is not unfair to one's colleagues because they can and do use them too. The victim of the practice is the institution.

Holds and other procedural devices that permit individual members to obstruct collective action reinforce the excessive individualism in which members do not do their share to support the institution. Abolishing or limiting such devices (perhaps even the not-so-silent filibuster) would improve institutional fairness not only by eliminating some actual abuses but also by encouraging changes in the attitudes of members and their staff. It could help sustain an institutional culture in which more members take more responsibility for the well-being of Congress as a whole. The gains of office would then come to include not only the personal and political advantage of individuals but also the public good of the institution.

Services of Office

Constituent service. To me, it's very important . . . if I think there is a cause where the government has mistreated a constituent, I'm going to do all I can, within the bounds of ethical conduct, to see that that government responds to this constituent.

In this opening statement to the Senate ethics committee during the hearings in the case of the Keating Five, Senator Dennis DeConcini portrayed the help he gave Charles Keating as an honorable part of the calling of a legislative representative.[1] It was, he suggested, just an instance of constituent service, the customary practice of "providing help to individuals, groups, and localities in coping with the federal government."[2] Such help includes services ranging from aid with immigration problems to assistance in applying for governmental grants. The beneficiaries are not only individuals but increasingly corporations, foundations, hospitals, universities, professional associations, and other organizations.

Unmentioned in the Constitution, unimagined by the Founders, and until recently unanalyzed by journalists, constituent service has become a major part of the job of most members of Congress. DeConcini was not alone in his exaltation of the practice. Some of the senator's colleagues, including members of the ethics committee, did not even acknowledge the "bounds of ethical conduct" to which DeConcini alluded. They seemed to assume that if what a member does is constituent service and breaks no law, it is always proper. If the service does not involve bribery, extortion, or an illegal campaign contribution, it is not only acceptable but admirable.[3] For its final report, the committee removed much of the discussion that the special counsel had included on limits on intervention.[4] Neither the House nor the Senate committee has ever applied sanctions against a member simply for intervening to help a constituent, no matter how questionable the merits or the manner of the intervention. The committees have acted only if they could find some kind of improper connection, as in a bribe, or a failure to disclose an improper connection.[5]

Yet the services that members provide and the way they provide them can corrupt the political process independently of any personal or political gains that members may receive. In personal ethics it may be better to give than to receive, but in legislative ethics the favors that members give are as fraught with ethical peril as the gains they receive. This chapter confronts that peril and explores the bounds of ethical conduct in the services that members provide. The main focus is on constituent service and the institutional corruption that results when that service is provided improperly. But to appreciate the distinctive nature of the institutional corruption, some attention must first be given to the individual corruption that the services of office can create.

Undeserved Service

In instances of individual corruption, what makes service improper is that it is not deserved: it violates general standards of justice as distinct from standards specific to the institution. The most obvious kind of violation would be helping a constituent evade the law. Such violations are relatively rare in Congress because most members are not inclined to help criminals and the few who might be tempted know that their complicity is likely to be discovered. In any case, the opportunities for a lone legislator to help a citizen evade the law are also fewer than those of judges and some administrative officials.

Nevertheless, some members have knowingly served the criminal purposes of their constituents, usually in return for a bribe or a contribution. In some instances what the constituent sought was itself wrong, independently of the bribe or contribution. One of the most egregious cases featured John Dowdy, who represented the second district of Texas, served on the House Judiciary Committee, and chaired the Subcommittee on Investigations of the Committee on the District of Columbia. During the 1960s he attempted to help the owner of the Monarch Construction Company escape prosecution for illegal sales and financing practices in the home improvement business. According to the federal court, "there was little question that Monarch and some of its principals had engaged in wholesale violations of the law." Evidently aware of the company's illegal practices, Dowdy still worked actively on the behalf of its owner. He expressed his personal interest in the case to officials in the Justice Department and the Federal Housing Administration, and also met with a prosecutor and the owner's attorney.[6]

Had Dowdy stopped there, his intervention would have been a pure case of individual corruption (a corrupt connection between personal gain and illegal service). The service was wrong because of its purpose, not because of its method. The officials at Justice and the FHA testified that at their meetings Dowdy asked nothing illegal or improper in itself. Had his constituent been a law-abiding citizen, the constituent service would have been perfectly legitimate. But he went further, and provided service that no member should provide for any constituent, even one with a just cause. He tried to arrange for Monarch's owner to testify before his subcommittee in a scheme to secure immunity, and he gave the owner internal documents he had subpoenaed from two federal agencies that were investigating the company.[7]

Dowdy did not succeed in protecting Monarch's owner from prosecution, but he nearly escaped prosecution himself. He argued that his activities had been "legislative acts" protected by the speech and debate clause of the Constitution.[8] On precisely this ground the appeals court reversed his convictions on all the counts involving the "service" he provided for Monarch. The court let stand the convictions for perjury, and he eventually served six months in prison. Thus Dowdy was convicted not for what he did for Monarch, not even for what he got from Monarch, but for lying about both.

The House ethics committee never took up the case. They stood aside while the legal process ran its course—as if to declare that what mattered was only the individual, not the institutional, corruption. After Dowdy was convicted the committee proposed a resolution that would have prohibited a member who is convicted of a serious crime (carrying a potential sentence of two or more years) from participating in committee business or House votes. But Dowdy promised he would not vote while appealing his conviction, and the House never acted on the committee's resolution.[9]

The case throws into sharp relief the difference between the two ways that service can be corrupt. Dowdy served an unjust cause according to general standards of the criminal law, and he also served it improperly according to the specific standards of legislative and administrative procedure. Because the cause was so clearly wrong, it can be more easily distinguished from the methods by which he tried to further it, some of which were wrong and some of which were not. The case also shows how the response of authorities to the two kinds of corruption can interact, in effect canceling out each other. The ethics committee evidently assumed that individual corruption is the more reprehensible and deferred to the courts, which seemed better qualified to decide questions of criminal responsibility. But the courts declined to probe Dowdy's conduct because they saw it as part of his institutional role. Judgment about his misconduct fell between two authorities.

Dowdy, it is true, did not completely escape. But that only underscores the point that almost any conduct that can be somehow associated with constituent service enjoys remarkable protection. Even in a case of individual corruption as flagrant as his, the courts struggled and ultimately failed to find a material basis on which to convict him for helping a constituent evade the law. One implication (to which chapter 6 returns) is that the criminal process is not well suited to dealing with corruption, whether individual or institutional, when it is closely associated with legislative duties. Another implication (pursued later in this chapter) is that the standards for judging individual and institutional corruption in constituent service should be clearly differentiated. Like the rules of war, which distinguish the justice of a cause from the justice of the means of fighting it, Congress needs rules to judge not only the merits of a constituent's case but also the methods a member may use to pursue it.[10]

Favoritism

Providing services can also violate general standards of justice through favoritism. Perfectly proper services may become improper if they are provided for some constituents but not for others who have equally compelling claims. Like any practice that reflects special pleading (for example, transition rules in tax legislation, or earmarking of grants for local projects), such services must overcome the presumption that they are unfair.

Ethics committees are not inclined to consider a service itself, no matter how zealous or exceptional, as evidence of favoritism. One of the charges of which the House committee exonerated Speaker Wright was providing "special favors or privileges" for Neptune Oil Company.[11] As a result of provisions of the peace treaty between Egypt and Israel, Neptune stood to lose future profits and most of its past investments in the Sinai. Egypt had resisted Neptune's claims, and the United States was trying to remain strictly neutral in the dispute. The principal owner of Neptune, a constituent whom Wright had known for many years, asked him to help. Wright arranged for him to meet with the U.S. ambassador at large for Egyptian-Israeli treaty negotiations and the Egyptian prime minister in Cairo. Wright also phoned and wrote to the secretary of state, the Egyptian ambassador to the United States and President Anwar Sadat. Neptune's attorney wrote to the State Department: "Wright will not let up on this—if the response to [his letter to the secretary] is negative, there will be several more go-arounds."[12]

Although Neptune did not completely succeed in its aims, the company did recoup its investment. Wright's efforts were extraordinary: he himself said he went "further than I do on some things."[13] Perhaps it is difficult to believe that members would do for any constituent what Wright did for Neptune's owner, but since members can almost always contend that the constituent's claim is special, it is usually difficult to establish favoritism just by pointing to unusual efforts. Although critics may believe that members favor the prominent and wealthy in their districts, in the absence of evidence of payoffs and quid pro quos they can rarely prove it.

The difficulty of proving favoritism in constituent service is further illustrated by the Senate ethics committee's treatment of one of the charges brought against Alfonse D'Amato in 1989. The charge, that he improperly intervened on behalf of Unisys, a defense contractor in his district, was the only one of the sixteen on which the committee, after a nineteen-month investigation, found grounds to sanction D'Amato.[14] They "rebuked" the senator for "failing to establish appropriate standards for the operation of his office." The offense was institutional, but it was treated so lightly that D'Amato could declare "the Senate Ethics Committee has found that I did nothing wrong."[15] The committee was frustrated in its efforts to probe some of the charges of individual corruption because about half the witnesses it subpoenaed invoked their Fifth Amendment privilege and declined to testify.

What prompted the committee's rebuke was not the senator's constituent service on behalf of Unisys. He had written several letters to executive branch officials, but they were "ordinary and routine."[16] He was rebuked because he neglected to prevent his brother, Armand, from using his office to lobby the Navy Department. A Unisys executive had hired Armand to help the company win multimillion dollar contracts for antimissile radar systems. Rather than lobbying too aggressively, Armand apparently did not do much at all. He was convicted of mail fraud for billing Unisys for services he never performed (the conviction was reversed on appeal).[17] The Unisys executive (though apparently not others in the company) thought he was buying access to the senator, and Armand did persuade the staff to write two letters of support for Unisys under the senator's signature.[18] Although nothing in the letters themselves was improper, the access that Armand enjoyed was unusual and could be construed as favoritism.

The senator denied knowing anything about the letters or his brother's use of his office for lobbying. During the senator's testimony before the ethics committee in secret session, fellow Republican Senator Warren Rudman, the vicechair, expressed doubts about his denial: "it is incomprehensible to me that a brother of a United States Senator, who is a lawyer and who is now representing a defense contractor, would come in and discuss, or do anything with relation to a defense contract, with the administrative assistant, without the senator hearing about it."[19] In the end, however, the ethics committee evidently accepted the senator's denial because it charged him only with negligence, not with knowingly providing favors to his brother or to Unisys.

Although fewer than 10 percent of citizens ever benefit from constituent service, members see it as one of their most important contributions to democracy.[20] The culture of Congress is so strongly imbued with the ideal of serving all constituents equally that members find it difficult to acknowledge any favoritism in such service. They believe, with evident sincerity, that they serve all equally. When it comes to constituent service, members preach an egalitarianism that would make Jean Jacques Rousseau proud. DeConcini expressed the prevailing ideology: "And when a constituent . . . walks into my office, we have no discrimination, whether they're Republican, Democrat, liberal, conservative, rich, poor . . . even if they're not registered voters . . . we listen to them."[21]

Given this belief, members are inclined to assume that in serving constituents, the worst offense—indeed, the only serious offense apart from bribery and extortion—is favoritism. As several members emphasized during the Keating Five hearings, it would be wrong (and perhaps evidence of corruption) for members to favor big contributors.[22] But if members can show that they do not play favorites, they can claim that they are simply doing their duty. No further questions can be raised.

That is why during the hearings of the Keating Five, members went to such great lengths to show that what they did for Keating they would do for any constituent. They seemed to accept this question as a reasonable standard: "Does the member typically intervene in this way for other constituents?" DeConcini made it a major part of his defense to show that his office responds to virtually any constituent who asks for help. He brandished a list of 75,000 constituents who could be called to testify, though to everyone's relief he settled for inviting only three. They were well chosen: a social worker for Hispanics, a drug-busting sheriff, and a handicapped veteran.[23]

Despite this heroic defense, the evidence still strongly suggested that what the senators provided to Keating was not typical constituent service. Five senators meeting in private with regulators on a specific case *is* unusual. During the entire hearings, no one could cite a sufficiently close precedent. Lobbying the Defense Department to support Apache helicopters, asking the Customs Service for an exception to trade restrictions, questioning the Justice Department about a potential indictment of a shipyard company—these instances, and all the others paraded before the committee, lacked some critical feature of the Keating Five case.[24] None involved pressure on independent regulators to give special treatment to a particular company in a quasi-adjudicatory process, and in none did the intervention continue after the member could reasonably have been expected to know that company's intentions were questionable, if not illegal.

If our only concern were the favoritism found in individual corruption, we would condemn the Keating Five only for denying this kind of zealous service to other constituents. But if we keep in mind the harms of institutional corruption, we will look beyond the justice of the constituent's cause and consider the methods that the member uses to pursue it. Instead of asking whether a member would provide this service equally for any constituent, we should ask whether the service should be provided in this way at all. Some ways of providing service damage the institution, either as a result of the single act of an individual or the collective consequences of many individual acts. In either case, legislative ethics must attend to the institutional dimensions of constituent service.

Institutional Consequences of Constituent Service

Members devote more time and allocate more resources to constituent service than their predecessors did and evidently gain more electoral advantage from it.[25] "The nice thing about case work is that it is mostly profit; one makes many more friends than enemies."[26] Serving constituents can also serve the public interest. It can provide a check on the abuse of power by executive agencies in individual cases. In effect, it fulfills the role of an ombudsman in some other political systems. If administrators are harassing a constituent, as some of the senators said they suspected in the Keating Five case, members may be obligated to intervene not only to protect the constituent but also to correct administrative procedures.

Furthermore, members can use what they learn in dealing with individual cases to carry out more effectively their responsibilities for oversight and legislation. Individual casework can help identify systematic problems in an administrative agency that require reform or systematic failure in government that calls for legislation. Relying on constituents to call attention to administrative abuses— what has been called "fire-alarm oversight"—is more common and probably more efficient than direct and continuing monitoring by Congress—"police patrol oversight."[27]

Much of the constituent service that members perform serves the public interest as well as the constituents' interests. No doubt many of the causes that members pursue are worthy, and many citizens would otherwise be denied justice from the government. One of the most dramatic examples is the case in which a medicare beneficiary was refused payments for his hospital stay because government records listed him as deceased. Only after repeated appeals by Congressman Gary Ackerman's office, culminating in a threat to bring the constituent to the insurance office in the flesh, did the government's agent agree to pay the bill.[28]

Even when administrators are acting in good faith to carry out a congressional mandate, members may still be justified in trying to correct unintended injustices that legislation may have produced. After Congress instructed the Education Department to clamp down on schools that had high default rates on student loans, many members continued to intervene to prevent schools in their districts from losing their eligibility. Senator Carl Levin of Michigan went to the defense of Jordan College, a nonaccredited institution with a default rate greater than the standard the Department had set. He succeeded saving it by arguing that it "serves 2,000 mostly poor minority students."[29]

As valuable as constituent service is in our democratic process, it can damage that process if unrestrained. The damage may result from the improper actions of an individual member (as when Jim Wright attempted to press a constituent's cause by threatening to expose the sexual orientation of an administrator). But even if the casework done by an individual member seems perfectly proper, the collective consequences of members' individual acts may not be salutary for the democratic process. This potential discrepancy between individual and collective consequences creates the need for institutional rules to prohibit conduct that individual ethics would permit. To lessen the risk of institutional harm, the ethical standards for individual conduct have to be adjusted. Once the standards are in place, conduct that otherwise would have been acceptable becomes unethical.

What are the risks of institutional harm that such standards should seek to reduce? First, as constituent service becomes such a prominent part of the job, legislative duties suffer. A growing proportion of members' staffs now spend almost all their time on casework. More than 40 percent of the House personal staff and 30 percent of the Senate personal staff work in the districts, where the main task is constituent service.[30] Even if the number of staff and the resources for legislative work have also increased, more members spend more time in their districts than before.[31] Moreover, voters tend to pay more attention to personalized service than to legislative records; as a result, political responsibility for legislation deteriorates.

Another danger is that by concentrating on righting wrongs against individual citizens, constituent service can favor particular remedies over general reforms. Ad hoc and local solutions do not necessarily produce changes in procedures or policies that benefit the public as a whole. In addition, to the extent that incumbents gain electoral advantage through constituent service, new members who could bring fresh policy views or offer new criticisms of government performance are less likely to make their way into the legislature.

Because constituent service is in these ways a mixed democratic blessing, we should be wary of the laissez faire attitude toward it that prevails in both chambers. Letting each member decide what is appropriate is not likely to produce the optimal institutional result. Any legislator who cut back on casework to devote more time to legislation would be at a competitive disadvantage. So would any member who declined to pursue constituents' cases as zealously as his colleagues. In interviews some members expressed reservations about some of the tactics they had used to pressure administrators but said that if they refused to use them, they would gain a reputation for being less aggressive than their colleagues.

Individual discretion also frustrates the institutional coordination necessary to control some of the harmful effects of casework. It is neither necessary nor desirable for all members to devote themselves all the time to programmatic work in the legislature. Some may attend to particular remedies while others work on general reforms. The harm to avoid is an institutional imbalance: too many members devoting too much time to constituent service. Similarly, there are times when zealous intervention is called for, perhaps even times when five senators should meet with regulators to plead a constituent's case. The danger is that some members would employ individual remedies in matters where they are not appropriate, and other members might decline to use them where they are appropriate.

These considerations point to the need for institutional regulation of constituent service. What ethics requires any member to do depends in part on what other members are doing. Ideally, the House and the Senate would establish a congressional office for casework, a professionally staffed agency, similar in status to the Office of the Legislative Counsel or the Congressional Research Service, that would handle all complaints brought by constituents. Some members have proposed similar reforms. One of the earliest and still one of the most constructive is Representative Henry Reuss's proposal for a congressional ombudsman, appointed by Congress and armed with subpoena powers, who would investigate complaints from constituents who claimed they had been unfairly penalized, denied a benefit they are due, or subjected to unfair proceedings.[32]

In the procedures outlined in most of these proposals, constituents would still bring problems first to members, and members would then ask the casework office to investigate the complaint and report back on the action taken. In this way members would keep in touch with their constituents and could still earn their good will for providing the service. Institutionalizing the process of investigating complaints and correcting abuses would make constituent service both more efficient and more ethical. Similar cases would more likely be treated similarly, particular remedies more likely lead to general reforms, and institutional imbalances more likely come to the attention of members and the public so that they could be corrected. Ethics committees would be better informed when they set standards for intervention and better positioned to enforce whatever standards they set.

Despite these clear advantages, the proposals have never won much support in Congress. Members are reluctant to give up any part of constituent service because they see it as a primary duty, because they fear the loss of some electoral advantage, or because they simply enjoy it. If, as some political scientists suggest, casework gives incumbents an advantage over challengers, members are not likely on their own to delegate part of the job to any agency, even one under their control.[33] Only pressure from challengers, the press, and the public is likely to cause Congress to consider such a change.

Even if Congress does not establish an office of casework or a congressional ombudsman, members might still come to see some advantage in adopting stronger standards for regulating constituent service, particularly interventions in administrative proceedings. Members could reasonably believe that without such standards some of their colleagues will abuse their discretion, creating greater public suspicion about intervention and deterring other members from performing legitimate constituent service.[34] The unregulated misconduct of a few could in this way have a chilling effect on the many. This effect results not from disciplining members for improper intervention (as some suggested during the Keating Five hearings[35]), but rather from failing to accept an institutional responsibility for regulating intervention.

Limitations of Legal Standards

In the American democratic system, legislators have a duty to oversee the decisions of administrators. Courts have repeatedly affirmed the constitutional importance of legislative oversight, and members individually and collectively routinely exercise it. Yet the courts have not taken a laissez faire attitude toward congressional intervention in the proceedings of administrative agencies. Beginning with *Pillsbury* v. *Federal Trade Commission*, courts have placed some limits on intervention, even by members acting within the authority of oversight committees. In *Pillsbury* a federal appeals court invalidated a Federal Trade Commission divestiture order against the Pillsbury company because during subcommittee hearings several senators had criticized the chair of the commission and his staff for taking a position favorable to the company in the preliminary version of the order. Even if the pressure had not actually influenced the commission, the appearance that it had was enough to deny Pillsbury due process. The court stressed that it was adopting this standard mainly because the proceeding was quasi-judicial or adjudicatory (involving a decision in a pending case). A more permissive standard, the court implied, might apply in quasi-legislative or rulemaking proceedings (those involving standards that apply to types of cases).[36]

Five years later, the District of Columbia Circuit Court made the distinction between adjudicatory and rulemaking proceedings explicit by providing a more permissive standard for rulemaking. An agency decision is invalid only if "considerations that Congress could not have intended to make relevant" actually influence the decision.[37] The consideration in this case was the threat by an appropriations subcommittee chair to withhold funds for the District's subway system unless the secretary of transportation reversed his opposition to a new bridge across the Potomac.

But the legal limits on intervention have turned out to be less potent than they seemed at first.[38] The decision to impose stricter standards on quasi-judicial proceedings makes sense, but the consequence, intended or not, has been that standards for other kinds of proceedings have been so weakened that they permit virtually any intervention.[39] The most significant shortcoming of these decisions or standards is that none applies directly to members of Congress. If a court finds that a standard is violated, it simply invalidates the result of the administrative proceeding and usually gives the agency an opportunity to try the case again. The member whose intervention caused the problem is not subject to any sanction, and indeed is not even a party to the legal action. The law even makes strategic intervention possible: a member could intervene in favor of a decision to which he is actually opposed in the hope that the intervention itself would cause a court to invalidate the decision.

Some judges have suggested that members might hold themselves to higher standards than the courts have been willing to impose. In one case in which a court declined to invalidate an agency decision that several members had sought to influence, the court nevertheless observed that the kind of conduct in which the members engaged was "improper and should be discouraged."[40] Still, the only substantial legal constraint that applies directly to members is the Sunshine Act's prohibition against ex parte communications.[41] Members must put on the public record any statement they make to a decisionmaker in a formal agency proceeding (which includes some rulemaking proceedings).

Although most of the law on intervention does not directly control the conduct of members, court decisions provide some guidance for standards that ethics committees could adopt. Standards could at minimum discourage appeals to irrelevant considerations or extraneous factors that Congress did not intend to affect the implementation of the legislation.[42] Greater restraints could be placed on chairs and members of a committee who could influence appropriations for an agency.[43] Standards could distinguish between requests that administrators expedite a case, which should be permitted, and requests that they decide it in one way rather than another, which should be restricted.[44] Interventions that create an appearance of impropriety could be prohibited even in cases in which the agency decisionmaker has not actually been influenced by the pressure from members.[45]

Although courts have applied some of these principles to quasi-judicial proceedings, ethics committees could extend them to other kinds. The committees should not limit their concern to rights of individuals in particular cases; they should also be concerned about the integrity of the decisionmaking process, because the public has an interest in substantive and fair deliberation. The principles of legislative ethics also support this broader application of the principles.

Limitations of Ethical Standards

When the Senate ethics committee concluded its report on the Keating Five, it noted that the Senate had no written rules specifically governing "contact or intervention with federal executive or independent regulatory agency officials on the behalf of constituents." The committee recommended that the Senate establish some. The lack of rules may have been one reason the committee did not impose sanctions on the senators for the methods they used to advocate Keating's cause. If so, it was a dubious excuse. As the special counsel showed and the committee itself acknowledged, some guidelines already existed, and the Senate's general rules could be interpreted as prohibiting the more flagrant forms of improper intervention.[46]

Nevertheless, the committee was right to urge the Senate to develop better standards for intervention, and what the task force produced and the Senate adopted in the next session of Congress represented a modest improvement.[47] For the first time, a Senate rule provided specific guidance on what members may do in responding to petitions for assistance from constituents. Following an advisory opinion that the House ethics committee had issued in 1970, the Senate rule authorized members to request information or a status report, urge prompt consideration, arrange for interviews or appointments, express judgments, and call for reconsideration of an administration response.

It is striking, however, that almost all of the Senate rule is devoted to stating what members may do. It begins by asserting their right to intervene and ends by reaffirming their authority to perform their legislative responsibilities. The only conduct specifically proscribed or even deemed questionable is providing assistance on the basis of contributions or services.[48] This prohibition is neither strong nor new: it essentially restates the law against bribery and conflict of interest. It says nothing about improper means independent of corrupt connections. Critics rightly pointed out that the rule fails to address a senator's responsibility to ensure that "the methods of intervening . . . are not themselves so inherently damaging . . . that they offset any public benefit that might be gained."[49] In response, the majority leader could only point to the protection afforded by the "larger system of ethical restraints and enforcement in the Senate." It was, of course, the inadequacy of that system that had led the ethics committee to urge a new rule in the first place.

The Senate paid the House a rare compliment by adopting part of one of its rules, and in fact the House committee's guidance still remains superior to anything the Senate has devised. The House advisory opinion includes some general prohibitions against favoritism that the Senate rule ignores and restricts somewhat more the grounds on which members may ask for reconsideration of an administrative decision. Also, the *House Ethics Manual* devotes a whole chapter to "Casework Considerations."[50]

Nevertheless, the advisory opinion advises against very little and prohibits even less. It is the staff authors of the *Ethics Manual* who on their own added the most substantial suggestions: members should not endorse the factual claims of constituents without checking them and should assure an agency that they are only seeking a result consistent with regulations and the law.[51] There is as yet no authority in House or committee rules for much of the rest of the sensible discussion of casework in the *Manual*, such as the caution against assisting nonconstituents, guidance on helping constituents with government grants, and advice on recommending candidates for government positions.

In the case of Speaker Wright the House's standards faced their greatest challenge, and they did not fare well. When the special counsel concluded that Wright's intervention with the Bank Board violated House rules, he rested his conclusion on the very broad language of the rule requiring conduct that reflects "creditably on the House" and on a relaxed interpretation of "undue influence" in the advisory opinion.[52] As a result, the ethics committee found it easier to dismiss the special counsel's conclusion and reaffirm its faith in casework. Wright may have been "intemperate," the committee conceded, but it insisted he was just doing his job as a representative of his constituents.

A closer look at Wright's interventions, however, justifies doubting whether this kind of conduct should be part of a representative's job. In one instance Wright asked Bank Board Chair Edwin Gray to replace the board's special representative, who had refused to restructure $200 million in loans to a Dallas-based real estate investor.[53] Until Gray agreed to appoint a new representative and the replacement also agreed to the restructuring, Wright put a hold on a recapitalization bill that the board desperately needed to fund the continuing bailout of the savings and loans. In another incident Wright pressured Gray into meeting with a major Democratic party contributor who, because of some legally questionable transactions, had been prohibited from operating any government insured association.[54] Gray testified that he would not have agreed to the meeting, which was against the board's rules, or to the appointment of a special counsel to examine the case, but for Wright's influence on the recapitalization bill.

In the most disturbing incident, Wright complained to Gray about H. Joe Selby, a regional director of the board who "had the reputation of being a tough regulator . . . and was feared and distrusted by many in the thrift industry."[55] According to Gray, Wright said

> that he understood that Selby was a homosexual. And he
> understood from people that he believed and trusted [that]
> Selby had established a ring of homosexual lawyers in
> Texas at various law firms, and that in order for people to

deal with the Federal Home Loan Bank supervision people, they would have to deal with this ring of homosexual lawyers. . . . He said, "Isn't there anything you can do to get rid of Selby or ask him to leave or something?"[56]

This time Gray refused to give in. Wright did not get his way, but surely his request to get rid of Selby goes beyond the limits of constituent service. If Gray's description of the incident is accurate, as the special counsel believed, it is not difficult to accept counsel's conclusion that Wright's action "greatly exceeded the bounds of proper congressional conduct."

These incidents reveal a form of institutional corruption that the committee declined to pursue. They further suggest the need for some standards less permissive than those assumed by the committee. The standard that the committee proposed for sustaining a charge of improper intervention was undue influence as shown by "probative evidence that a reprisal or threat to agency officials was made."[57] Inferences from circumstance or the technique and personality of the legislator, the committee said, should not be the basis of any such finding. Instead of balancing the "constant tension between the . . . desires of legislators . . . and the actions of agencies," the committee resolved it in favor of the legislators.

Toward Stronger Standards

The principles of legislative ethics must acknowledge the critical value that vigorous intervention represents in our political system. But they also suggest that there should be a better balance between the actions of legislators and administrators than current standards imply. If constituent service were performed in part by a congressional ombudsman, the standards could be more readily modified to preserve the optimal balance. But even without such an office, the standards should enable members to promote the legitimate claims of constituents while respecting the integrity of legislative and administrative institutions.

Intervening on the Merits

The principle of independence prescribing that legislators act on relevant reasons provides a standard that would regulate intervention. It requires that the intervention be appropriate to the substantive merits of the constituent's case. Such a standard would not prohibit members from acting aggressively on behalf of constituents, but it would direct them to consider the substance of constituents' claims in deciding whether and how to intervene. It would proscribe practices that evidently prevailed in Senator Cranston's office. According to his aide, Carolyn Jordan, "unless you have a complete kook . . . the number one rule of this game is you never kiss a constituent off. That's the rule in our office. And you never tell them no unless they're asking you to do something that is just so far from the beaten path."[58] Jordan also testified that she was never asked and never did investigate the validity of Keating's claims and evidently did not usually do so in other cases.

Members may have a duty to support meritorious claims, but they should not press claims that they have, or should have, reason to believe are without merit. Furthermore, the higher the stakes, the greater the responsibility to investigate the merits of a claim. By the same token, the stronger the claim appears, the more vigorous the intervention may be. To promote claims without any regard to their merits is to promote a policymaking process moved more by considerations of power than purpose.

The standard does not make impossible demands on members. It does not require members to investigate claims fully and try to adjudicate them. It only requires what Senator Paul Douglas long ago urged his colleagues to do: members "should not immediately conclude that the constituent is always right and the administrator is always wrong, but as far as possible should try to find out the merits of each case and only make such representations as the situation permits."[59]

The Keating Five case again illustrates how such a standard might be applied. Keating's claim, it is now known and could have been known then, lacked merit. John Glenn and John McCain made some effort to find out about the case before they went to the meetings with Gray and the regulators. Giving the senators the benefit of the doubt, one might say that, under the pressure of time, they took all the steps one could reasonably expect before they intervened with the regulators. The senators did, after all, have some evidence at the time (a statement from the firm of Arthur Young and a letter from Alan Greenspan, former chair of the President's Council of Economic Advisers) that appeared to lend credibility to Keating's complaints.

But once the senators heard about the regulators' intention to make a criminal referral, they had adequate notice that Keating's claims were questionable. Although criminal referrals are not unusual and do not constitute clear evidence of wrongdoing, a conscientious senator (indeed, even a prudent one) would have looked more closely into the merits of Keating's case before continuing to assist him. The two who continued to pursue his case, DeConcini and Cranston, did not. This is partly why their conduct should be criticized more severely, as the special counsel suggested. But the ethics committee, lacking a specific standard of the kind proposed here, was more equivocal in its criticism.

A satisfactory standard would require not only that members consider relevant reasons in deciding whether to intervene, but also that action on any matter be based solely on the merits. This aspect of the standard would include all of the misconduct covered by current prohibitions against undue influence, such as personal threats, arbitrary reprisals, and other considerations, that should not be germane to the administrative decision. "Relevant reasons" or "merits" provides a more satisfactory basis for those prohibitions and also extends the scope of the standard to conduct that is not now covered.

"Undue influence," as typically used, focuses on the effects of pressure and takes an inquiry down the wrong path. It invites questions about whether a particular administrator was too sensitive or not sensitive enough to pressure and whether the administrator took any actions in response to the pressure. Even with a more objective criterion (the "reasonable" or "typical" administrator, for example), the focus on influence still misses the target. The aim should not be to control how much but what kind of pressure a member brings to bear on an administrator, not how effective but how appropriate the influence is. If the pressure consists of claims that should not be germane to the case, such as promises of support for increased appropriations to the agency, it may be wrong, however mildly or ineffectively expressed. If the pressure consists of reasons that are relevant (the constituent did not receive a fair hearing), then it is justified almost no matter how vigorously brought to bear.

"Relevant reasons" also captures more misconduct than does "undue influence." It covers cases in which the member is not pressuring the administrator at all but simply providing cover for the administrator to do what he wanted to do anyhow. Alfonse D'Amato did not have to exercise undue influence to get the Department of Housing and Urban Development to fund local projects for his political supporters. The Republican secretary of the department, Samuel Pierce, was all too eager to help. The ethics committee did not find any violation here—at least none within the committee's jurisdiction.[60] The investigation and perhaps the outcome would have been different if they had been looking at the merits of claims that D'Amato backed.

Similarly, the House committee might have taken a more critical view of Wright's interventions with the Bank Board had they been looking for relevant reasons. Even if Wright's constituents had legitimate complaints against H. Joe Selby, even if Wright did not make any threats, the reasons he gave—the effects of Selby's homosexuality—were not appropriate. The committee would have been better positioned to condemn this kind of intervention had they been able to apply a relevant reasons rather than the undue influence standard.

Underlying the tendency to treat constituents' claims as infallible is a general view of the role of a legislator as advocate rather than representative. To the extent that members see themselves as advocates, they may not recognize ethical problems in the way they intervene. They take their role to be like that of a lawyer, whose duty, they assume, is to fight for a client without regard to the merits of the case.[61] The only alternative role they seem able to imagine is that of judge, which they rightly reject because it allows no scope for partiality toward constituents.

But the role of the representative in a legislature is not that of either a lawyer or a judge. Unlike a judge, representatives may give special consideration to their own constituents. But unlike a lawyer they must take into account the effect of their actions on other citizens and on the political process. Not only should they consider the merits of the claims, but they should weigh those claims against any likely harm their advocacy may do to democratic procedures. In the absence of a genuine adversary system, a member is not justified in assuming that opposing claims will receive their due.

Intervening in Fairness

The practice of constituent service should also be guided by the principle of fairness. The principle tells legislators to adopt and follow institutional rules that establish terms of fair cooperation to protect constituents, administrators, and colleagues.

Who are the constituents who should receive service? The answer is not so obvious, as the Keating Five case illustrates. It points to what might be called "the problem of too many representatives." Only DeConcini and McCain could claim Keating as a constituent in the electoral sense. The other three senators count as his representatives mainly by virtue of his business interests in their states. It is true that business interests may deserve representation, and geographical districts need not define the limits of representation, even of constituency service. Also, the senators from California, Michigan, and Ohio could reasonably claim that they were acting for the constituents in their own states who would benefit from Keating's business activities there.

This kind of representation, however, ceases to be constituent service and should be evaluated, like legislative activity, from a broader perspective, one that takes into account all a representative's constituents. From this perspective the benefits that these senators were providing to some of their constituents may not have well served most others, specifically taxpayers and depositors. Those constituents may understandably object to multiple representation if the extra representatives always go disproportionately to citizens with greater financial resources. This form of unfairness, of course, goes beyond what ethics rules can and should impugn. Whether any instance of disproportionate representation is unfair is a matter of legitimate political disagreement. But precisely for that reason the practice should not be treated as just another form of constituent service, immune from further challenge as long as it satisfies the standards of ordinary constituent service.

What ethics rules can and should address is the further unfairness that the system of casework itself introduces. A standard prescribing that members give priority to constituents would be warranted. Such a standard is already implicit in the unofficial advice offered in the *House Ethics Manual*: "As a general matter ... a Member should not be devoting official resources to casework for individuals who live outside the district. Where a Member is unable to assist such a person, the Member may refer the person to his or her own Representative or Senator."[62] Any standard based on this advice would, of course, apply only to individual cases, not general policies. Subcommittee chairs, for example, would not be constrained in any way from dealing with citizens from any part of the country who had complaints about whole programs or agencies under the subcommittee's jurisdiction.[63]

Another institutional standard would better protect the privacy of communications between members and constituents. Many of the requests that members receive concern sensitive matters such as medical, family, and financial difficulties. Constituents may reasonably expect members to treat this information as confidential, and most members have done so. However, the Privacy Act, which prevents the disclosure of similar personal records by governmental agencies without permission of the citizens who are the subject of the records, does not apply to congressional documents or correspondence.[64] Congress needs a similar privacy rule to provide the protection that constituents have a right to expect.

The internal fairness of administrative proceedings is well protected by administrative law, but intervention by members has the potential to undermine that fairness. This is so particularly when agencies are deciding disputes between two or more parties. The administrative law regulating adjudicatory proceedings may be helpful here, but the congressional rules should go further. They should prohibit members from intervening in any way in any adjudicatory dispute while it is still under timely review by legally designated authorities. The current rules permit members to "express judgment" in such cases, a privilege that can easily be abused, as can the request for information, which is also permitted. Under stricter rules, if a constituent complains about undue delay by an agency, members could properly ask for a status report and could urge prompt consideration. Once the agency had reached a judgment, members could ask for reconsideration on substantive grounds.

Some of these distinctions may seem subtle, but they are not so different from informal norms that are already recognized by members and their staff. One of McCain's aides faced intense questioning, evidently intended to shake her confidence, about whether she could distinguish proper from improper conduct in interventions with the Bank Board in the Keating case. She responded, "it is very simple . . . what we were talking about was raising issues to determine whether or not there was fairness. That is not taking steps to negotiate. That is also not working towards a resolution."[65] Experienced administrators also say that they have no trouble in recognizing the difference between a status report and an improper request, even when they are expressed in similar language.[66]

In the Keating Five case, the senators evidently did not recognize any difference between what would be an appropriate intervention in rulemaking proceedings and what would be appropriate in quasi-judicial proceedings. The Lincoln case more closely resembled the latter.[67] In a quasi-judicial proceeding, there is generally more procedural protection for constituents and less legitimate scope for disputes about policy.[68] Some political bargaining is necessary in the administrative process, but at least some of the senators in this case went beyond what might be called the normal range of acceptable political pressure. They did more than make status inquiries. The repeated interventions of DeConcini and Cranston looked to the regulators, and probably would have looked to an objective observer, like attempts to produce a decision favorable to Keating.

Although rules should give special attention to protecting quasi-judicial proceedings from legislators' intrusions, they should not de facto give unlimited license for legislators to intervene in other kinds of proceedings. The relative independence of administrative agencies is guaranteed by the constitutional doctrine of separation of powers, itself a manifestation of fair procedure. A chief purpose of this separation is to maintain the appropriate level of generality in decisionmaking by assigning to branches other than the legislative the responsibility of applying the laws. Legislative actions that are proper in the process of making laws are not always legitimate in the process of administering them. Standards of legislative ethics therefore should prescribe that any intervention be appropriate to the nature of the administrative proceeding in question.

Finally, ethics standards should recognize that intervention can be in various ways unfair to colleagues. When members try to outdo each other in providing more and more aggressive service, generating the spiral effect described earlier, the result can be unfair. Those who decline to join this competition are disadvantaged. Other kinds of actions against colleagues can be even more insidious. Some of the problems in the Keating Five case resulted from only partly submerged tensions among the senators themselves. McCain barely concealed his anger at DeConcini for putting his name on a letter inviting Riegle to the meeting with Ed Gray.[69] Several of the other senators' defenders suspected that Riegle may have initiated the first meeting and then deliberately failed to show up for it.

The experience of the Keating Five case may discourage joint interventions in the future, but if they take place, the purpose and agenda of the meetings should be made clear to all participants. In addition to unfairness to specific colleagues, members can be unfair to all their colleagues, in effect to the institution as a whole. Using the excuse of "everybody does it," as some of the Keating Five did, reflects badly on Congress, and unfairly so because it was not true that all members did what all the Keating Five did.[70] Some clearer standards and a central office for constituent service would render such excuses less plausible and less frequent, but a rule specifically condemning actions and statements that recklessly slander the institution might still be necessary (see chapter 6).

Intervening on the Record

A third standard, based on a principle of accountability, would require that interventions take place in a manner that enables the public to assess whether they satisfy the other standards. (Another aspect of this standard dealing with the appearance of impropriety is considered in the next chapter.)

The interventions for Keating, though not strictly secret, fell short of meeting the accountability standard. The pattern of the interventions—after-hours meetings, the absence of aides, early morning phone calls to regulators at home, the vagueness of records—made it difficult to reconstruct the events. (The only exception was the "transcript" of the April 9th meeting prepared by one of the regulators, and that was hardly standard procedure.) The circumstances warranted a reasonable suspicion that the discussions were never intended (at least by the senators) to be accessible for public review. Similarly, the absence of records and the conflicting testimony made it difficult to determine the extent to which Wright's interventions were more than "intemperate." In the case of D'Amato's many interventions, the public has no record at all because the ethics committee did not release any substantial information about its investigation or any of the testimony it took.

It is neither practical nor desirable that all interventions be formally on the record and made public at the time they occur. Considerations of privacy, for example, may justify keeping confidential some parts of complaints that citizens bring to members. But interventions should not be so clandestine that the member and the agency cannot be held accountable in the future should the actions of either be called into question.[71] The standard should go beyond what the current law against ex parte communications requires. It should apply to all kinds of proceedings involving individual constituents, formal or not. It should direct members to keep records of all their contacts with administrative agencies on behalf of constituents and generally make those records publicly available at regular intervals.

Some agencies, such as the Food and Drug Administration and the Federal Communications Commission, have adopted regulations that obligate their officials to log and disclose the substance of virtually all communications with members of Congress and their staff.[72] Some members already keep similar records of their contacts with administrative agencies. A general recordkeeping requirement does not therefore seem burdensome, and it could also serve to protect members from false suspicions and unfair accusations. If citizens knew that the records of such contacts were available, they might be more likely to trust that the interventions were proper, even if they never bothered to examine the records.

The "bounds of ethical conduct" for constituent service are thus more circumscribed than DeConcini and his colleagues assumed. In the American system of government, members do democracy's work when they help citizens who have problems with their government. But unless they establish and observe adequate ethical standards to govern the way they provide this help, they do democracy harm. They serve some constituents at the expense of others and ultimately weaken the capacity of the legislature to serve all citizens.

Corrupt Connections

*This legislation [the Gifts Reform Act] says that for $20 and
1 penny . . . we are not to be trusted. . . . I am not for sale, and I do
not believe others in this body are for sale.*

When Senator Malcolm Wallop
spoke these words against the proposed ban on gifts in the Senate,
he expressed a view shared by many members as well as by many
longtime observers of Congress.[1] Most members do not trade their
votes or services for gifts, he argued, so banning gifts is not necessary to prevent corruption.[2] The premise of Wallop's argument is
surely right: most members are not for sale in the way he has in
mind. But the conclusion does not follow. Gifts and other contributions to members do give rise to corruption—not usually the individual corruption that marks the most notorious cases, but the
institutional kind that emerges in the practices of everyday legislative life.

This chapter examines the *connections* between gains that members receive and the services they give. In the current practice of
legislative ethics, connections are typically presumed innocent until
proven to fit the model of individual corruption. Bribery is the paradigm. At the same time, it is presumed that individual corruption
must be defined narrowly so that some common exchanges in politics, especially campaign contributions, do not turn out to be bribes.
If these presumptions are not examined, many ethically questionable connections escape scrutiny. Legislative ethics should take a

broader view and recognize that institutional tendencies as well as individual motives may constitute a corrupt connection.

In individual corruption the connection runs through the mind of the individual legislator.[3] A member acts because of, or in exchange for, a thing of value: the gain causes or tends to cause the member to provide the service.[4] Because the gain *moves* the member, the connection is regarded as a corrupt motive. Apart from the connection, the gain itself does not have to be otherwise improper. The gain can be either personal (typically a gift) or political (a campaign contribution).[5]

In institutional corruption the connection runs through the practices and norms of the legislature. The connection is an institutional tendency that short-circuits the democratic process, violating the principles of legislative ethics. An individual member may (even knowingly) contribute to such a tendency without having the corrupt motive that characterizes individual corruption. Although a member does not provide service because of the gain, his or her actions create other connections between the gain and service that should be regarded as corrupt.

Corrupt Motives

It is not surprising that Wallop's conception of corruption is individualist. He served as chair of the Senate ethics committee, which in the early 1980s had to decide the fate of Senator Harrison Williams, one of the members caught in the FBI sting operation known as ABSCAM.[6] Under the direction of the Justice Department the operation deployed some one-hundred FBI agents in an elaborate two-year undercover investigation of legislative corruption. Some of the agents posed as Arab businessmen who offered bribes in return for political favors. Eventually, seven members of Congress were caught in the sting, their improprieties captured on videotape for the public to see.

Williams's actions fit the standard pattern of individual corruption. Not only did his gain seem to be personal rather than political, but also (and more to the point here) the gain was closely connected to the service. Months before the ethics committee announced its conclusions, a federal jury found Williams guilty of bribery, among other crimes. The primary evidence for both the jury and the committee was a videotape showing Williams agreeing to help an Arab sheik (an FBI agent in disguise) secure a government contract and a resident visa in exchange for stock in a Virginia titanium mine.

Williams did not brazenly stuff money in his pocket, as did Republican Congressmen Richard Kelly, who was caught in the same sting operation. Nor did he declare, as Democrat John Jenrette did, "I've got larceny in my blood."[7] But Williams never objected to the proposal the bogus sheik made. He boasted of the influence he could exercise on the sheik's behalf ("[I am] in a position to go to ah well, you know, right to the top on this one"), and gave the sheik an "absolute pledge [to] do everything in my power" to advance his cause.[8]

For both the committee and Williams, the issue turned on motives. Williams said he "never *intended to* do anything that would bring dishonor to the Senate." He took no money and said he believed the stock the sheik offered was worthless. The committee concluded that Williams agreed to use his influence "in order to elicit a commitment" from the sheik for financial compensation. Williams "actually *intended* to use his influence to attempt to obtain government contracts."[9] On the floor, Vice Chair Senator Howell Heflin emphasized the importance of motives. "Senator Williams did not hesitate to link his willingness to perform an official act—to help the sheik with his immigration problems—if it would result in the sheik's favorable response on the titanium deal. . . . This [was the] critical nexus, [the] incriminating link. . . ." Williams "acted in an official capacity out of motives for personal financial gain. . . . As to his motive, one can only surmise that it was greed."[10]

Although few members doubted that Williams's conduct was corrupt, many still had difficulty supporting expulsion. During his twenty-three years in the Senate Williams had won the respect of his colleagues for his conscientious legislative work and the support of liberals for his efforts on behalf of progressive causes. Many members also thought that the FBI had acted improperly in the sting operation. They sympathized with Williams's defense that he had been entrapped.[11] Williams exploited this sympathy, trying to shift the focus from individual conduct to an institutional fault, conforming to the dynamic of legislative corruption. To his colleagues he said: "It is not only Pete Williams that stands accused or indicted; it is all of us, the entire Senate."[12]

Contrary to the recommendation of the committee's special counsel, the Senate decided to postpone further action until Williams had exhausted his appeals in the courts. In a prophetic casting of roles, the special counsel urging more immediate action was Robert S. Bennett, who would become special counsel in the Keating Five case. It was Senator Alan Cranston who, as if anticipating his own later fate, led the effort to reduce Williams's punishment from expulsion to censure. Even Heflin thought at first there was a "good chance" that Cranston's resolution would succeed.[13] Unlike expulsion, which requires a two-thirds majority, censure needs only a simple majority. No senator had been expelled since the Civil War, and none on charges of corruption.[14] By the time the Senate was ready to vote, however, the stigma of Williams's criminal conviction loomed large. As one member said, the fact that he was a convicted felon "hangs over the Senate like a cloud."[15] Just as the Senate was about to vote on his expulsion, Williams resigned.

Thus even in an almost pure case of individual corruption, it took unusually explicit evidence and confirmation provided by a criminal conviction to bring the Senate to the point of imposing its ultimate sanction. In most cases the accused's motives are less evident and his colleagues' judgment less severe. As the corruption moves further from individual paradigm, colleagues are more reluctant to find serious violations.

Because the book deals of Durenberger and Wright lacked a corrupt motive linking services and gains, they were treated as less serious than Williams's conduct. The special counsel in the Durenberger case (Bennett again) explicitly distinguished Durenberger's conduct from Williams's: "The essential difference is that there is insufficient evidence supporting a finding that Senator Durenberger acted with *criminal intent*, malice or with specific intent to break the law."[16]

The organizations and individuals that bought the books were not trying to bribe Wright or Durenberger. Most were responding to requests from the members' offices, and some resented what they saw as pressure to buy the books. Arguably, the deals might be seen as a kind of low-keyed extortion.[17] But the investigations turned up no specific promises or threats, and the evidence fell far short of establishing any criminal motive in either case. The circumstances of the gifts (limousines for personal travel) that Durenberger accepted from organizations with an interest in legislation may have come closer to providing the corrupt connection a criminal conviction would need. But again, in the absence of evidence of any explicit exchange the committee found Durenberger guilty of only the lesser violation of the gift rule (which requires no motivational link between the gift and any favors the member might provide).

In Wright's case the House ethics committee declined to find any basis at all for action against the Speaker in his two oil well deals with the Neptune Oil Company (the same corporation that benefited from his vigorous interventions described in chapter 4). In the first oil well deal, a principal of the company bought back, on unusually favorable terms, Wright's interest in a well. The committee agreed with the special counsel that Wright did not intervene for Neptune "because of [any] promise that a favor would be done."[18] The fact that the deal took place several years after intervention seemed to convince the special counsel and the committee that there could be no corrupt connection between the deal and the intervention. They looked at individual acts, not patterns. In the other incident, in which Neptune gave Wright the opportunity to buy an interest in a well on favorable terms not available to others, the special counsel believed Wright had violated the gift rule.[19] But the committee rejected their counsel's conclusion. Its members not only denied any connection between a gift and service but even doubted that the interest in the oil well was a gift at all. They found the record ambiguous and resolved the ambiguity in favor of Wright.

The search for corrupt motives, as these cases illustrate, is likely to be frustrating. It is rare that the evidence clearly shows a member acted or intended to act because of a benefit received from an interested citizen. Given the ambiguity, colleagues understandably give the member the benefit of the doubt. It is easier to show that a member accepted "a thing of value" from a citizen with an interest in legislation. But even here, in the absence of any evidence that the member intends to do anything for the citizen, colleagues find it difficult to judge the member corrupt. The preoccupation with motives deflects attention from institutional corruption.

Certainly, when ethics committees find the motives corrupt, as in the ABSCAM cases, they should find the offenders guilty. Certainly, motives are relevant in the minimal sense that to be found guilty a member must violate a rule knowingly or at least negligently. But ethics committees should not try to force all kinds of connections into the mold of individual corruption. They should not assume it necessary to show that a member acted out of a motive such as greed or because of anything an interested citizen gave in the past or promised in the future. Members do not have to be bought in any of these ways in order to warrant the charge of corruption. Whatever their motives, they may still be perpetrators of institutional corruption. Congress needs standards to govern that kind of corruption.

In the case of gifts these considerations argue for a gift rule that is simple, strict, and broad. First, the rule should have few exceptions, and none based on the supposed virtuousness of a motive. During the Senate debate on gift reform, many members urged that expenses for travel to charitable events should be exempt.[20] No one noted the ironic implication of this suggestion: if members are less in danger of being corrupted by gifts for charity than by for gifts for themselves, they must care more about personal gain than philanthropic causes. The only exceptions that should be allowed are those that are necessary for members to carry on their legitimate political activities (meals taken in conjunction with their official duties, for instance) and those typical of normal social and family life (such as customary birthday gifts to their children from friends). Some members may need to be reminded what a normal life is. During the debate Senator J. Bennett Johnston challenged Senator Paul Wellstone, one of the sponsors of the gift bill: "Do you say you should not go to the symphony ball, ambassador ball, National Guard, the opera ball, what have you?" Wellstone replied: "I would say you can go to any opera you want to; you pay for it. Just like regular people pay for it when they go to the opera. It is that simple."[21]

Second, the gift rule should assess the seriousness of the offense partly in terms of the harm the practice causes, not exclusively in terms of the viciousness of the motive. Wright's routine acceptance of gifts from oil interests should not necessarily be treated as less serious than Williams's one-time acceptance of titanium stock.

Third, the restrictions should apply not only to members and their staffs but also to lobbyists. The ban on accepting gifts should be accompanied by a ban on giving gifts. The whole burden of changing the culture of coziness should not fall on members. An important part of this effort must also be disclosure rules, requiring a broader range of lobbyists than are now covered to report their contacts with members.

If Congress is prepared to ban gifts, why not contributions from political action committees? Senator Glenn remarked: "It is a little hypocritical for members to say they could be bought for a $21 lunch, yet turn around and pick up a phone to a PAC and ask for a contribution over 200 times that amount." In this spirit, members found it difficult to resist when Senator Frank Murkowski proposed an amendment that banned gifts from PACs. "My amendment," he said, "merely adds [to the gift] prohibition . . . a very important type of gift, a political contribution."[22]

But contributions are not exactly the same as gifts, and if they are to be treated the same, reform has to go much further than members are prepared even to consider. Senator William Cohen pointedly distinguished the different roles of senators: "We are looking for symmetry between what we can do as candidates and what we can do as Senators. But there is no symmetry. The Senate has gone on record in favor of [reducing] the value of a gift . . . down to zero. If you follow the logic and apply it to campaigns, then you eliminate all contributions to campaigns other than through public financing."[23] Many reformers believe that Congress should follow that logic, and they may be right. But as Cohen observes "there are very few [members] who are willing to take that step." As long as candidates must raise funds for campaigns, legislative ethics must find ways to control the conditions under which they receive contributions. To understand better what the conditions should be, it is necessary to consider the further difficulties of finding corrupt motives in cases in which the gain is political rather than personal.

Mixed Motives

Establishing a corrupt motive is more difficult when the gain is political. The greater difficulty partly stems from the fact (emphasized in chapter 4) that political gain is part of the job of a legislator. A gift of an interest in an oil well or a free limousine trip seems less necessary and less respectable than a contribution to a political campaign. But the connection between the gain and the service itself poses a further difficulty. The corruption cannot be found in the motives of members because of a fundamental feature of representative government: legislators act on *mixed* motives.[24]

In any electorally based representative system, legislators are required to take into account many different kinds of considerations in making decisions. They act for the benefit of particular constituents, for the good of the whole district or state, for the good of the nation, and for their own interest in reelection or future political goals. Some of these motives may be more admirable than others, but none is illegitimate in itself and all are in some measure necessary in our democratic system.

Given the circumstances of mixed motives, it is difficult for any member, however conscientious, to separate proper from improper motives or to find a reasonable balance of motives in making any particular decision.[25] It is harder still for citizens, even well-informed nonpartisan ones, to judge at a distance whether the official has actually found the balance. In the design of a representative system or in the practice of judging representatives, therefore, one cannot in general rely on being able to evaluate motives in individual cases.

The problem is not merely psychological, one that could be overcome if politicians were only more self-aware or if citizens could only see more deeply into the minds of politicians. The difficulty is built into the structure of representative government. The role of representative requires legislators to connect the political support they receive with the service they provide. Citizens in turn must be free to use their financial resources to support the candidates of their choice. Citizens would rightly be disappointed if representatives never acted in response to the political support they received or expected to receive. In this sense, representatives act because of, even in exchange for, political support, including campaign contributions.

Stated at this level of generality, the connection is not only acceptable but desirable: it expresses part of the essence of democratic accountability. Only when the connection becomes too specific should we begin to worry. But how specific? The point at which accountability to constituents turns into corruption is not easy to discern either in theory or practice. The implications of this difficulty can be seen in the efforts to distinguish campaign contributions from bribes.

Congressional rules and federal law prohibit members from providing services on the basis of, because of, or in exchange for campaign contributions.[26] Such a connection seems to fit the familiar mode of individual corruption: the motive is corrupt. In one respect such prohibitions do not go far enough because they ignore institutional patterns. But in another respect they may go too far. The difficulty is that this kind of corrupt exchange does not seem so different from many of the other kinds of deals that go on in politics. Politics is replete with quid pro quo's: you vote for my bill, and I'll support yours; you raise funds for my primary campaign, and I'll endorse you in the general election. Without such exchanges, political life could hardly go on at all. Why are campaign contributions different?

The conventional answer, favored by ethics committees, most politicians, and many courts, is that only some campaign contributions are different from other political exchanges. Only a few relatively rare contributions count as corrupt. By insisting on narrow criteria for what counts as a corrupt link, advocates of this view believe they can condemn improper contributions without casting suspicion on the contributions that make up the vast majority of the support that members receive. Only when the connection between the contribution and some service is especially close should there be any reason to worry about corruption. In this approach the connection between the contribution and the service must be close in two senses: proximate in time and explicit in word or deed.

Temporal proximity is assumed to tighten the connection because it permits fewer intervening causes to occur. Explicitness is presumably a reliable indication that the public official recognizes the connection. This condition may help explain the otherwise puzzling belief that financial gain is the only kind of gain that counts as corruption.[27] Financial gain makes the connection closer than other kinds of political gains (such as promises of future support or political endorsements) because both its value and its motive are more determinate. Everyone can more easily appreciate what my

$5,000 contribution to your campaign is worth and why I am giving it than what my promise of political support is worth and why I am offering it.

In the case of several of the Keating Five, the connection between the contributions and the service were, even by these standards, close. The connection was especially close in Cranston's case, which was one reason the committee singled him out for special criticism. In this "mutual aid society," Cranston regularly solicited contributions from Keating while he was also working to help Lincoln Savings and Loan with its problems. His chief fundraiser combined discussions about regulations and contributions. Favors and contributions were also linked in memos and informal comments.[28]

The committee found the contributions and services to be "substantially linked" through an "impermissible pattern of conduct," but it stopped short of finding "corrupt intent."[29] The connection, it would seem, could hardly be closer. Why did the committee decline to find corruption here? (It might also be asked why the committee did not find the pattern impermissible in the case of Riegle and DeConcini.) Since "corrupt intent" is the language of the bribery statutes, the committee did not dare suggest that campaign contributions could be bribes. The line between contributions and bribes must be kept bright.

But *is* the line so bright? "Almost a hair's line difference" separates bribes and contributions, Russell Long once testified.[30] Certainly the courts have not been able to provide a principled way of distinguishing the two.[31] The confusion that arose in *U.S.* v. *Brewster*, a leading court case on public corruption, illustrates how difficult the conventional distinction is to sustain. Senator Daniel Brewster was indicted for bribery in 1970 because he had accepted or solicited payments from a lobbyist, some of which went to his campaign fund. The appeals court ordered a new trial for Brewster because the trial judge's instructions attempting to distinguish innocent campaign contributions from bribes were "indigestible."[32] But the appeals court itself failed to explain the difference.

More recently, in *McCormick* v. *U.S.* a majority of the Supreme Court overturned the extortion conviction of a West Virginia state legislator who had accepted contributions from a group of foreign-trained unlicensed doctors lobbying for the right to continue to practice medicine in the state. The jury had been instructed that no explicit promise or quid pro quo by the legislator was necessary to turn a campaign contribution into an illegal payment. But the Supreme Court majority said that an explicit promise *is* necessary. Otherwise, elected officials would be too vulnerable to criminal charges in the normal course of political activity. The broader standard would "open to prosecution . . . conduct that in a very real sense is unavoidable so long as election campaigns are financed by private contributions or expenditures, as they have been from the beginning of the nation."[33]

This appeal to national traditions does not establish any principled basis for distinguishing contributions from bribes. It begs the question of whether contributions *should* count as bribes. The most cogent argument for denying that they should is based on the value of encouraging competition for political support. A broad concept of bribery would have a chilling effect on potential contributors as well as politicians. But this argument at most shows only that some other value (political competition) outweighs the cost of corruption, and only under current conditions. It does not show that the only, or the most important, kind of corrupt connection is that defined by the narrow definition of bribery.

There is, furthermore, no good reason to believe that connections that are proximate and explicit are any more corrupt than connections that are indirect and implicit. The former may be only the more detectable, not necessarily the more deliberate or damaging, form of corruption. Corruption that works through patterns of conduct, institutional routines, and informal norms may leave fewer footprints but more wreckage in its path.

Are we driven, then, to accept the view of some critics of our political system who regard all contributions as corrupt?[34] This approach does have the virtue of highlighting serious structural flaws in the current system of campaign finance. But it does not encourage the kinds of distinctions necessary in the kind of politics the United States actually has now and is likely to have in the foreseeable future. This approach provides no basis for judging some forms of corruption worse than others and therefore no guidance in deciding which reforms should have higher priority. Treating corruption as so pervasive obscures important moral differences in the kinds and degrees of wrongdoing in which politicians may engage. It would imply that an explicit proximate bribe is morally equivalent to a regular $1,000 campaign contribution to one's longtime party favorite. We need some standards that would draw more nuanced distinctions among the various connections that link service and contributions.

Short-Circuiting the Democratic Process

A common reaction to another aspect of the Keating Five case points toward the basis for such standards. Many people thought there was something peculiar about Keating's lavishing support on senators whose political views he so strongly opposed. Cranston and Keating were an odd couple: an archconservative Arizona businessman, devoted to the free market and opposed to pornography and abortion, teamed up with one of the leading liberals in the Senate, a former candidate for president who had called for a nuclear freeze and higher social spending. The two differed even on government policy toward the financial services industry.

The common reaction that this ideological incongruence is odd, that it does not constitute the kind of political support appropriate in democratic representation, is correct, but not for the reason commonly assumed. The reason is not that the incongruence exposes the cynical motives of Keating and Cranston, proving that they were acting out of material self-interest. This may make them less admirable, but it does not make them corrupt because self-interest is not sufficient and actual motives are not a reliable test.

Ideological incongruence is significant not because it exposes cynical motives but because it reveals apolitical practices. Specifically, it identifies a type of contribution that serves no public political function. A contribution given without regard to the political positions of the candidate only incidentally provides political support; its primary aim is to influence the candidate when in office. In its pure form it has no function other than to translate the private desires of a contributor directly into government action. In effect, it short-circuits the democratic process.

Contrast this kind of contribution with that given to support a candidate with whom a citizen shares a general political orientation or agrees on issues that he or she thinks salient.[35] A contribution of this kind directly serves a political function: its aim is to help a candidate get elected, and it works through the political process.[36] Rather than bypassing the process, the contribution animates it.

The basis of the distinction is the principle that citizens should influence their representatives and representatives should influence policy only in ways that can be contested through public deliberation and political competition in a democratic political process. This principle is consistent with conceptions of representation ranging from delegate to trustee. It requires only that representatives act on behalf of policies and persons that they have defended or are prepared to defend in a public forum—and at the risk of political defeat. The problem with the Keating-type contribution is not that it makes a representative an agent of individual constituents but that it makes the representative an apolitical agent. The objection should be not that the contributions come with strings attached but that the strings have no political substance.[37]

Ideological incongruence is common in current campaign finance as big contributors hedge their electoral bets. It is not itself a necessary or sufficient condition of corruption. Neither does its absence make an otherwise questionable practice acceptable. However, its presence in any particular case suggests that corruption may also be present. And further, when corruption is present, incongruence becomes a component of it. The incongruence thus points toward a more comprehensive criterion for identifying corrupt connections. The connection between contributions and benefits is corrupt if it short-circuits the democratic process. When legislators help private interests use public authority without submitting their claims to the full test of the democratic process, they are agents of corruption. They pollute the public with the private.

There are, of course, many different ways in which contributions might be regarded as bypassing the democratic process, and the ways that are considered corrupt will depend on what conceptions of democracy are accepted. The principles of legislative ethics identify the connections that should raise serious concerns for almost any conception of democracy. They point to institutional tendencies that produce corruption independently of any corrupt motives that members may have. The principles suggest that a connection is more likely to be corrupt the less closely the contribution is connected to the merits of conduct it is intended to influence, the less fairly distributed the services are, and the less accessible the connection is to publicity.

The significance of these principles is best seen by considering their implications for the role of money in the legislature, specifically campaign contributions. Because the main concern here is ethics *in* Congress, we must put aside most of the issues in campaign finance and concentrate on what if anything is ethically distinctive about the effects of money on the conduct of legislators.[38]

The Root of Some Evil

Many social critics suppose that money is necessarily corrupting in politics. Political power and political office, it is said, ought to be among the things that money cannot buy; dealing in political goods should be a "blocked exchange."[39] It is a mark of political progress when societies do not allow votes and offices to be sold. Putting a price on political goods turns them into commodities, corrupting their meaning and ultimately their value. Thus money should not influence politics.

Clearly, there is some truth in this view. Political competition should not be just like economic competition. Acquiring political office should not be like buying stock in a company. But the claim that money by its very nature corrupts politics is too broad. The problem cannot be money itself. Public office is not something, like a baby or a kidney, the acquisition of which should never depend on money. Politics is more like the wide range of activities, such as creative work or professional practice, in which the influence of money is limited but not excluded. Money is not only necessary to support artistic and educational projects, it can also stimulate higher levels of achievement in these domains. Artists or teachers are not corrupted by accepting money for their work. They are not regarded as corrupt even if they are motivated mainly by the money they receive, as long as their art and teaching continues to satisfy independent standards of esthetic and pedagogical excellence. It is to these standards that one looks to set limits to the role of money in activities. The point is to try to keep money from undermining the quality of the results of creative endeavor.

Politics is similar in the sense that money can corrupt the quality of decisions and policies of government. But money can also corrupt the process, even when it is not possible to point to specific ways in which the outcomes of the process are corrupted. This is not because the standards for judging the outcomes are more contestable or indeterminate in politics than in art or education. It is rather because the connections between the influence of money and the outcomes are harder to trace in detail, and because the process itself has independent value as an activity in which all citizens are supposed to be able to share.

As in other activities that have noneconomic purposes, politics can be degraded or dignified by money depending on the conditions of its use. This is why some of the political theorists most hostile to political corruption could favor the sale of offices. Under certain conditions, money can serve as a check on corruption. The Baron de Montesquieu and Jeremy Bentham saw the aristocracy and the monarchy as the most serious source of corruption in their societies and believed that the sale of offices would combat this traditional corruption by opening up politics to the rising commercial classes.[40] Although their particular problem is not ours, their general point is still relevant. We should try not to eliminate the use of money in politics but to control the way it is used.

Despite the "many cries of 'too much'" from both voters and candidates who complain that the cost of campaigns has become exorbitant,[41] it is by no means obvious that as a society we are spending more than is appropriate for such a socially important activity as choosing our representatives. In an age of mass media, an informative and competitive campaign is expensive, and even larger amounts of money than we now spend—if spent more fairly and effectively—could enhance the democratic process. A careful assessment by two political scientists concludes the problem is not only "how much is spent on congressional elections, but also the distribution of that spending between challengers and incumbents."[42] Too much is now spent by incumbents but too little by challengers. Instead of only limiting the amounts, we should try to regulate the effects and sources—and specifically in the case of legislative ethics the connections between the sources of funds and the conduct of legislators.

Impairing Independence

If we take the first principle of legislative ethics seriously, we will try to minimize the influence of money on the judgment of legislators. Money is a corrupting kind of political support when it bears no relation to the substance of the politics it seeks to influence. Here its capacity to take on the colorings of any political view is the root of the evil. This does not mean that members should not seek contributions, but that they should seek contributions from citizens who want them to do what they would have good reason to do.

As far as legislative votes are concerned, contributors probably do not have much direct influence. Political scientists have not generally found strong correlations between contributions and roll call votes. Where correlations appear, the policy areas tend to be narrow, and the effects tend to be weaker than other factors such as constituency and ideology.[43] Furthermore, the evidence does not determine the causal direction: contributors may simply give to those legislators whose policy positions they favor.[44]

But if money does not buy votes, it may still buy access.[45] Many contributors care less about influencing roll call votes than about securing informal assistance from a member. Putting the contributor in touch with staff of a key committee, facilitating an approach to the head of an executive agency, publicizing the contributor's cause, writing a transition rule, or offering an amendment in committee—these and similar services go to citizens who have access to members. Some members acknowledge what one would expect: given limited time, they are likely to return phone calls and grant appointments to their major supporters first.[46] The influence of money on committee work may be the most striking effect. In a careful study of three House committees, two political scientists found that although PAC money did not purchase members' votes, it "did buy marginal time, energy, and legislative resources" during formal markups and committee action behind the scenes.[47]

To the extent that contributors receive priority, money buys attention. Contributors receive more of the time and energy of members than they otherwise would. Their problems are likely to be more prominent on the members' political agendas than they would otherwise have been. A pattern of access that favors contributors could thus over time influence the judgment of members about legislative matters. This kind of influence operates not through any conscious motives or individual exchanges but habitual actions and institutional routines.[48]

If this influence only reinforced priorities that members already have or positions they take in the competitive campaigns, then it would not be so troublesome. It would be subject to review in the democratic process. But members usually do not and probably could not separate those contributors who are simply providing political support from those who are mainly buying access for their own private interests. Therefore, to limit the institutional effects of the Keating type of influence, Congress will have to find better ways to disconnect contributions from services and legislative activity in the daily institutional life of members.

If the only goal were to minimize this kind of influence, members could be required to make decisions behind a veil of ignorance that prevented them from knowing who had contributed to their campaign.[49] Some writers have actually proposed reforms that would have just this effect. One proposal would require that all contributions to candidates go through an official agency such as the Federal Elections Commission, which would transmit them in lump sum payments to candidates, without any indication of the amounts that individual contributors gave. "When the large contributor loses the power to prove the size of his contribution," the advocate of this scheme writes, "he is reduced to the same status as any other contributor."[50]

But while this scheme might well eliminate most corrupt contributions, it would also drastically impair the capacity of candidates to raise legitimate funds. Citizens who simply wanted to support a candidate and expected nothing in return could of course still contribute. But even if there are many such citizens, candidates could not effectively target their fundraising efforts and would lack adequate information about the effects of their efforts on legitimate supporters. Contribution-blind schemes of this kind would throw out the baby of political competition with the bathwater of political corruption.

A more promising approach would impose a less impenetrable veil. Members would continue to know who their contributors are, but their legislative and service staffs would not. The fundraising and the legislative functions in their offices would be separated. The tasks would be performed by different staffs whose communications would be limited and documented for the record and accessible to ethics committees under certain circumstances. (As chapter 3 showed, such separation is also desirable to prevent the use of official resources for campaign purposes.)

The functions of fundraising and legislative staffs of course overlap in various ways, and a complete separation is probably not feasible. But some members—several in response to the Keating Five hearings—have organized their offices to minimize the interaction.[51] Even those who have not formally divided their offices have established rules that try to keep the activities distinct. Asked if he had any policy or standard that he and his staff followed with respect to even the discussion of substantive matters and contributions' activity by particular individuals, Senator Glenn responded, "Yes. We have a rule that if we are talking substantive matters, or people are in the office on an issue, that we will not get into any discussion of contributions, potential contributions, at all."[52]

Although no division of labor of this kind can or should completely sever the connection between contributions and services, it should help break some of those institutional habits that give contributors more influence than they ought to have. It should also provide some institutional mechanisms that would give improper influence more publicity than it now receives.[53] It would discourage mixing fundraising and substantive legislative or regulatory issues in the way that, according to the Senate ethics committee, Cranston allowed. This mixing, the committee said, was carried out largely by staff, especially by Joy Jacobson, Cranston's chief fundraiser. She regularly attended meetings with contributors to discuss legislative or regulatory problems, and "revealed an attitude that contributors were entitled to special access to and actions from the Senator"[54]

Formal rules for organizing offices are not likely to be sufficient. Changes in informal practices will probably also be necessary. In a culture that habitually connects service with support, staff will have to learn how to draw lines more carefully. After an official act is taken, "often the next thought on people's minds . . . is 'How can we benefit from what we've done in terms of the upcoming election?'"[55]

Senator Frank Lautenberg, one of the champions of stronger ethical standards in Congress, also has one of the strictest policies against mixing campaign and official business. "ANYONE who calls regarding a fundraising event, even if it's only time, place, etc.—the appropriate answer is 'Senate staff is not involved in the Senator's fundraising activities. . . . NO EXCEPTIONS.'" Yet Eva Lubalin, the chief of staff who prepared this statement, herself wrote memos that could be read as advising campaign fundraisers to target people who had received help from the senator. Urging fundraisers to approach an investment banker whom Lautenberg had helped, she noted, "Just did something nice that made him very $$."[56] A month later the banker contributed $1,000 to Lautenberg's campaign. In another memo on the planning of a fundraiser, she wrote of a prominent Washington businessman that Lautenberg had "helped him out on a number of things lately and he should be called for an event in this area." Another memo recommended seeking contributions from leaders in the railroad and airline industries, whose interests were affected by the Appropriations Subcommittee on Transportation that Lautenberg chaired.[57]

Lautenberg said he regretted Lubalin's choice of words but insisted that her memos violated no rule. Invoking the narrowly drawn Senate rule, he insisted that no "assistance of any kind provided by my office was made in expectation of, much less in return for, a commitment of future contributions or services to my campaign."[58] Lautenberg's campaign manager explained, "the people who support you and agree with you on issues is where you have to raise your money."[59] Furthermore, the "nice thing" Lautenberg had done for the investment banker was merely supporting a grant for a program called Cities in Schools, which did not benefit the banker financially. Thus since there was no individual corruption (no quid pro quo, no personal gain), there was nothing to worry about. The ethics committee took no action.

But an editorial in *Roll Call*, a newspaper far from hostile to members, was "compelled to compare Lautenberg's behavior to the Keating Five." The editor wrote that the memo "crosses the line— by citing specific acts the senator had taken and seeking to capitalize on them."[60] Whether or not the line was crossed, several members quickly asked their staffs to review their procedures to make sure they would not write any such memos.[61] Lautenberg himself announced that he would issue "reinforcing instructions" to keep fundraising and legislative activities separate in the future.[62]

This case is instructive, but not because it shows, as Lautenberg's opponent in the Senate race claimed, that "the person who's talked about being a saint seems to have developed the capacity to sin."[63] Rather, it illustrates how difficult it is in the current culture even for conscientious members to keep the proper degree of separation between the role of campaigner and the role of representative. Because the gray areas are so expansive, the rules may have to be more rigid than might otherwise seem necessary and the education of staff more assiduous than it has been in the past. To these ends the ethics committees could provide some model descriptions of office procedures for staffs of various sizes and offer some regular training programs for staff specifically on these problems. More boldly, Congress could consider prohibiting the acceptance of any campaign contributions from lobbyists.

Subverting Fairness

It was Lautenberg who during the Senate debate on the gift rule appealed to a principle of fairness. He was the only senator in the debate who explicitly raised the possibility of systematic bias in otherwise legitimate connections or exchanges:

> The cumulative impact . . . is to bias the system. Most so-called average citizens do not get to spend an hour, or 2, or 3, a weekend, or 2 days, with a Senator. Average citizens often do not get to build a personal relationship this way with a Senator or a Representative. Average citizens do not have the access—the opportunity to present their case and explain their concerns is just not available—as lobbyists do get it.[64]

To his credit, Lautenberg recognized that cumulative effects can produce corruption even in the absence of corrupt motives. The practices of individual members may be biased without their being aware of it, and the practices of Congress may be biased without the actions of any individual member being biased. Neither of these kinds of bias alone constitutes an ethical violation unless the institution establishes standards to control it. But the harm that this bias causes to the democratic process points to the need for some such standards, and once in place their violation would count as a form of institutional corruption.

This kind of institutional corruption is probably the single most insidious effect of money on congressional life. It is the most difficult to detect and the most difficult to prevent because it is partly the result of inequalities in the distribution of resources in society. Some of the inequality is no doubt justified, and some of the greater access that money buys may also be justified. Citizens should be able to use their discretionary income to support their political goals. But in our imperfect society, many inequalities are not justifiable and are criticized by conservatives as well as liberals. Even if individual members cannot do much about these underlying injustices, they surely have an obligation to minimize their effects on their own conduct of legislative business. Injustices that are inevitable are no excuse for encouraging further unfairness in the access to political power within the legislature itself.

The strict separation of campaign and legislative routines, designed to promote the principle of independence, should also help further the principle of fairness in at least one respect. Members would be less likely to favor contributors because their legislative and service staffs would be less likely to know who they are. Conscious and perhaps some unconscious biases would be minimized. However, even this rather thin veil of ignorance could also prevent members and their staffs from detecting patterns of bias that no one intended, those that result from institutional practices. A device designed to protect against bias could become a barrier against correcting bias.

Therefore a regular review of patterns of access and service should be instituted for offices of members. A similar review should be conducted for each chamber as a whole, either by an office of ombudsman such as that proposed earlier or by the ethics committees. The aim of these reviews would be to discover and correct any systematic biases that members or the chamber as a whole may be showing toward contributors. Where the reviews find bias, they would not recommend denying access to contributors but could propose ways of improving access for ordinary citizens. The identities of particular contributors, the exact nature of the services, or (in the case of the institutional review) the name of the office would not be significant and perhaps would not have to be made public. The review would focus on patterns and trends that contribute to a corruption that most members do not intend.

Endangering Accountability

Money is in one respect *more* likely to satisfy the principle of accountability than are other kinds of political influence: money can be quantified, publicized, and objectively reviewed. This is why there are elaborate and precise rules about financial disclosure but nothing comparable about the names of friends, colleagues, and groups who provide other kinds of support for members. In other respects, however, money poses formidable difficulties for accountability.

Open, direct contributions are not the only important kind of financial influence in politics. No less significant is the capacity of those with money to promise support (or threaten to withdraw it) in campaigns as well as other political activities. Many of these promises and threats are only implicit, and the countless financial transactions that sustain them usually take place behind the scenes. The complexity and flexibility of modern financial institutions with their national and international connections make it hard to follow the paper trail of their transactions and often impossible even to raise enough questions to prompt an investigation. Most of the time political money makes its rounds quietly, without raising any specific suspicions and without offering opportunities for democratic accountability.

A division of labor in congressional offices should increase the likelihood that some ethically troublesome uses of money will receive more publicity. So should regular reviews of contributors' access. Broadened disclosure rules could also help expose some patterns of support and prompt further questions and investigations. (Such rules are also desirable for other reasons; see chapter 6.) But given the serpentine paths and clandestine corridors through which money can travel, citizens may rightly insist on holding members accountable for more than the types of connections so far discussed. It is not enough that citizens have access to information that would permit them to discover connections that indicate corrupt motives. It is not even enough that citizens can discover connections that reveal distortions and biases in institutional practices. Citizens should be able to call members to account for connections that *appear* to link gains to services in these first two ways, whether or not citizens have evidence of any actual link. The need for this kind of accountability is this chief reason that congressional ethics must take seriously the so-called appearance standard.

The Importance of Appearances

In the thicket of codes, rules, and statutes that regulate ethics in government, no standard is more common than the one that admonishes public officials to avoid the appearance of impropriety.[65] Yet the standard is often misunderstood.[66] The word *appearance* itself invites the misunderstanding. It encourages a contrast between the mere appearance of an ethical wrong and a real ethical wrong. The violation of the appearance standard is taken to be a minor, lesser offense, a sort of pale reflection of the real offense. The standard then comes to be regarded as merely prudential, a piece of political advice that if not followed is seen as grounds for a charge of mistaken judgment rather than an ethical wrong. Recall that the ethics committee found that DeConcini and Riegle had created an appearance of impropriety but found them guilty of showing only "insensitivity and poor judgment."[67] A former director of the Office of Government Ethics was even more explicit: "Our attitude is, when there is an appearance problem, that the persons involved have done no wrong, have committed no improprieties, and are presumed to have acted ethically. It is an appearance only."[68]

Properly interpreted, the appearance standard identifies a distinct wrong, independent of and no less serious than the wrong of which it is an appearance. It would be better called a tendency standard because it presumes that under certain institutional conditions the connection between contributions and services *tends* to be improper. It is in this respect like the institutional tendencies already discussed. But it adds a further presumption: when confronted with a connection that exhibits these tendencies, citizens cannot be reasonably expected to obtain the evidence they need to judge whether the connection is actually corrupt.

Thus the more judicious versions of the appearance standard do not refer to appearances at all but instead cite considerations such as conduct that does not "reflect creditably on the House" or "circumstances which might be construed by reasonable persons as influencing the performance of governmental duties."[69] In terms of the principles of legislative ethics presented here, the standard specifies that a connection between contributions and services should be regarded as corrupt if it takes place under conditions that would lead citizens reasonably to believe that the contributions are causing services to be provided without regard to substantive merit or appropriate fairness.

The appearance standard has two general aims. First, it seeks to reduce the occasions on which the connection between gain and service is actually improper in both the ways already examined—those that operate through corrupt motives and those that work through institutional tendencies. By prohibiting a broader range of circumstances than do standards that focus only on these two connections, the appearance standard is more likely in practice to capture more of these very connections. It is also more likely to capture some conduct that is not corrupt in either of these ways. Like many rules, it is in this respect overinclusive.[70] It could, for example, condemn a member for accepting a contribution even when the member's legislative judgment was not influenced in the slightest. This might be grounds for charging that the appearance standard is unfair if it did not have a second purpose.

The second and more distinctive aim of the standard is directed at maintaining public confidence. The standard seeks to decrease the occasions on which the connection is reasonably perceived to be improper. Like the rules based on the institutional tendencies discussed earlier, this perception is grounded on general knowledge of the conditions that tend to produce actual improper connections. But the distinctive wrong that the appearance standard seeks to prevent is a different, further kind of moral failure. When a legislator accepts large contributions from interested individuals under certain conditions, whether or not the legislator's judgment is actually influenced, citizens are morally justified in believing the legislator's judgment has been so influenced and in acting on that belief.[71] The legislator is guilty of failing to take into account people's reasonable reactions. The conduct displays a form of the traditional vice of "giving scandal."[72]

In a democracy the obligation to respect the reasonable reactions of other people has political implications. The obligation is both more difficult and more important to fulfill in public than in private life. It is more difficult because citizens cannot easily collect the evidence they need to judge the motives of politicians in particular circumstances. Without such evidence, they have to judge presumptively. The obligation is generally more important than in private life because it goes to the core of the role of a representative. Citizens have a right to insist, as the price of trust in a democracy, that officials not give reason to doubt their trustworthiness. This is so no less for a trustee than for a delegate conception of representation. Representatives must avoid acting under conditions that give rise to a reasonable belief of wrongdoing. When they fail to avoid doing so, they do not merely appear to do wrong, they do wrong. Appearances matter ethically, not just politically.

The conditions to which the appearance standard refers may be specific to the case. For example, Cranston's accepting a $250,000 contribution from Keating in the whip's office and then immediately agreeing to call the chair of the Bank Board on Keating's behalf constitute reasonable grounds for citizens' believing he was improperly influenced, even if he was not actually so influenced, or even if those who witnessed the events or those colleagues who knew him well believed that he was not so influenced.[73] The conditions may also be more general. When members routinely provide preferential access and service to organizations that make large contributions to their campaigns, citizens have reasonable grounds for believing that legislative independence and fairness are not being well served.

Because appearances are usually the only window that citizens have on official conduct, rejecting the appearance standard in general is tantamount to denying democratic accountability. This was dramatically demonstrated in the objections regularly raised during the Keating Five hearings by several of the senators and their attorneys. Cranston's lament was the most unequivocal. He kept objecting to the suggestion (strongly urged by Special Counsel Bennett) that his conduct should be judged by how it appears to a reasonable person. That is a "mythical person," Cranston said; the only real person who can judge is the senator himself. "You were not there. *I* was there. And *I* know that what I knew at the time . . . convinced me that my [actions] . . . were appropriate."[74] If pressed, Cranston might have included his constituents among the "real persons" who could judge his actions. But this concession would still leave his colleagues and many other citizens without a way to hold him accountable for the ethical integrity of the Senate (even for conduct that could reasonably undermine public confidence in the institution). Electoral accountability is, as chapter 6 argues, no substitute for collegial accountability.

The most common objection to the appearance standard is that it is too subjective: what appears wrong to some people does not appear wrong to others. Defending his peripatetic chief of staff, John Sununu, President Bush complained: "Nobody likes the appearance of impropriety. On the other hand . . . you shouldn't be judged by appearance. You ought to be judged by the fact."[75] Although like any other rule of ethics, the appearance standard requires interpretation, it is, just as much as any other rule, based on facts. The standard is justified by empirical regularities: observed correlations between certain kinds of practices (accepting large contributions) and certain forms of corruption (granting favors). Appearances, rightly understood, are based on inferences from objective circumstances to subjective motives and institutional tendencies. An appearance standard, rightly applied, assumes that the inferences are made by citizens who are as well informed and as unbiased as possible, given the inherent limitations of their position. That is the point of the requirement that the judgment of impropriety be "reasonable."

Some of the inferences that an appearance standard would warrant can be codified: for example, rules that prohibit legislators from voting on matters in which they have a "direct personal or pecuniary interest."[76] These and other conflict-of-interest rules are simply the way some violations of the appearance standard are made more specific. Conflicts of interest can be thought of as appearances of wrongdoing made categorical. No appearance standard would be necessary if we could codify all violations by means of the comprehensive rules like those proscribing conflict of interest. But not all appearance violations involve conflicts of interest, and in any case such detailed specification is neither possible nor desirable. It is not possible partly because of the familiar problems of codification, the difficulties of specifying in advance all the possible violations. Further, the rules would have to specify not only all the primary offenses but also the secondary offenses that are defined by the range of conditions under which the primary offenses may reasonably appear to have been committed.

But even if comprehensive codification were possible, it would undermine two desirable features of our representative system.

First, an elaborate set of rules would limit the discretion of representatives that a democratic system rightly grants to facilitate necessary compromise and desirable political change. It would also make members more vulnerable to technical violations, which could be exploited by their opponents. The appearance standard is of course also subject to abuse because of its indefiniteness. But this danger is somewhat mitigated by another consequence of the very same indefiniteness. Because the mere charge that a member has appeared to act improperly is indefinite, it is not likely to have much harmful effect until it is further specified by an ethics committee or similar authority. (Although appearance violations cannot be completely specified in advance, they can and should be more fully specified in judging particular cases. It is this kind of specified appearance that legislators and citizens should take seriously.)

A second feature of representative government also argues against codification. Elaborate conflict-of-interest rules are not consistent with the rationale of a system that assumes a coincidence of interests between representatives and at least some of their constituents. Because representatives have some of the same interests as their constituents, the range of impermissible conflicts of interest has to be kept limited. An appearance standard is therefore even more appropriate for legislative than for executive ethics.

These disadvantages of codification provide part of the answer to another familiar objection to the appearance standard. Some critics object that the standard is unfair because it imposes ex post facto punishment. Members are judged on the basis of interpretations of a standard they cannot know in advance. But even granting that the appearance standard is less definite than most other rules and laws, members should still appreciate its advantages compared to the alternative—greater codification. There is a direct trade-off between these two approaches. The more that members resist general rules like the appearance standard, the more reason citizens have to insist on adding more and more specific prohibitions to the codes. The appearance standard provides an ethically justifiable ways to lessen the growing burden of detailed rules with their multiple exceptions.

Furthermore, the standard is not less determinate than many other rules of ethics and provisions of the law. The law is shot through with concepts that require interpretation: equal protection, due process, due diligence, reasonable precautions, and the like. As case law develops, the implications of the concepts become clearer, and officials and citizens know better what conduct falls within their scope. There is no reason that a similar process should not work in legislative ethics.

Yet another objection to the appearance standard is that it makes style more important than substance. Politics is already too much dominated by appearances: images, sound bites, code words. What is needed, the critics say, is more concern with the substantial reality that lies behind these superficial appearances. The criticism of the quality of political debate certainly has merit. Superficial appearances are hardly what should inform the judgment of democratic citizens. But these are not the kinds of appearances to which the appearance standard refers.

The appearances that count in ethics are well-grounded perceptions: what appears to be the case to a well-informed and unbiased citizen. They are not the images and illusions that the critics correctly condemn. Both ethics committees, the Office of Government Ethics and the *Code of Ethics for Government Service* now explicitly adopt the criterion of the "reasonable person."[77] This concept too, as Senator Cohen has pointed out, is common enough in the law and should cause no more difficulty in congressional ethics.[78]

Rather than reinforcing the superficiality of political debate, appearances in the sense assumed by the appearance standard are the source of substantive criticism. It is mainly on the basis of well-grounded appearances that citizens are able to criticize politicians for being superficial, for failing to deal with the substance of issues. By the same token, it is mainly on the basis of such appearances that critics can reprove both politicians and citizens for misjudging the kinds and degrees of corruption in Congress, and especially for exaggerating the individual and neglecting the institutional kind.

Some version of an appearance standard is necessary to fulfill the demands of democratic accountability and further to protect the values of independence and fairness. Whether an appearance standard, even rightly understood, can work effectively and fairly depends ultimately on who is authorized to interpret and apply it. Who should decide what conduct citizens would reasonably proscribe?

Who should decide when a member has engaged in that conduct? Such questions go beyond the domain of the appearance standard. To answer them, it is necessary to shift from considering what conduct is wrong to considering who should decide what conduct is wrong. The next chapter therefore turns from the content of the standards of legislative ethics to the procedures of their enforcement.

Tribunals of Legislative Ethics

You have members sitting in judgment of other members with whom they have to work day by day. . . . There is a kind of innate conflict of interest when members of the Ethics Committee are called upon to judge their colleagues.

While insisting that he was only "being a bit of a Devil's advocate," Representative Lee Hamilton in testimony before the Joint Committee on the Organization of Congress exposed the conflict of interest at the heart of efforts to enforce legislative ethics.[1] The Constitution assigns Congress the responsibility for disciplining its own members.[2] Yet principles of legislative ethics cast suspicion on any process in which members discipline themselves. How can ethics committees claim to judge an individual conflict of interest when they themselves stand in a position of institutional conflict of interest? The chief constitutional instrument for enforcing ethics seems itself to be ethically compromised. Members judging members raises reasonable doubts about the independence, fairness, and accountability of the process.

This chapter explores the difficulties that this institutional conflict creates for congressional ethics. The difficulties cannot be overcome simply by relying on the electoral process and the system of criminal justice, the other principal tribunals of judgment. Some changes in the way the ethics committees conduct their business are necessary. Most important, both chambers need to establish a new body, composed of citizens who are not members and who enjoy some independent authority. Such a body is especially needed to cope with the increase in cases of institutional corruption.

131

The Deficiencies of Self-Discipline

"No one should be the judge in his own cause."[3] This maxim has guided judges of controversies and makers of constitutions since ancient times. It expresses fundamental values of due process and limited government, providing the foundation for the separation of powers, judicial review, and federalism in the U.S. Constitution. It is the principle that the authors of the *Federalist Papers* invoke at critical junctures in their arguments for the Constitution. Both James Madison and Alexander Hamilton apply the principle to institutions—the states, Congress, the federal government as a whole—not only or mainly to individuals. Madison commented, "no man is allowed to be a judge in his own cause, because his interest would certainly bias his judgment, and, not improbably, corrupt his integrity. With equal, nay with greater reason, a body of men are unfit to be both judges and parties at the same time."[4]

In what sense is the Senate or the House a party to the cause when it judges the case of an individual member charged with an ethics violation? Although neither chamber is literally on trial in any particular case, their interest is closely connected to the fate of the individual member. The perspectives of the judges and the judged are not so distinct as they are in a judicial trial or even in disciplinary hearings such as those conducted in some other professions. The distinction between judge and a party to the cause in a legislative institution is blurred in three ways, all of which tend to bias the judgment and corrupt the integrity of both the members and the institution. These effects operate in cases of individual corruption, but they become even more potent in cases of institutional corruption.

The first way in which the distinction breaks down is the result of collegial interdependence. More than officials in most other institutions (even in the other branches of government) and more than members of most other professions, members of Congress depend on one another to do their job. They have worked together in the past and they must work together in the future. The obligations, loyalties, and civilities that are necessary, even admirable, in these circumstances make it difficult to judge colleagues objectively or to act on the judgments even when objectively made. Furthermore, the less that a charge seems to resemble individual corruption, the harder it is for colleagues to come to a severe judgment even if it is warranted. The member implicated in institutional corruption, showing no obvious signs of a guilty mind or unusually selfish motives, is seen as simply doing what the job requires or at least permits. Under such circumstances the sympathy of colleagues is maximized and their capacity for objectivity minimized. The circumstances are not favorable for the principle of independence, which calls for judgment on the merits.

The attitude of "we are going to protect our own" that Lee Hamilton criticizes can produce bias against members as well as in favor of them. "Protecting our own" when the "own" are members of one's party or faction may lead not only to defending guilty members but also to attacking innocent ones. In an interdependent and partisan legislature, ethics charges can become a political weapon, setting off the cycle of accusation described in chapter 2. In the succession of charges and countercharges that followed the judgment against Speaker Wright, both judges and those they were to judge found themselves the objects of charges.

A second way members are judging themselves when they judge their colleagues refers to the institution itself and poses special difficulties for the principle of fairness. In many cases a key question is whether an accused member's conduct has departed from the norms of the institution. The conduct of the members who are judging can thus become an issue when the accused member claims that what he has done is no different from what other members have done. It is not fair to single him out. This was a familiar plea in the case of the Keating Five. Although this plea could not be sustained, it put other members, including members of the ethics committee, in the awkward position of having to defend themselves. Their ability to do so directly affected the judgments they could make about their accused colleagues. Unless the committee members could show how their own conduct differed, they either had to acknowledge their own guilt or declare their colleagues innocent.

In other cases the conduct of most members may not in fact differ from that of the accused, and the committee may readily accept the defendant's plea without considering whether the conduct, and the standards that seem to permit it, should be criticized. The House committee could not bring itself to criticize the ways Wright intervened on behalf of a Dallas real estate investor or the Neptune Oil

Company. Committee members may have assumed that he had only done what some of them had done in the past and what others might wish to do in the future. In their effort to be fair to Wright, they neglected to ask whether, from the perspective of the democratic process as a whole, the norms that permitted his conduct were fair to citizens.

Even when committees stand firm, their members may find themselves devoting as much attention to defending their own actions as to investigating the misconduct of an accused member. The committee and its procedures become the issue. During the fall of 1993 the entire Senate spent two full days on the case of Senator Bob Packwood.[5] The debate ignored the charges of sexual harassment and intimidation of witnesses that had been raised against him. The only subject was Packwood's challenge to the subpoena for his diary that the ethics committee had issued as part of its investigation of the charges. The substantive business of the chamber ceased while senators debated extensively a claim of privacy that, if made by an ordinary citizen, no court would take seriously.[6]

The third way the positions of the judges and the judged converge in congressional ethics affects the principle of accountability. Members who are judging their colleagues know that they themselves will be judged by the public. The political pressures that build during the disposition of ethics cases are potent, often more potent than judicious. In the Keating Five case, Vice Chair Rudman believed that "the public had decided [for] the guillotine at dawn on the Capitol grounds. That was the atmosphere in which the Ethics Committee was operating. . . . Capital punishment would be just about right."[7] Some members also thought that some of their colleagues may have been too sensitive to public opinion because they were facing reelection in November.[8]

To avoid these kinds of pressure, the committee can conduct its investigation in private, as it did in the case of D'Amato, which occupied its attention at almost the same time as the case of the Keating Five. The committee held no public hearings on the charges against D'Amato and did not release transcripts or summaries of the testimony. At the conclusion of the investigation it issued a brief report that provided scarcely any account of the events in question. The committee thereby insulated itself from improper public pressure, but at the price of excluding proper public concern and arousing greater public suspicion. The conclusion and the process continued to be the subject of public criticism long after the committee reached its conclusion.[9]

Because of the political nature of a legislature, it is difficult, and not even desirable, for members to act purely as judges, focusing only on the case at hand. Legislators have obligations that judges do not have. They must take seriously the reactions of constituents and consider the effects of their decisions on the health of democratic political institutions, including Congress itself. Ethics committees must determine whether a member has conducted himself or herself "in a manner which shall reflect creditably on the House," or has avoided "improper conduct which may reflect upon the Senate."[10] In judging colleagues the committees must assess not only their institutional norms and practices but also public confidence in those norms and practices. Balancing the scales of justice in these circumstance would try the skill of Solomon.

Because of all these factors, when a legislative body investigates, charges, and disciplines a member, it is not observing the principle that one should not judge in one's own cause. It is not in the best position to reach an impartial judgment on the merits, treat members with fairness, and maintain public confidence in the process.

Similar considerations have persuaded most other professions to move away from self-regulation. The model rules and codes that govern the ethics of lawyers, for example, are mostly enforced by the courts. Lawyers are increasingly subject to other kinds of sanctions, such as liability suits for breach of ethical duties, institutional controls, and administrative regulations affecting representation before government agencies. Still, some of the most thoughtful commentators on legal ethics are challenging the adequacy of the present system, calling for more outside controls (though tailored to specific contexts).[11] Even accountants and business executives face many more controls on conduct that only their peers or their consciences once regulated. External agencies such as the Securities Exchange Commission now set ethical standards and punish violations.

The practice of medicine is highly regulated by state agencies, and health care reform eventually is likely to lead to still more control. Physicians also face the threat of malpractice suits if they fail to meet professional standards of care and sometimes even if they meet them.[12] The profession has not distinguished itself in dealing with those few areas of medical ethics for which it still retains primary responsibility, in particular, conflict of interest and self-referral.[13] The American Medical Association has only recently adopted, evidently under the threat of legislation, rules against self-referral. But the rules remain vague and without enforcement mechanisms, even though there is growing evidence of abuse. As a result, governments are beginning to regulate self-referral.[14]

Two other professions that have traditionally insisted on regulating their own ethical conduct, academics and the clergy, also face increasing demands for scrutiny by outside authorities. Professors in many institutions are now required by state legislatures and other agencies to disclose sources of funding for their research, report their outside activities, and follow certain procedures in making appointments to the faculty.[15] The enforcement of ethical standards among the clergy is probably the most varied, ranging from completely laissez-faire systems in some Protestant denominations to the relatively rigid controls in the Catholic Church.[16] But revelations of sexual misconduct in the priesthood have cast doubt on the efficacy of even those controls.

The profession that has most successfully resisted outside regulation of its ethics is journalism. It typically wards off evil by waving the First Amendment before its attackers. Compared with most other professions, journalism also has few institutional mechanisms for enforcing ethical standards. Even moderate proposals that would limit the speaking fees journalists can accept from organizations they cover have been met with powerful opposition within the profession.[17] Journalists, like legislators, think they can regulate themselves well enough and indeed see no need for much regulation of any kind. It is ironic that the only professionals who affirm their right to self-regulation as strongly as legislators do are also those whose ethics many legislators most distrust.

During the hearings of the Senate Ethics Study Commission, Senator Thomas Daschle observed: "We wouldn't stand for doctors or lawyers or insurance agents or any others forming a group with which to discipline themselves and accepting that as the sole determinant as to whether or not someone is appropriately within his bounds."[18] He asked why are senators different? The question is germane, and more difficult to answer than is usually assumed.

Letting Voters Decide

The most prominent difference between legislators and members of other professions is that legislators have to run for office. They must defend their performance in public and at regular intervals let voters judge their success. Because of this electoral connection, they are more directly accountable than other professionals who exercise power over other people. They can be trusted to run their own disciplinary procedures, it is said, because they are subject to the most fatal form of discipline of all for a politician—loss of office. "You are not your brother's keeper," a House member once said. "He is answerable to the people in his district just as you are."[19]

Disclosure

Because legislators stand for election, some question why any further accountability is necessary at all. "We ought to disclose what we do," Senator J. Bennett Johnston suggested during the debate on the gift ban, "and let the voters decide."[20] Others have proposed that Congress should replace its elaborate regulations on conflict of interest, acceptance of gifts, and allowable outside income with a simple set of rules requiring only disclosure of financial interests.[21] Ethics committees would make sure that members disclose what the rules required, but only voters would decide whether members were guilty of any ethical improprieties.

This approach is deficient in principle and practice. As a matter of principle it relies on a mistaken view of democratic representation. It assumes that the constituents in one district or one state should have the exclusive authority over the conduct of the representative from that district or state. This kind of representative system may be appropriate for a transient convention, what Edmund Burke called a "congress of ambassadors from different and hostile interests."[22] But it is hardly adequate for a permanent legislature, a congress of members who can pursue their different interests only if they preserve their common interest in the integrity of the institution. A true legislature cannot leave the ethical fate of the whole body to the mercy of a few members and their constituents.

Because legislative ethics provides (as chapter 1 emphasized) the preconditions for all legislative action, citizens rightly take an interest in the ethical conduct of all members, not only that of their own representatives. In this respect their concern about ethical conduct differs from their interest in any particular piece of legislation. Even on delegate conceptions of democratic representation, constituents in *any* state or district may quite properly instruct their representative to seek, through procedures of the representative assembly, standards to govern the ethical conduct of *all* representatives. That is part of the rationale for the disciplinary authority of the ethics committees and ultimately for Congress's constitutional power of expulsion. That is also why letting members disclose and voters decide is in principle not sufficient.

In practice in the current system, disclosure serves only a limited function.[23] Each year members and high-level staff are required to file an elaborate report listing virtually all their own and their spouses' financial holdings and indicating the range of value (as in "greater than $1,000, but not more than $2,500," one of eight possible categories for income alone).[24] Because the forms do not correspond to any familiar pattern such as an income tax return, members and the public often find them confusing. Furthermore, although ethics committee staff usually examine the forms and notify members of discrepancies, there is no independent audit, not even a review of the kind conducted by the Office of Government Ethics for executive branch officials who are subject to essentially the same requirements. It is therefore impossible to know whether the tougher penalties adopted in 1989 (doubling the maximum civil fine to $10,000 for violating disclosure rules) has improved compliance.

Members who have been caught violating *only* disclosure rules rarely suffer any serious sanctions from their colleagues, let alone voters. Only three of the sixteen cases involving disclosure violations considered by the committees since 1977 involved no other charges.[25] Of the seven cases in which a committee decided to impose a sanction, only one did not involve other charges. Only two of those receiving sanctions were defeated for reelection.[26]

Like mail fraud and income tax evasion, disclosure offenses are sometimes used to reinforce charges that investigators regard as more serious but for which they have less conclusive evidence. In the only case in which a sanction was imposed after a member was charged with only a disclosure violation, the House reprimanded George Hansen in 1984 for failing to disclose $334,000 in loans and profits received under suspicious circumstances, but only after he had been convicted of federal felony and sentenced to prison.[27] Even when other serious charges have been made and a member has violated disclosure rules, committees do not always impose any sanction. In 1987 the House ethics committee found that Fernand St. Germain had repeatedly violated disclosure provisions of both the House code and the Ethics in Government Act, but concluded that the "identified improprieties do not rise to such a level warranting further action by this committee."[28]

Another deficiency of disclosure is that it does not cover at all some conduct that raises serious ethical questions. It cannot satisfy legitimate concerns about the jobs that members take after they leave office, the province of postemployment rules. Disclosure here simply comes too late. For some other misconduct, such as conflict-of-interest violations, disclosure reveals too little. These violations often come to light only after careful investigation of complex financial relationships. Neither voters nor reporters are usually in a position to conduct such investigations.

What is disclosed is generally not used effectively. Stories on the financial resources of members are rarely presented in a way that would best help voters make balanced judgments about the ethics of members. The press is often most interested in who the wealthiest members are, how much their spouses make, or who takes the most expensive trips paid by corporations.[29] A few reporters try to show connections between political action committee contributions and legislative committee memberships, but given the ambiguity of those connections, the stories can usually do no more than raise suspicions. This effect points to yet another limitation of disclosure. By itself, disclosure may merely further undermine confidence in government, causing citizens to suspect the motives of legislators but providing no constructive ways to restore trust. Disclosing a possible conflict of interest merely reveals a problem without providing any guidance for resolving it.

If the limitations of disclosure were more fully appreciated, both members and citizens might come to expect less from it. They would not only be less tempted to rely on it exclusively, but they might also be more inclined to look for ways to combine it more effectively with other forms of enforcement. For example, the ethics committees could regularly review the financial activity of members, identify potential problems, and recommend measures to correct them. They would publicize information only if members failed to correct the problems. Committees could ask for much more information than is now disclosed, but most members would have to make much less public. (As always, leaks would be a risk, but both ethics committees have unusually good records in protecting confidential information.) Furthermore, the information could be targeted more specifically to the problems that particular members may have. More relevant than the range of amounts of members' holdings is their history of relationships and patterns of investments. In particular, ethics committees could request more specific information about members' holdings that might be affected by the committees on which they serve, especially those they chair.

The Electoral Verdict

In practice the current system of enforcement consists of two decisions: a finding by Congress and a subsequent verdict by the electorate. (Expulsion is so rare in modern times that it has little practical effect even as a threat.)[30] Colleagues declare a judgment and voters deliver the final verdict. When voters have the last word, what do they say?

Of the twenty-three members on whom an ethics committee imposed sanctions from 1978 to 1992 for corruption offenses, five (22 percent) were defeated in their bid for reelection and four (17 percent) decided not to run again.[31] During the same period the average rate of defeat for all members facing reelection was 7 percent and that of retirement 10 percent.[32] This comparison does not, however, indicate whether the ethics charges actually contributed to the retirement or the failure to win reelection.[33]

The most systematic study of the effects of charges of corruption on voting behavior in more than one election found that accused candidates suffered a loss of 6 to 11 percent from their expected vote in reelection races.[34] A significant number of accused candidates lost the primary or resigned rather than risk defeat in the general election. (The study covered all races in which a candidate's alleged corruption was an important issue, not only races in which a candidate had been charged or had a sanction imposed by an ethics committee.) Although voters evidently do not ignore corruption, they do not protest unequivocally against it at the polls. More than 60 percent of all those accused won reelection. Of the accused candidates who reached the general election, nearly three-quarters prevailed.[35] The voters most likely to vote against the accused candidates may be those least likely to have the classic characteristics of good citizenship: strong issue orientation, party identification, active participation, and commitment to the democratic rules of the game.[36] If this is so, relying on the electoral verdict puts the health of the democratic process in the hands of the least reliable citizens.

Neither do electoral judgments discriminate among types of corruption in a way that satisfactorily tracks their effects on the democratic process. Individual corruption is punished much more severely than offenses involving institutional corruption. Campaign and conflict-of-interest violations produced losses on the order of 1 percent of the expected vote, while bribery charges led to losses of about 12 percent. Members charged with morals offenses suffered the most: they lost more than 20 percent of their expected vote.[37]

Doubts about depending on voters to punish corruption are further reinforced by studies of the effects of the House Bank Scandal.[38] A political disaster for members but a professional windfall for political scientists, the scandal provided a rare natural experiment: "a new, exogenous, accurately measured and potentially powerful independent variable."[39] Because a large number of members were charged with different degrees of the same offense at the same time in a late phase of the election cycle, political scientists could more accurately assess the electoral effects of the scandal. The more bad checks a member had written, the more likely he or she was to retire, fail to win the nomination in the primary, or lose the general election.[40] The best estimate is that the scandal reduced the reported vote for incumbents by about 5 percentage points.[41]

The scandal influenced the vote primarily through its effect on the decisions of a relatively small group of voters (about 7 percent). Those who were most inclined to punish the malefactors were also the least disposed to believe that their own members had written bad checks, even when they had. Voters who were not sure whether their incumbents were guilty tended to assume they were. In general, "ignorance and misperception" limited the electoral effects of scandal. Only 43 percent of voters could correctly say whether their representative wrote any bad checks.[42]

Even more troubling than voters' misperceptions are the distorted priorities that the electoral verdict expresses. Voters acted with much more effect against the culprits in the House Bank scandal than against the perpetrators of many other more serious scandals, such as the savings and loan crisis or irresponsible budget deficits. The Bank scandal should not even count as corruption in the sense most voters assumed (see chapter 3). Insofar as the scandal revealed corruption, it was institutional. The problem was administrative negligence by members (particularly the leadership) rather than fraud against the taxpayers, the kind of individual corruption that most voters assumed had occurred.

To criticize these misperceptions and mistaken priorities is not necessarily to criticize voters. Their behavior was perfectly sensible under the circumstances. The information about the House Bank was kept secret for many years and then came out in a fragmentary and confusing form. Only the reports of the investigations, not the details of the investigations themselves, were made public. The special counsel released his report only after the election. Few reporters bothered to try to put what information was available into perspective. As for their priorities, voters could not "measure their representative's personal contribution to the savings and loan fiasco or budget deficits, but they [could] know who wrote overdrafts."[43]

More generally, when voters choose their representatives, they may understandably take into account factors other than ethics. They are often willing to forgive lapses in ethical behavior if the member looks after constituents. As one of D'Amato's supporters observed, "Here [on the streets of Island Park, Long Island]—this is where I know Al D'Amato. He's been here when he had to be here. The rest of it—that's stuff that happens in Washington."[44] For others, a representative's party or position on policy issues weighs more heavily in their decision than any charge of corruption.[45] Voters do not necessarily think that party or policy matters more than honesty; they may discount the corruption simply because, unless a case goes to trial, they usually do not have enough information to assess the validity of the charges. Most of the charges investigated by ethics committees remain confidential, and even those that result in investigations and sanctions do not include public hearings like those held in the cases of Durenberger and the Keating Five. Finally, even with full information and discerning judgment, voters have only one sentence they can impose: the political equivalent of capital punishment.

The considerations that explain why voters should not be blamed also underscore why the ethics process should not rely mainly on the electoral verdict as it currently operates. Voters have, of course, the final word in any democratic system, but before they give that word the process should provide more and better information than it does now. Some of the proposals considered later in this chapter to strengthen the ethics committees could improve the quality and efficacy of the verdicts voters deliver in the electoral tribunal.

Letting Courts Decide

During hearings on the organization of Congress, Senator Richard Lugar surprised some of his colleagues by suggesting that "one solution to the ethics committee problem is not to have one." Persons who file complaints could be told to "see the local court system or State court or the Federal court, and let them try your case." Other members have from time to time made the same proposal. Its attractions are plain. The legal process has the permanent expertise to investigate the complaints effectively and the procedures to adjudicate them fairly. As a legislature, Congress has neither. Although the ethics committees have hired outside counsel a dozen times since 1978 and codified their own procedures (some forty pages for each chamber), the "perception of many of our trials here," Lugar observed, is that "we're amateurs flailing about."[46] The perception does not do justice to the professional competence that the staffs (and some members) of both ethics committees have demonstrated over the years, but it does reflect an institutional fact: because the congressional ethics process stands closer to the political process, it is not likely to be as orderly and stable as legal proceedings.

To some extent Lugar's proposal has already been put into practice. Many of the most serious charges against members are prosecuted in the criminal justice system. More than half the cases in which ethics committees have taken action since 1978 have also been the subject of criminal investigation.[47] In other cases, such as those of Harrison Williams or Mario Biaggi, the courts have provided the only sanction because members resign before Congress can act. The ethics committees have not taken any action on the fourteen cases since 1977 that involved members who were indicted or convicted for offenses committed while in office.[48] Why then not let the courts take over all the cases involving corruption charges against members?

As was suggested in chapter 3, cases involving general offenses are better left to the criminal court system. Although reserving the right to take up a case at any time, the committees could declare as a matter of policy that they would let the courts deal with these offenses. Ethics committees are increasingly postponing action until courts reach a judgment or at least prosecutors conclude their investigation. A case like that of Durenberger, in which Congress acts before the courts, is now less common than one like that of Representative Dan Rostenkowsi, in which the ethics committee declines to act until the courts conclude their work. In practice, the ethics process is moving toward Lugar's proposed solution, or at least toward the moderate version he also suggested: violations of ordinary law should go to the courts, and violations of "higher standards" should be heard by the committees.[49]

Although the courts can in this way play an important role in some ethics enforcement, they are not an appropriate tribunal for many charges against members and should not be the sole or final tribunal for any ethics charge. Because the aims and methods of the criminal process and the ethics process differ in principle, the two must remain distinct in practice. In simplest terms, the ethics process seeks to determine whether a member's conduct has harmed the institution; the criminal process judges whether a citizen has harmed society. In this respect the ethics rules and committees, as two experienced members once observed, are "like the professional standards and the disciplinary board of a medical or bar association." They explained: "just as the question for such a board is professional integrity and performance as prescribed by the standards, so the question for the committee is [congressional] integrity and performance as prescribed by the Code."[50]

The punishments imposed by the ethics process are also more limited in scope than those imposed by criminal law. An ethics sanction does not deprive a citizen of life or liberty. The criminal courts can do both, and can also deny a member the right to hold public office again.[51] In a colloquy with Lugar, Hamilton emphasized yet another important difference: "the standards for serving in Congress ought to be higher than whether or not you have committed a felony."[52] Whether or not they are higher, many are different. Ordinary citizens do not have to disclose their personal finances to the public, and most are not subject to restrictions on gifts they can accept. Even more significant for the purposes of legislative ethics is the whole range of offenses that produce institutional corruption, such as giving special help to big campaign contributors or putting improper pressure on federal regulators. The reason most of these offenses are not crimes is not that only legislators can commit them but that they involve ambiguous conduct, difficult to define in advance and awkward to condemn after the fact. This kind of conduct lacks the corrupt motive that criminal prosecution usually requires.

Because some of the offenses differ, so should some of the procedures. When disciplining members, Congress and its ethics committees are not bound to observe the procedural protections of the criminal process. Accused members do not have access to all the testimony and evidence gathered by the committees (although committees often make much of it available). More significantly, the standards of proof, especially in the earlier and usually most critical phase of an inquiry, require much less than a conclusion beyond reasonable doubt. Only "substantial credible evidence" is necessary to impose some sanctions and to initiate a formal investigation. (The hearings for the Keating Five constituted only a preliminary inquiry).[53] The committees may even legitimately pursue a case against a member who has been justly acquitted in court on the same charge.

For many institutional offenses a criterion of strict liability or at least a standard short of criminal negligence may be appropriate. Senator D'Amato was rightly rebuked for permitting his brother to use his office improperly, even though the committee had no evidence that the senator knew about his brother's conduct. Ethics committees may also legitimately decide to move more quickly to a conclusion for reasons that would not be appropriate in court, for example, because of the need to settle a case before the next election or to resolve the chairmanship of a critical committee. (This is an important reason the committees should not totally relinquish their jurisdiction over even general offenses.)

Some members would create a sharper division between Congress and the courts than these considerations suggest. They object, for example, to the Justice Department's using testimony or documents that accused members have provided in the course of an ethics committee investigation. They argue that such use will discourage members from cooperating with the committees and that it violates the "speech and debate" clause, which protects members from being "questioned in any other place" than Congress for their legislative statements and actions. On these grounds Durenberger persuaded a federal district judge in 1993 to dismiss an indictment against him for submitting false claims to Congress for travel reimbursement.[54] The prosecutors had used several pages of the ethics committee report in their presentation to the grand jury.

This decision and the objection carry the separation too far. The committee report in question was part of the public record and therefore potentially available to members of the grand jury anyhow. It is difficult to see why under these circumstances prosecutors should be barred from using it. (They should not of course mislead the court, as the judge in this case accused them of doing; they had explicitly told the court that they had not submitted any of the report to the jury.) Durenberger was reindicted, but this time the prosecutors avoided using any documents from the ethics committee, and the courts refused to dismiss the indictment.[55]

In another case, a federal appeals court held that the Justice Department's use of ethics committee testimony did not violate the speech and debate clause and did not interfere with the congressional disciplinary process. The ethics committee had sent Representative Charles Rose a formal and public letter of reproval for violating the financial disclosure provisions of the House rules and the Ethics Act. Contrary to the committee's wishes, the Justice Department began its own investigation and filed a formal complaint against Rose for violations of some of the same provisions. (Unlike the committee, the department charged that the violations were "knowing and willful.") The appeals court held that testimony given in a personal capacity to a congressional committee does not count as a legislative act protected by the speech and debate clause.[56] The court explicitly criticized the decision in the Durenberger case for misreading Supreme Court precedent on this point. There was no violation of separation of power or interference with committee processes, the appeals court said, because Congress itself delegated to the Justice Department part of the responsibility for prosecuting violations of this act, and Congress itself could always change the law.

Although the appeals court generally drew the boundaries between the two processes in a sensible way, one aspect of the decision is troubling. The court commented in passing that if the ethics committee had wished to prevent the Justice Department from using any part of its proceedings to prosecute Rose, it "could have declined to issue a report or issued one in redacted form."[57] Such a practice might well protect the committee and the accused member, but at the price of diminishing public confidence in the ethics process.

Strengthening the Ethics Committees

Although both elections and courts serve as important tribunals for the enforcement of the standards of conduct for legislators, neither can substitute for Congress itself. Ethics committees are here to stay, and Congress must look for ways to make their procedures better fulfill the principles of legislative ethics. The most important reform would establish a new outside commission, as described later in this chapter. But even without this commission, a number of changes could improve the way the committees conduct their business. Even with such a commission, the other changes could help the committees do their job better. In either case the committees would still play a major role in enforcing ethics standards because Congress retains final authority for imposing ethics sanctions on its own members. To recognize the deficiencies of self-discipline is not to call for the abolition of the ethics committees.

Partisanship and Prejudgment

Partisanship is the first fear that comes to members' minds when the independence of the ethics process is challenged. The Senate created a strictly bipartisan committee in 1964, partly in response to the partisan disputes over the investigation of Bobby Baker, the secretary of the majority, who was later convicted of criminal charges involving the misuse of his office and campaign contributions. The House followed suit in 1967 after the controversial case of Adam Clayton Powell, who was "excluded" by the House but was later reinstated by the Supreme Court. To avoid partisanship, the ethics committees have an equal number of members from each party, the only congressional committees to have such balanced representation. The members chosen for service are generally known as moderates and are usually less partisan than their colleagues. Members rarely volunteer for service on these committees.

The public decisions that the committees have reached generally do not seem to be partisan.[58] The final votes are almost always unanimous and dissenting opinions are rare. The committees have imposed sanctions on more Democrats than Republicans in the past decade and a half, even though the Democrats controlled Congress during most of this period. On average Democrats made up two-thirds of Congress but four-fifths of the total of members who received sanctions.[59] There is no reason to believe that Democrats are more corrupt than their higher rate of sanction implies. Rather, it appears that the offenses they are more likely to commit are those most likely to receive more severe sanctions. Democrats are more often charged with bribery and related offenses; Republicans are more often accused of conflicts of interest.[60]

Although the ethics committees have probably provided a less partisan forum than other committees in Congress, their independence has come at a cost in accountability. One of the reasons they have been able to maintain a spirit of cooperation is that they have done much of their business in private. To the extent that the proceedings take place in public, partisanship is more likely to break out. In the future the committees may find it more difficult to maintain the traditions of bipartisanship, even in private. There are already some ominous signs. Some members with long experience on the Senate committee say that during the Keating Five case partisanship intruded into their proceedings for the first time. Most of the members of the House committee in the 1990s are new, as are the chair and ranking member, and the tone of these meetings is also becoming more partisan, according to staff and former members.[61] As comity deteriorates in Congress, the committees cannot expect to escape its effects.[62] To the extent that they are creatures of Congress, the committees will partake of the characteristics of Congress. A body for deciding ethics charges that is more removed would provide better insurance for independent judgment.

A different threat to the independent judgment of the committees comes from the structure of the process itself. The committee that decides whether there is sufficient evidence to go forward with a case is the same committee that decides whether the accused member is guilty and should be punished. It is as if the prosecutor, grand jury, jury, and judge were combined in a single body. Committee members themselves have said that it is difficult under these circumstances to avoid prejudging a case.[63] For the accused member and for the public, the preliminary judgment is often regarded as the final judgment.

To avoid these difficulties, House committee rules now provide that the preliminary inquiry be conducted by a subcommittee and the final adjudication be settled by the rest of the committee.[64] But the new procedure has yet to be tested, and some observers do not think it is likely to overcome the problems of prejudgment. The committee chair and ranking member serve ex officio on the subcommittee, and the same staff serves both the subcommittee and the full committee. A reform proposed by Senator Rudman would avoid this problem in the Senate by establishing a separate adjudicatory committee; it would be composed only of senators who are not members of the ethics committee and who serve only once to decide a single case.[65] This proposal would probably lessen the problem of prejudgment, but it might well create new problems of continuity. Because its membership would change from case to case, the adjudicatory committee could not develop any traditions or common experience and would be less likely to reach consistent judgments over time. The Senate Ethics Study Commission could not agree on any proposal that would assign different members to different phases of an inquiry. It restricted itself to recommending that the current multistep process be reduced to two basic steps, investigatory and adjudicatory.[66]

These proposals move in the right direction. The multistep process was intended to dispose of false or frivolous charges expeditiously and thereby serve fairness, but it has had the opposite effect. It gives prominence to charges earlier and for a longer time before any final judgment is reached. A two-step process would reduce unnecessary delay and duplication and create less confusion about the meaning of findings at each stage. It is likely better to serve the interests of members and the public.

In the ethics committees of both chambers, therefore, investigation should be separated from adjudication.[67] Investigation should include the power to make a preliminary finding (for example, whether there is substantial credible evidence that a violation of standards has occurred). Different members with different staffs should serve on bodies performing each function, and some continuity of membership should be maintained. Even if no other changes were made, the separation of these functions would improve on the present process, especially in the Senate.

Another protection of independent judgment is the power to appoint a special counsel. Under the present system in which only members judge members, the counsel is essential. Special counsel should be appointed not only in unusually time-consuming or complicated cases in which the committees lack resources or staff to conduct an adequate inquiry, but also in cases in which citizens have special reason to doubt that members could judge their colleagues, notably in those that have strong partisan overtones or that include allegations of institutional corruption.

In any two-step process the appointment of a special counsel should be required in the investigatory phase unless there is a compelling reason to the contrary. This is close to the present de facto procedure in the Senate.[68] In the first phase the counsel would act primarily as a fact finder and legal adviser. The counsel should also normally continue in the adjudicatory phase, but the role here would be that of an advocate for the committee's conclusion reached in the first phase.

Fairness to Members

Another purpose of separating investigation and adjudication is to enhance the fairness of the process. Other changes may also be necessary to ensure that accused members are treated fairly. Fairness does not require that members be granted the same rights an ordinary citizen would receive in the criminal process. They should not enjoy the same kinds of rights of privacy, for example. Nor should members demand greater rights than other citizens: like an ordinary citizen in a criminal proceeding, a senator must comply with a subpoena for his diary.[69] But fairness does call for some basic procedural protections for the sake of members as well as for the public interest in the rights of all public officials.

The current rules of both committees grant certain rights to accused members, but the rights are not complete and their exercise is wholly subject to the discretion of the committees.[70] The full Senate and House should guarantee members some basic protections. They should be notified promptly of the content of any complaint against them and of any decision by the committee to proceed with an investigation. They should have the right to be represented by counsel once an investigation begins and throughout the rest of the process, up to and including action by the full Senate or House. Members should have the opportunity to see (in an appropriate form) the evidence available to the committee and the opportunity to be heard by the committee and bring further evidence to its attention. None of these protections need delay or obstruct an otherwise legitimate proceeding. All are necessary not only to ensure fairness but also to expedite the dismissal of unfounded or frivolous allegations and to improve the quality of information that the committees receive.

Probably the most disturbing unfair treatment comes from the effects of a false charge. The mere making of a charge, whether it has merit or not, is sometimes enough to damage a member's reputation and career. Even if the member is exonerated, the damage often has been done. The charge can cause serious damage to the institution as well. One of the most egregious cases—the one most often mentioned by members in interviews—was the charge in 1982 by two former pages that some thirty members had had sexual relations with pages. After a yearlong investigation, a special counsel concluded that the original charges had no foundation.[71] Many of the members who had been falsely accused believe that far more people noticed the accusation than the vindication.[72] (In the course of investigation the special counsel did discover two other cases of improper sexual relations with pages. The members involved, who had not been named in the original accusations, were censured by the House.)[73]

In the current system the principal protection against false charges is the requirement that any individual who submits a complaint to the committee must swear to its truth and satisfy several other procedural requirements. In the House the complainant must try to get three members to sign the complaint before going to the committee.[74] One staff member acknowledges that "we have made it more difficult for ordinary citizens to file a complaint."[75] The strategy seems to be to keep the threshold for making complaints high in the hope of discouraging unfair charges. If so, it is misguided. The threshold fails to block some ill-founded charges that the committee should not consider and may suppress some well-grounded ones that it should consider seriously.

Formal complaints are not the only the basis for starting an investigation. The committees find it impossible to ignore some serious charges made in the press or in public forums, whether or not any formal complaints are filed.[76] In the past, committees have begun an inquiry simply on the basis of a report in the press, as the House committee did in the 1987 case of St. Germain.[77] In general, barriers to bringing complaints should be kept low for several reasons. First, public confidence in the process will be undermined if citizens think that complaints are dismissed for technical reasons or that one has to be a lawyer to get the attention of an ethics committee. Second, if the barrier is high, valid charges may escape investigation. Formal requirements do not reliably separate valid or serious from invalid or trivial charges. An anonymous submission of documents could turn out to be more substantial than a sworn complaint as the basis of a serious charge. Neither should committees have to wait for a complaint from any individual: some of the offenses most damaging to Congress have no identifiable victims.

A low threshold may actually better protect members. Although it permits more spurious complaints to be presented, it provides a more effective way of resolving them. If a complaint is rejected for technical reasons, the public will continue to harbor suspicions. Complaints thus rejected do not usually die; they fester in the press. The lower threshold also makes the initiation of action by a committee more common and therefore less damaging. A higher threshold gives any complaint that meets it greater legitimacy.

Rather than raising the threshold, Congress should consider raising the cost of making false charges. The committees, or preferably a semi-independent commission, could issue a formal criticism of members who deliberately or negligently make false charges.

In some cases committees could impose more serious sanctions on such members. Although the First Amendment prevents Congress from punishing private citizens or members of the press for making false charges, it does not prevent ethics committees from criticizing them. It is of course often controversial whether a charge is false or frivolous, but in flagrant cases there should be enough agreement to make sanctions credible.

Another potential source of unfairness is the breadth of the standards by which members are judged. Standards that refer to conduct that "shall reflect creditably on the House" or the avoidance of "improper conduct which may reflect upon the Senate" do not themselves provide much guidance.[78] As noted earlier, similar concerns arise about the appearance standard. Some members object that broad standards subject them to something like an ex post facto law. They do not provide fair notice of what conduct is prohibited, and they invite politically motivated charges.

Nevertheless, this kind of broad standard is important and should be retained. No specific code could capture the full range of conduct that, in the changing circumstances of political life, could damage Congress. A code would inevitably fail to capture some conduct that should be prohibited and could impugn some innocent conduct by failing to recognize explicitly some of the special circumstances under which members work and the environment of the institution. Protections against institutional corruption are especially difficult to codify.

Furthermore, the more comprehensive a code is, the more complicated it becomes and the more easily subject to neglect by members or abuse by those who would make false or politically motivated charges. A broad general standard permits more charges, but it also gives fewer of them immediate legitimacy. A charge under a broad standard will have little public impact unless it identifies a genuine and serious wrong. It must appeal to a distinct sense that the conduct in question violates some widely shared moral principle, not simply some obscure technical rule of the Senate or House. Institutional corruption could be brought under such a general moral principle by emphasizing the damage it causes to the democratic process and thereby to the rights and welfare of all citizens.

Fairness is a matter not only of the rights but also of the obligations of members. A duty of fair play, doing one's part to make the institution work, imposes institutional responsibilities on all members.[79] They are responsible for accepting unpleasant assignments (such as service on the ethics committees), for trying to improve the institution rather than just attacking it, and for calling colleagues to account for misconduct. Failure to take responsibility for collective problems poses serious dangers to the capacity of the institution to function and contributes to the erosion of public confidence in it. If each member looks only after his or her political fortunes, no one is left to look after the institution's ethical integrity.

It is neither realistic nor fair to expect any individual member to fulfill these institutional obligations in the absence of some reasonable assurance that other members will do the same. The logic of collective action, much studied by social scientists, shows why. If a collective good such as institutional integrity is being provided, then any individual can benefit from it without contributing to it. The member can be a free rider. If a collective good is not being provided, it is not in the interest of any individual to contribute to it, not only because the contribution may not make enough difference, but also because making the contribution may work to the individual's disadvantage. Members who spend more time than others do on institutional chores have less time for electoral pursuits. Also, defending Congress when colleagues and challengers are all attacking it is not usually a winning strategy. Relying on voluntary contributions to the collective good is therefore not likely to be sufficient. Members may need some further encouragement—some "selective incentives"—if they are to take their institutional responsibilities seriously.

It is bound to be difficult to implement reforms that would institutionalize such incentives in Congress. The same logic that makes the incentives necessary also makes their institutionalization less likely. It is not usually in the interest of individual members to devote themselves to carrying out this kind of reform. Nor is it easy to find incentives powerful enough to overcome the political pressures working in the opposite direction. Nevertheless, some members are dedicated to making the institution work better and are prepared to take political risks to do so. They may provide the leadership necessary to undertake reforms of this kind. Although many failures of institutional responsibility are probably beyond the reach of internal discipline, some are not. For a start the chambers could establish a rule, once proposed by the House ethics committee but never adopted, that would require any member and employee who becomes aware of any ethics violation to report it in writing to an ethics committee.[80] Some of the measures discussed in chapter 3 could also help: for example, denying members certain committee assignments or eliminating procedural devices that invite abuses.

The incentives need not be only punitive. A more positive approach is worth considering, at least as a supplement. Members should look for ways to balance the almost wholly negative character of ethics enforcement so that it would depend more on reward. Jeremy Bentham, that diligent theorist of legislatures, noted long ago that reward serves better to produce "acts of the positive stamp" and is more likely to be self-enforcing because officials have an incentive to bring forward the necessary evidence.[81] We should care as much about honoring faithful legislators as condemning felonious ones. For example, some independent body might be authorized to formally recognize members who have exceptional records in fulfilling their institutional responsibilities. The body would have to guard against the natural tendency to pass out so many of these awards that they would come to mean little. But if judiciously selected and effectively presented, they could serve not only to recognize the contributions of individuals but might also eventually improve the reputation of the institution.

Accountability to the Public

It has already been shown how accountability places some limits on what fairness might otherwise require. Now further implications of members' duty to account for their conduct need to be considered.

In a legislature that is the most open in the world, the ethics committees are relatively closed.[82] The Senate committee has held public hearings on charges only five times since 1977 and the House only three.[83] The rules of procedure of both committees contain many provisions to prevent unauthorized disclosure but few to ensure legitimate publicity. The largest part of the committees' work takes place without any public record at all. Members, often only the chair and vice chair or ranking member, deal with most of the complaints and conduct preliminary reviews when necessary. The staff spends most of its time giving advice to members, only a small part of which ever becomes part of the record in the form of advisory opinions. Several former staff members with long experience in providing such advice said that they were often told not to be so hard on members and to tell them "how to do what they want to do." The kind of common law that develops under these conditions of confidentiality, one staffer said, is "parochial and permissive."[84]

The committees have the power to convene executive sessions at any time. In the House the committee is required to make public only a brief statement of an alleged violation and any written response from the accused member once a formal inquiry has begun. In the Senate the reports of staff and special counsel are treated as confidential.[85] The special counsel's report in the Keating Five case became public only because one of the committee members made it part of his own report. Some other members even brought charges against him for leaking a confidential document. When the committees do issue public reports, they are often too brief to be informative. From reading only the Senate committee's report on the D'Amato case, even well-informed readers would have difficulty in discovering what conduct led to the charges, let alone why the committee thought the conduct did not violate any standards.[86] Although critics later raised questions about D'Amato's testimony, the committee never released the transcripts of the hearings.[87]

Some of this secrecy is understandable. It not only protects the rights of members and witnesses, it also encourages citizens to bring forward complaints and enables committees to investigate them effectively and objectively. If a semi-independent commission took over the early phases of the process, perhaps confidentiality would be more acceptable. But in conjunction with the problem of members judging members, secrecy undermines public confidence. It tilts the balance too far against accountability.

If the present structure of the ethics process is not changed, the ethics committees should be required to make public the content of all complaints and their disposition. If the complaint is dismissed, reasons should be given. Committees should issue a full report at the end of any investigation and at the conclusion of any adjudication. If a special counsel is appointed at any stage, he or she should be required to prepare a report, which should also be made public at an appropriate time. The need for accountability and public confidence outweighs any increased burden of work and any risk of harm from leaked reports. Furthermore, if citizens knew that a full report would be made public at some stage, they could more easily accept the fact that some of the proceedings would be kept confidential in the earlier stages.

Another aspect of accountability is the length of time in which members are answerable for their actions. How far into the past are ethics committees entitled to probe? The Senate committee has no statute of limitations, a policy reaffirmed by its Ethics Study Commission. The House committee generally does not consider any allegations of conduct that occurred before the third previous Congress.[88]

These practices are more defensible than they might at first appear. Fairness does not require committees to refuse absolutely to consider allegations of violations that occurred in the past. A statute of limitations for ethics violations could even deny a member the opportunity of vindication in the face of old charges. It would also prevent action against offenses such as crimes of violence that could seriously impair collegial relations and could further undermine public confidence. But statutes of limitations in general serve some important purposes. They help prevent the prosecution of cases in which the evidence is unreliable because of the passage of time. They also provide an incentive for law enforcement officials to carry out their investigations expeditiously. Further, they provide a sense of security by ensuring that no citizen has to live indefinitely under the threat of possible prosecution for an offense that may or may not have been committed.

For public officials, however, the value of statutes of limitations is reduced or outweighed by other factors, particularly by accountability. Evidence against public officials is likely to have a longer shelf life than evidence against other citizens; it is likely to remain reliable for a longer period of time. Many charges against public officials rest heavily on documents, for example. Besides, the committees could take into account the reliability of evidence before proceeding to a full investigation. The passage of time may be a reasonable basis for dismissing cases in which the most important evidence consists of testimony of eyewitnesses or participants. Similarly, committees need not pursue charges that have lost their relevance because of the passage of time, such as conflict of interest violations when a member's financial circumstances have changed significantly.

A statute of limitations may be desirable in a system in which a large number of prosecutors deal with a large number of cases. But it is an unnecessarily crude instrument in the more limited and more visible system that constitutes the ethics process. This is also why the incentive to pursue investigations expeditiously is less relevant. Finally, legislators should not (and indeed most do not) expect to enjoy as much protection from public scrutiny of their past lives as ordinary citizens reasonably demand. Part of the price of public service is the sacrifice of some of this security.

The ultimate instrument of accountability inside Congress is the power to discipline members; yet the range of sanctions available to the ethics committees and the chamber as a whole is limited. Because expulsion is rarely used, public criticism ranging from censure to reproval is the principal mode of discipline. (In recent years, fines have occasionally been imposed, as in the Durenberger case.) In the Senate the absence of fixed terminology of criticism has led the attorneys of accused members, evidently armed with thesauruses, to negotiate for the mildest possible language. Senators Herman Talmadge and Durenberger preferred to be "denounced" rather than "censured," and the ethics committee complied. The proliferation of terms—confusing to members as well as to the public—has probably contributed to suspicions about the fairness and openness of the process.

The Senate Ethics Study Commission's recommendation to simplify the schema of sanctions (bringing it closer to the one used by the House) could help alleviate the problem.[89] Committees themselves should take more responsibility to clarify the meaning of the sanction in each case they decide. In addition to specifying the level of severity and the rule or standard that was violated, a formal judgment by a committee could describe the kind of injury to individuals and the kind of damage to the institution at stake.

Measures could also be taken to give the committee (or at least the chamber as a whole) more authority over what can be one of the most potent sanctions: the loss of positions of power within Congress (chairmanships, ranking memberships, and seniority). At present the Senate committee can only recommend these sanctions to party conferences, which have never imposed any such discipline.[90] In the

House since 1980 the Democratic Caucus has required members who are indicted in the criminal process to step down from chairmanships. Republicans have been more reluctant to discipline members under such circumstances. The party refused to remove Joseph McDade from his position as ranking member of the Appropriations Committee long after he had been indicted in 1992 on charges of bribery.[91] Because party organizations in Congress have not acted as vigorously as they should, prohibitions should become part of the chambers' rules, and ethics committees should be given the authority to impose these sanctions. The positions from which members would be removed are properly considered offices of the institution, not the private property of the parties or individual members. All citizens and therefore all members have a legitimate interest in making sure that those who hold these positions live up to the ethical standards of the institution.[92]

The Need for Ethics Commissions

No matter how much the ethics committees are strengthened and their procedures improved, the institutional conflict of interest inherent in members judging members remains. Most other professions and most other institutions have come to appreciate that self-regulation of ethics is not adequate and have accepted at least a modest measure of outside discipline. Congress should do the same.

Proposals to establish an independent body that would supplement and partially replace the functions of the ethics committees are not popular in Congress. In 1994 the Senate Ethics Study Commission considered and rejected all proposals that would involve outsiders in the process.[93] Nevertheless, support for them is growing. Members in both houses have introduced resolutions—at last count, five—that would establish some version of an independent body.[94] Many state legislatures have set up independent ethics commissions, many of which regulate conduct of legislators as well as campaign practices and lobbyists.[95] Some city councils have created similar commissions.

The advantages of delegating some authority to a relatively independent body should be clear. They mirror the deficiencies of self-regulation discussed earlier. An outside body would be likely to reach more objective, independent judgments. It could more credibly protect members' rights and enforce institutional obligations without regard to political or personal loyalties. It would provide more effective accountability and help restore the confidence of the public in the ethics process. An additional advantage that should appeal to all members: an outside body would reduce the time that any member would have to spend on the chores of ethics regulation.

The need for an outside body is especially important in cases of institutional corruption. Here the institutional conflict of interest is at its most severe. When members judge other members for conduct that is part of the job they all do together, the perspectives of the judge and the judged converge most closely. The conduct at issue cannot be separated from the norms and practices of the institution, and the judgment in the case implicates all who are governed by those norms and practices. The political fate of the judges and the judged is also joined together. Even if they are of different parties, they face similar political pressures. Especially when the institution is implicated in the corruption, some of those who judge the corruption should come from outside the institution.

There are many different ways of involving nonmembers in the process, and some are more likely than others to achieve the needed improvements.[96] In general, the better methods keep the roles of the members and nonmembers separate. Any such reform should also be consistent with a two-step process of investigation and adjudication and with the principles of legislative ethics. Here is one version of an enforcement process that meets these criteria.

A Model for Ethics Commissions

Two bodies in each chamber would be responsible for enforcing standards of ethics in Congress: an ethics committee resembling the present body and a semi-independent ethics commission. (A possible variation would establish a single commission for both chambers.) The commissions would investigate charges against members to determine whether there is substantial, credible evidence that a violation of the chamber's ethics rules has occurred. The proceedings of the commissions would not normally be public, but they would publicly report their findings to their respective ethics committees. The commissions' membership, budget, and the standards they enforce would all be under the control of their ethics committee or each chamber as a whole.

Each commission would consist of seven distinguished citizens with a knowledge of legislative ethics and congressional practice. Three would be appointed by the majority leader or Speaker and three by the minority leader of each chamber. The seventh who would serve as chair, would be chosen by the other six from a list of three proposed by the ethics committee of the relevant chamber (with a random procedure for breaking ties). Commission members would serve six-year, staggered terms. No sitting members, family or business associates of members, lobbyists, or others with close current connections to Congress could serve.

The number of former members who might serve should be limited, perhaps to a maximum of two, although few former members would be likely to meet criteria set out above and also be willing to serve. No more than one or two former members would probably be needed to make sure that the commissions are adequately informed about the customs and practices of congressional life. More would be likely to dominate the process, as professionals typically do on ethics committees and disciplinary boards that include lay representation. Further, it is important to keep this part of the process as independent as possible, primarily to inspire public confidence. Also, the more independent the commissions are, the more acceptable the confidentiality of the proceedings is likely to be. With relatively independent commissions, confidentiality could be consistent with accountability and promote fairness and independence at the same time.

In addition to investigating cases, the commissions could also take over the advisory and educational functions now exercised by the ethics committees. They could also oversee the audit of the financial disclosure reports. The staffs of the commissions would operate more like a congressional service such as the Congressional Budget Office. The aim would be to develop a professional staff as independent as possible from the partisan divisions and collegial pressures of the Senate and House. The commissions would also be well placed to review not only individual conduct but also institutional practices and make recommendations for institutional reforms.

The Role of the Ethics Committees

Under this proposal the composition of the ethics committees would not necessarily change, but their functions would be significantly modified. They would hear and decide cases only after the commission had found credible evidence of a violation. They would then make a final judgment or a recommendation to the full chamber. If the work of the commission and its report were as through and fair as it should be, a committee's task would be much simpler than it is now. Many cases could probably be settled without any hearings, and in those that could not, the hearings would probably be much shorter.

It is true that in cases in which a committee disagreed with a commission's finding, the committee could feel forced to conduct extensive hearings itself. But these hearings would not likely be any longer than those in the present system or those in any of the other proposed systems, and on this plan they would be less frequent. The committees would still have the final authority on any changes in the standards, although the recommendations could come from the commissions and their staffs.

Simplifying the tasks of the ethics committees in this way would make many of the questions that critics have raised about the present system less urgent. There would be no need to expand the number of members. More senior members might be persuaded to serve. Rotating terms (which reduce continuity) would be less necessary. There would be no problems about the status of nonmembers on a congressional committee. Other tensions in the present system, such as the conflict between confidentiality and accountability, would also be reduced.

Objections to Ethics Commissions

But would this proposal ease the problems of the ethics committees only to create greater problems for the new commissions? Some critics argue that assigning any significant part of the ethics process to outsiders would be an abdication of congressional responsibility.[97] The constitutional provision (Article I, section 5) granting Congress the authority to determine rules and punish members implies that only members should discipline other members for ethics violations. Any attempt to dilute that authority, it is argued, would be irresponsible and perhaps unconstitutional.

This objection has some force, and ultimately provides the main reason Congress should not create a completely independent agency or commission to enforce ethical standards. Congress must have the final authority for disciplining its members. This seems a reasonable inference from the Constitution, and a necessity given the limitations of alternative tribunals. Neither voters nor judges can do the job alone. It is therefore not likely that any single body could.

But the objection does not go as far as the critics think. That Congress must have final authority does not mean that it must have continuous control of the process. In the first place, Article I, section 5 does not literally prohibit the delegation of this authority. It says only that Congress "may" determine rules and punish its members, not "shall," the term used in some other clauses to express nondiscretionary standards. In addition, no authoritative court decision has interpreted this clause in a way that would prevent Congress from establishing an outside body for enforcing ethics rules. One of the few cases bearing on the clause points in the opposite direction. The decision held that a lower court did not have jurisdiction over a claim made by House members that they were denied their share of seats on committees.[98]

Virtually all the proposals under consideration leave to Congress the power of appointing members to the outside body and the authority to make the final judgment in any particular case. The proposals differ chiefly in how much of the process prior to final judgment (investigation, hearing, formal charge) they would assign to the outside body. Within this range of alternatives, considerations of political prudence and administrative convenience may reasonably play a role in designing the proper procedure.

If Congress delegated some authority to the ethics commissions described here, it would not be abdicating responsibility but fulfilling it. Congress would be demonstrating confidence in itself by entrusting part of the process of enforcing ethics rules to citizens who would be more independent than any member could be, not by virtue of their character but of simply their status: they would not be judges in their own cause. The logic of the proposal to establish the commissions is very much in the spirit of other principles inherent in the Constitution. It is a constitutional principle that seeks to separate as far as possible the judges and parties to a cause.

A second common objection to proposals that would establish ethics commissions is that outsiders are not likely to know enough about Congress and its customary practices and are not likely to appreciate the pressures under which members work.[99] It is true that the composition of the proposed commissions favors independence and objectivity over knowledge and sympathy. It is also true that the members of an outside commission should understand well the practices and pressures of life in Congress. However, there is no reason that commission members, especially respected citizens who have followed Congress from the outside for many years, could not learn what they need to know about life inside the institution.

Virtually no one making the objection that outsiders do not know enough ever provides a specific example of knowledge about Congress that could not be conveyed to at least some nonmembers. Pressed in interviews to give such an example, most responded along the lines of "I can't think of anything specific, more a general feeling about the institution. Maybe I will think of something as we go along." Only one of the members interviewed offered a specific example: "an outsider might not appreciate how important it is for members to challenge abuses by the bureaucrats in the executive branch."[100]

The implications of the general objection, if taken seriously, are more far-reaching than may be recognized. If outsiders (even the well-informed citizens that all these proposals assume would be appointed) lack the necessary insight into the legislative service to serve responsibly on a commission, the prospects of the public's learning to trust the decisions of any ethics committee are even more bleak than they seem now. To the extent that no one but insiders can truly understand the customs and practices of Congress, one of the chief purposes of legislative ethics—maintaining public confidence—could never be fulfilled. Legislators could not be held accountable for ethics of the institution as a whole.

A third objection to these commissions is that their members would not be accountable in the way that members of Congress are and therefore would be less likely to make sure that any decision they made could withstand public scrutiny.[101] This would be more troublesome if the commissions were made up of former members or others with close ties to Congress. A commission might then seem to be just a device for letting those with nothing to lose electorally take the political heat. But for truly independent citizens of character and discretion, the absence of electoral accountability would leave room to take public opinion into account to the extent that it is well informed and unbiased. They would have less inclination and less need to respond to political pressures created by special interests or irresponsible media. There is no reason to assume that such citizens are not available or would not serve. Regulatory commissions, special counsels, presidential panels, and many other such bodies attract distinguished and highly competent citizens to government service. Surely Congress can expect no less.

These objections may tell against more extreme proposals that would transfer entirely some of Congress's authority for disciplining its members to a completely independent body. But the objections are not fatal to more moderate proposals that, like the model outlined here, leave Congress with the final authority for enforcing its standards of ethics. Such proposals avoid the vices of not only the more extreme proposals for reform but also the more familiar practices of the current system. A properly designed and adequately staffed outside body could begin to overcome the "innate conflict of interest [that exists] when members of the Ethics Committee are called upon to judge their colleagues."[102]

Conclusion

Institutional corruption is not new, but it is newly prospering. It thrives in a political world where private greed mixes insidiously with the public good, where the difference between serving all citizens and serving supporters blurs, where public officials can evade responsibility for institutional failure. In the United States the executive branch has provided fertile territory for this kind of corruption. Many of the major government scandals of recent years have involved a large measure of institutional corruption—most notably, Watergate, Iran-contra, and the assortment of scandals commonly known by their initials, HUD, BCCI, and BNL.[1]

But it is in Congress that the problem has become most critical because the conditions that nourish institutional corruption are built into the very role of the representatives. To do their job, legislators must seek the support of private interests, provide service for constituents on whom they depend for campaign contributions, and defend their record to voters who care more about what they have done for the district or state than what they have done for Congress or the country.

These demands conspire with the growing complexity of the legislative environment to promote institutional corruption. As the job of the legislator becomes more complicated, opportunities for—and suspicions of—institutional corruption multiply. Acting from perfectly proper motives and simply trying to do their job, members increasingly find themselves in ethical difficulties. Sometimes they are unfairly accused, sometimes unfairly excused. In the mists of ambiguity that surround judgments about institutional corruption, some critics are too eager to make charges, some colleagues too ready to offer apologies. Both take advantage of the grey areas of ethics, to the disadvantage of the integrity of the institution and ultimately the democratic process.

We can better guard against the cunning ways of this form of corruption if we stay alert to its distinctive characteristics. In its pure form it differs in each of its elements from individual corruption, the more familiar variety. In institutional corruption the *gain* that the legislator seeks is political rather than personal. Political gain is part of the job, and when properly pursued is not only acceptable but admirable. What makes it improper is not that it promotes the narrow self-interest of legislators at the expense of the general public interest, as did the personal gains of David Durenberger or Harrison Williams. It is improper because it violates institutional norms that protect the democratic process. Using congressional office staff to help run a reelection campaign is a typical form of improper political gain. The line between personal and political is not always sharp, and where it should be drawn is a central concern of legislative ethics. What benefits should count as legitimate perquisites of office, for example, depends in part on what legislators need to do their job.

The *service* that a member provides to a constituent counts as individual corruption when the constituent does not deserve it. Providing it to the constituent violates general standards of justice. John Dowdy's assisting the criminal schemes of Monarch Construction, or Alfonse D'Amato's letting his brother use his office for lobbying exemplify this kind of improper service. In institutional corruption, what makes the service improper is not the merit of the cause but the manner in which the service is provided. It violates norms of the institution and thereby undermines the democratic process. Even if Jim Wright's oil company constituents had a just complaint against bank regulators, he should not have pressured the Bank Board's chair by using his power to put a "hold" on the recapitalization bill. In many cases the merit and manner of the service are closely related: when members fail to consider the merits of a constituent's cause, the manner of their intervention is improper, even if it turns out that the cause is meritorious. Even if Charles Keating's cause had been just, no senator should have pressured the Bank Board to decide in his favor in a quasi-adjudicatory proceeding.

The *connection* between the gain and the service that creates individual corruption runs through the mind of the individual legislator. It is a corrupt motive. Members need not have, like ABSCAM defendant John Jenrette, "larceny in [their] blood." Nor need they act out of greed, as Howell Heflin assumed Harrison Williams did in the same sting operation. But in instances of personal corruption a member acts because of or in exchange for a thing of value. The paradigm is bribery, though more indirect exchanges such as the book deals of Durenberger and Wright also qualify.

In institutional corruption, the connection is made through the practices and norms of the legislature. The connection consists of an institutional tendency that damages the legislature and the democratic process in various ways. Even when members do not knowingly provide a service because of a gain, their actions may create other connections between the gain and service that cause institutional damage. The appearance of impropriety for which the Senate ethics committee rebuked Dennis DeConcini and Donald Riegle displays this kind of connection. So does the special access gained by corporations and lobbyists who provide members travel and entertainment. It is not the motives of members but what Frank Lautenberg described as the cumulative impact of patterns of influence in Congress.

Despite its growing importance, institutional corruption has not received the attention it deserves. First, because it is so closely related to conduct that is part of the job of the modern representative, members take institutional corruption less seriously than its harms warrant. Ethics committees are more comfortable condemning colleagues for isolated and intentional wrongs. That kind of misconduct is less likely to raise questions about the institutional practices in which committee members themselves also participate.

To some extent this hesitancy is understandable. An overly zealous campaign against institutional corruption could have a chilling effect on many perfectly legitimate practices that promote healthy political competition: making deals to win political support, helping citizens fight bureaucratic abuses, taking stands against the party or chamber leadership. Yet it is precisely the danger of this chilling effect that should lead members to pay more attention to institutional corruption, to define its boundaries more carefully. It was partly the failure to face up to this kind of corruption, to formulate standards to deal with it and institutional routines to guard against it, that brought on the troubles of the Keating Five.

A second cause of the neglect of institutional corruption is the dynamic of corruption conversion. That dynamic forces institutional corruption into the pattern of individual corruption. The Senate could finally reprimand Alan Cranston because his conduct came closer than that of others of the Keating Five to the model of individual corruption: he helped Keating in exchange for contributions. The other four escaped the wrath of the full Senate because their offenses took on a more institutional cast.

Even when charges of institutional corruption are made, they often have the effect of diminishing its significance. The House ethics committee's rare finding of an institutional violation in Wright's case (the appearance of impropriety in accepting gifts from George Mallick) seemed to result more from doubt about the charge of individual corruption than from any conviction about the seriousness of the institutional corruption. More often accused members make charges against the institution to divert attention from their own misconduct, as Bob Packwood used the issue of the Senate ethics committee's subpoena to try to forestall further investigation into the charges against him. Another variation was Durenberger's attempt to legitimize his speaking fees by invoking the institutional authority of the Federal Elections Commission.

A curious convergence of defenses and criticisms of institutional corruption is another source of its neglect. The claim that all members do what the Keating Five did, though invoked for different purposes by their critics and defenders, leads to the same conclusion: there is nothing to be done about this kind of conduct. That it is so pervasive must mean either that it is excusable, perhaps even justifiable, or that it results from deep structural flaws in the system for which no individual is responsible. Despite the different attitudes toward the conduct (one sees healthy competition while the other sees debilitating corruption), both defenders and critics encourage the same undifferentiated approach toward it. Because for both views it is ethically speaking all the same, there is no point in trying to devise ethical standards and institutional reforms that would discriminate among the individual actions that produce the conduct.

One consequence of this way of thinking shows itself in the familiar assertion that all the major problems of congressional ethics are the result of the system of campaign finance. Until that system is radically reformed, it is often said, there is no point in tinkering with the ethics process. Certainly, the need to raise large amounts of money to mount an effective campaign is a major source of the corruption in the legislature, especially institutional corruption. But as the earlier discussions of political gain (chapter 3) and corrupt connections (chapter 5) indicated, money is the root of only some evil. Even in the unlikely event that Congress were to provide public funding for all serious candidates, plenty of problems of institutional ethics would remain. In the absence of radical reform of campaign financing, plenty of opportunities for improvements in institutional ethics remain. The improvements suggested here, as well as reforms others have proposed, could make a significant moral difference because they directly affect the integrity of the democratic process. Just because the political system falls short of our moral ideals in one sphere is no excuse for failing to try to make improvements in another sphere. That should be true even for those who believe that the system is deeply corrupt. There are relatively good and bad ways to behave even in a corrupt system. Institutional corruption may reveal another dark side of American politics, but we can still try to recognize degrees of darkness. We should aim for a kind of moral chiaroscuro.

Another reason that institutional corruption does not get the respect it deserves is the dominance of the criminal law model in the ethics process. Despite the repeated statements by ethics committees and testimony by others emphasizing the differences between ethical standards and criminal laws, even a senator as thoughtful as Richard Lugar can still urge that all ethics charges should be handled by prosecutors and the courts. In a legislature heavily populated by lawyers and a political culture deeply imbued with legalism, the pressure to force all cases into a criminal mold is almost irresistible. But the requirements of a criminal process—the need to find guilty minds, corrupt motives, proof beyond a reasonable doubt—militate against discovering, let alone condemning, corruption that takes the institutional form. That is why it was so hard to condemn the Keating Five, each of whom could have said accurately, "I am not a crook."

Even in cases of individual corruption the criminal process may distort the nature of the harm. Durenberger's receiving reimbursement for rent on his own condominium is not exactly the same as an ordinary citizen's defrauding the government. In some respects Durenberger's offense was worse (public officials should set an example, follow a higher standard) and in others more understandable (legislators have to maintain two residences). Neither point is likely to receive the attention it deserves in the criminal process.

The tendency to resort to the categories of criminal law can lead to the neglect of both individual and institutional corruption at the same time. That is a lesson of the John Dowdy case, in which the House ethics committee let the courts deal with what it evidently regarded as the more serious charge of individual corruption, while the courts declined to probe conduct that could have been part of his institutional role. In this interaction between the two processes, perpetrators of corruption of both kinds are likely to escape, as Dowdy did on the main charges of individual and institutional corruption.

Yet another source of the neglect of institutional corruption is public opinion itself. The complexity of institutional corruption does not make for the kind of stories that the press or the public savor. In reporting on Congress the media concentrate more on the drama of personal scandal than analysis of institutional processes.[2] More citizens attribute the problem of corruption to failures of individual members than to any defects of the congressional system.[3] Furthermore, the more closely misconduct fits the model of individual corruption, the worse most citizens think it is. This tendency shows up not only in surveys, but also in public reaction to prominent cases such as the House Bank scandal. The public's belief that members who overdrew their accounts cheated taxpayers and its disregard of the administrative failures that led to the abuses are symptoms of a preoccupation with individual corruption.

The reaction to the House Bank scandal also shows why no one should take any comfort in the public's neglect of institutional corruption. It is true that if citizens ignore institutional corruption, its growing prevalence cannot directly undermine public confidence in government. That might seem an ironic but happy consequence for legislative ethics, because one of its aims is to maintain public confidence. Indeed, for precisely this reason some friends of Congress might even be tempted to urge that legislative ethics remain focused on individual corruption. Congress is already in disrepute, and it hardly needs to give citizens yet another reason to distrust its members.

This temptation should be resisted. It represents a short-sighted view of what is necessary to maintain public confidence. The kind of confidence that legislative ethics seeks to create is founded on accurate information and understanding of the conduct of members and the practices of government. To try to appease the public by concentrating its attention on individual corruption is to invite the kind of misinformed reaction that the response to the House Bank scandal exemplifies. The public will not ignore the effects of institutional corruption but will simply view them in a different and ultimately more destructive light. The best hope for sustaining public confidence is to encourage citizens as well as public officials to develop a better informed and more discriminating understanding of the nature of political corruption, institutional as well as individual.

The preceding chapters have surveyed the damage that institutional corruption can do to the democratic process and have suggested changes that could help diminish the damage it is likely to do in the future. By way of conclusion, the character of that damage and the shape of the proposed changes can be clarified by considering the implications of both for the role of the representative in the contemporary Congress.

Like all political corruption, the institutional kind involves the improper use of public office for private purposes. Corruption shows itself when officials or citizens pursue private interests by circumventing the democratic process. The principles of legislative ethics, rooted in the purposes of the institution, can help identify violations of the democratic process that especially produce institutional corruption. The agents of institutional corruption are still individuals, but their corruption can be understood only in the context of the institution. In this respect the idea of institutional corruption joins the structuralist concerns of traditional political theory with the individualist modes of modern political science.

The principles of legislative ethics deal with the reasons on which representatives act, the terms on which they cooperate, and the methods by which they are held accountable. The principles imply a conception of the proper role of the representative. They can therefore help show how institutional corruption distorts that role and what reforms could restore its integrity. Many of the reforms therefore consist of measures that would separate one aspect of the role from another (for example, fundraising and casework). Some reforms locate different functions in different persons, some apply different standards to different functions, and others simply help members keep their various duties distinct in their own minds and the minds of their constituents. All try to cope with the multiple and conflicting demands that democratic government places on legislators by putting each demand in its proper place. If as a result representatives suffer from ethical schizophrenia, the therapy of choice aims not to induce them to eliminate the conflict but to enable them to keep each distinct and all in balance.

Tensions in the role of the representative come not only from conflicts between principles of legislative ethics and the circumstances of contemporary politics but also from conflicts among the principles themselves. The principles express different values, and therefore the reforms they prescribe may sometimes clash. For example, fairness may be better served by secret proceedings, but accountability calls for publicity. The balance of considerations in this instance favors accountability (chapter 6). In other instances the conflict can be shown to be less severe than it seems at first. Although broad standards (for instance, prohibiting "improper conduct which may reflect upon the Senate") may put members at risk for violations they did not foresee, narrow standards subject members to harsh consequences for technical violations (p. 153).

Nevertheless, the most far-reaching reforms proposed here promote the values of all three of the principles of legislative ethics at the same time. The proposed ethics commission is the prime exhibit (pp. 160–61). An outside body of this kind would alleviate the institutional conflict of interest in which legislators inevitably find themselves when they judge colleagues. The commission would also be in a better position than a congressional committee to assess objectively the need for institutional changes to promote ethical conduct. By at least partly separating the judge from the judged, the commission could help keep the minds of members concentrated on the primary duties of a representative. In this way it would act to block pressures that threaten independent judgment, fair procedure, and public confidence. In the absence of such a commission, the two-step process that the House has adopted offers similar advantages, though in a diluted form.

The proposals to establish other new bodies proceed in the same spirit. The congressional ombudsman or office of casework (pp. 87–88) is designed to increase the chances that interventions would be based on the merits of a case and that all the parties would be treated fairly. Because its officials would stand apart from legislators, it should also increase public confidence. The advisory commission on the perquisites of office (p. 64) has a similar rationale. It is intended to produce a distribution of privileges that is fairer to citizens, challengers, and other members.

The inclination of some of the Keating Five to assume the role of zealous advocate for their constituent illustrates a distortion of the role of representative that offends the principle of independence. When legislators act like lawyers, they do not give sufficient consideration to the merits of their clients' causes and they press their cases beyond the bounds of ethical propriety. They should conduct themselves as representatives, who balance multiple and conflicting demands, taking into account all the particular and general interests that bear on the merits of the issue. When they take advocacy beyond the proper limits of their role, they instigate institutional corruption.

The demand to balance all relevant reasons is not so extravagant as it might seem at first. What it asks is what most members claim they are trying to do, and to a remarkable degree actually try to do.[4] Some of the changes proposed here in the norms and practices of the institution could make it more likely that members would succeed more often in attaining a balanced approach. In general, changes should focus on institutional patterns in which personal or political gain are likely to influence legislative judgment, rather than on isolated instances of personal gain, as is often the case now. The changes should take into account the fundamental feature of representative government—that members act on mixed motives.

Adopting standards that define some conflicts of interest in terms of specific roles (pp. 57–58), strengthening postemployment rules (pp. 58–60), and modifying the gift rules (pp. 107–08) to break up the culture of coziness between members and lobbyists could better concentrate the minds of members on the merits of legislation. So could standards that emphasize "relevant reasons" rather than "undue influence" in regulating members' interventions in administrative proceedings (pp. 94–96). The separation of fundraising and casework within each member's office (pp. 118–21) could be even more important. The practice would help preserve the integrity of not only casework but also of campaign contributions, discouraging Keating-type contributions. Other separations in the ethics process itself would serve a similar purpose.

Other proposals to change institutional practices are intended primarily to support the rights and obligations of members, the province of the principle of fairness. Again the method is to differentiate the various roles of representatives more clearly. Some changes try to create more distance between the role of legislators and prosecutors by letting courts adjudicate general offenses (pp. 52–55) and by subjecting members to all the laws they impose on other citizens, such as employment regulations Congress only recently applied to itself (p. 65). Other changes would promote fair competition by preventing members from taking advantage of their official positions. That is the rationale for preventing former office staff from joining their member's campaign immediately after leaving their jobs (pp. 73–75).

Fairness also demands that as caseworkers members do not use private information from constituents for other purposes—for example, to promote their own political causes or campaigns (p. 98). Fairness is also part of the purpose of the proposed restrictions on interventions in adjudicatory and rulemaking administrative proceedings (pp. 89–90). The proposal for a regular review of citizen access to members (pp. 121–22) is meant to expose practices that give some citizens an unfair advantage, whether members intend it or not. Such a review could suggest changes that would better insulate decisions about access from other decisions in which political factors may be more appropriate.

Collegial obligations are more likely to be fulfilled if they too are not completely at the mercy of the pressures that follow members from their other roles. To protect the rights of members from such pressures, they should be formally guaranteed by each chamber (pp. 150–51). Also because of these pressures, authorizing stronger sanctions against members who make false charges should be considered (pp. 151–53). Because electoral pressures do not support collegial obligations, ethics committees must look for other ways to encourage members to do their fair share of the collective chores of the legislature and to do their part in maintaining procedures necessary for collective cooperation (pp. 72–76, 153–55).

Representatives can hardly escape the demands of the principle of accountability. They are only too well aware that all who wish to continue to serve must face the voters in the next election. But the electoral process does not provide an adequate tribunal for making the judgments that legislative ethics requires. An ethics committee or its equivalent is necessary to hold members accountable to their colleagues and to all citizens for conduct that affects the integrity of the institution as a whole. By enforcing the other principles of legislative ethics, the committees also promote accountability.

But the principle of accountability makes its own distinctive demand: representatives should act so as to maintain public confidence. The appearance standard, better construed as a tendency standard that recognizes that citizens and legislators may reasonably make different judgments about official conduct, is a principal means of fulfilling this obligation (pp. 124–30). It too may be seen as sharpening a division in the role of the representative, but by distinguishing grounds of judgment rather than by dividing functions. The standard separates the reasons for acting from the conditions under which members act. It asks representatives to acknowledge that acting for the right reasons is not the same as acting in ways that would enable a citizen reasonably to believe that they are acting for the right reasons. In this respect the conscientious representative must be of two minds. Yet both are morally motivated: the obligation to take into account the reasonable reactions of citizens is no less an ethical duty than the obligation to satisfy one's own conscience.

No less important than giving the appearance standard its due is making sure that the appearances on which it relies are correctly understood and competently judged. Media sound bites and survey statistics are hardly adequate to enable people to judge appearances.

The body that applies the standard therefore should be insulated from the immediate pressures of public opinion. The appearance standard also respects representatives' need for discretion in deciding how to interpret their roles. One of the advantages of the appearance standard, properly applied, is that it reduces the need to adopt increasingly detailed codes.

Most of the specific changes suggested here to promote accountability may be seen as ways to reassure citizens that representatives are properly balancing their many roles and keeping one from contaminating another. This is the point of urging that the whole process of administrative intervention be more public than it is at present (pp. 100–01). It is also the reason that disclosure rules should be tailored more closely to the specific responsibilities that members have in the legislature (pp. 57–58). Making it easy for citizens to bring ethics complaints (pp. 151–52) and making the content of complaints and their disposition public (pp. 155–57) should increase public confidence in the ethics process. So should the policy of giving fuller explanations of the meaning of sanctions and more often imposing the strong sanctions of loss of institutional status, such as committee seniority (pp. 158–59).

Some might argue these and other efforts to win the confidence of the public are futile.[5] The public, especially the news media, will never be satisfied, no matter how many reforms Congress makes. Congress has added more and tougher standards and imposed sanctions on more members in recent years, yet public confidence continues to decline and demands for reform continue to increase. Why bother to try to satisfy such apparently insatiable demands? The first answer must be that Congress has no realistic alternative. In a democratic system, legislators cannot do their jobs without seeking to win the confidence of citizens. Even if individual members manage to win reelection in the face of widespread cynicism about Congress, they will still suffer the effects of ethical controversy, as it implicates their colleagues and interferes with the conduct of legislative business. If members do not continue to try to improve the ethics process, they will find themselves and the institution increasingly deflected from legislative duties.

The loss of confidence in Congress does not mean that the reforms of recent years have had no positive effect. The decline is no doubt the result of many causes unrelated to ethics and might even have been worse if Congress had taken its ethics less seriously than it did. Furthermore, the improvements, modest though they may have been, have not gone without notice. Informed observers and other opinion leaders believe that members are more honest and the institution less corrupt than it used to be, which is likely to have a favorable effect on public opinion in the long run. Finally, some of the continuing distrust may be warranted. Citizens are surely right to be suspicious of some practices of ethics committees, such as refusing to release testimony and reports. Also, some reforms may not have gone far enough or may not have been focused precisely enough on the ethical problems that should be of most concern. The recommendations throughout this book have not called simply for more rules of the same kind but for more specifically targeted rules and for different, more credible bodies to enforce them.

No reforms alone can restore public confidence or promote legislative independence and fairness unless both citizens and their representatives come to understand better the nature and importance of ethics in the modern Congress. The obstacles to progress do not lie only in the political circumstances of government but also in the ethical beliefs of citizens and officials. Changes in the way we think about the ethics of representation are just as important as changes in the structures of representative government. Our beliefs inform our political customs and institutional routines, sometimes without our being aware of their influence. The beliefs shape judgments about what ethical conduct is most important and what should count as ethical misconduct. It is a set of beliefs that reinforces the preoccupation with individual corruption. In the habit of thinking in an individualist mode, citizens and their representatives too often look only for corrupt motives, undeserved service, and proximate connections; they overlook more far-reaching forms of wrongdoing that distort democratic representation. It is these forms that the idea of institutional corruption seeks to capture and the measures proposed here seek to correct.

Because the way we think about the ethics of representation is so important, congressional efforts to educate its members and the public about ethics are essential. During the hearings on the organization of Congress, Senator Paul Sarbanes urged more ethics education in Congress. He suggested that Congress should seek programs that would "sensitize [members to ethics questions] early . . . lay out a lot of practical examples in order to give them a real feel for the standard" and "really push their members to a higher level."[6]

Perhaps the first step should be to make sure that citizens and public officials know that ethics committees exist. During cross-examination in the Keating Five hearings, Bank Board Chair Edwin Gray was asked why, if he thought the conduct of the senators was unethical, did he not report it to the ethics committee. "You want the real answer?" he responded. Vice Chair Rudman assured him, "We always want the real answer to everything, Mr. Gray." So Gray continued: "Fine. The real answer is, I didn't know there was a Senate Ethics Committee, with all due respect to you gentlemen."[7]

Congress should sponsor training sessions and other educational programs to help members, staff, lobbyists, and the press better understand not only the current standards and procedures but also the dilemmas that members face in the current political climate.[8] The staffs of both ethics committees already perform a valuable educational function by providing advice when members ask specific questions. But the advising function would be more valuable if members used it more often for ethical enlightenment than for political cover. The ethics committees could also increase their programs to train the staffs of all members and those of legislative committees. At present some of the most effective ethics training is conducted by outside agencies, most notably the Congressional Management Foundation, a nonprofit group that runs sessions mainly for congressional staff. The benefits of such sessions could be greater if Congress required some regular ethics training for all staff, encouraged members themselves to attend such sessions, and cooperated with other organizations (perhaps even including the press) in arranging forums for various groups and the public.

As part of these educational efforts, ethics committees should try to develop a more accessible statement of existing standards, interpretative rulings, and ethics procedures. In their current form they are neither member friendly nor citizen friendly. Both ethics committees should undertake a review of all their standards with the aim of clarifying their purposes and meaning for members as well as for citizens. The *House Ethics Manual* is a step in this direction. The Senate should emulate it. At the same time, the handbooks and the statements as well as the training should emphasize more than they do now the aspirational standards of ethical conduct and the higher ideals of legislative service.

Finally, ethics education is important because ethics enforcement should aim more at prevention than at punishment. Better understanding of ethics is useful in preventing any kind of corruption of the democratic process, but it is especially useful in preventing the institutional kind. Following the trail of institutional corruption often leads into the grey areas of legislative ethics and therefore calls more frequently for the illumination that education offers. Its pitfalls are also likely to be less familiar to new members and staff than are the dangers of individual corruption.

The most important general lesson this education can teach is that the ethical standards that guide our representatives define the democratic process that governs our public life. The standards express our shared understanding of what we demand of those who represent us: the hopes we hold for their virtue and the limits we set for their vice. Both the hopes and the limits take their meaning from and have their effect on the practices of the legislature and the democratic process as a whole. When legislators fulfill our hopes, they honor their office. When they transgress the limits we set, they betray our trust. The more closely the ethical standards track the core values of the institution, the more commendable the virtues and the more condemnable the vices. That is why institutional service and institutional corruption must have a prominent place in legislative ethics.

Montesquieu, the most institutionally astute of political theorists who have written about corruption, warns that a state will "perish when its legislative power becomes more corrupt than its executive."[9] Some observers of the American executive in recent years might conclude that if Montesquieu is right, the American state is in no danger of perishing. How could Congress possibly compete with the Watergate or Iran-contra affairs? Others might argue that the continuing scandal of campaign finance has done more damage to democracy than all the executive misdeeds combined.

Neither comparison is reassuring. We should not take any comfort from a belief that one institution is less corrupt than the other if both suffer from more corruption than is good for the health of democracy. We should take Montesquieu's warning in a different spirit, as a reminder of the critical place of the legislature in our political system. By their actions, individually and collectively, its members shape the standards that define the ethical relations between citizens and representatives and determine the ethical quality of our democratic government. That is ultimately why legislative ethics deserves a prominent place in our public life.

Appendix:
Charges of Ethics Violations
Considered by Congress,
1789–1992

The lists that follow include all
ethics charges of which Congress took official notice by issuing a
statement, report, or by taking some formal action. Some charges
that were dismissed or not proven are therefore included. Charges
that ethics committees may have considered but for which they produced no public record are not included. Neither are criminal
charges or convictions on which Congress took no action. Also excluded are cases involving treason (twenty-five), election qualifica-
tions not involving corruption (fourteen), and decorum on the floor
(twenty). All but fifteen of these cases occurred in the nineteenth
century.

The classification by type of corruption is based on the three-
element definitions presented in chapter 2. Corruption in which the
gain is personal, the service undeserved, and the connection based
on a corrupt motive is treated as purely individual. Corruption in

182

which the gain is political, the service procedurally improper, and the connection based on institutional tendencies is defined as purely institutional. In impure cases, if two of the three elements are individual, the case is counted as individual corruption; otherwise it is treated as institutional corruption. Cases that involve several charges, such as that of James Wright, are assigned to the category that fits the largest number or the most salient charges. The entries under "charges" and "sanction" are simplified or abbreviated and do not necessarily use the language of the code or law in question. When different bodies imposed different sanctions, they are recorded in this order: committee/chamber/court.

The information in the lists is based on Mary Ann Noyer, "Catalog of Congressional Ethics Cases," Brookings, 1993, which provides more complete information about the cases. A copy of the catalog is available at cost from the Brookings Institution Library, 1775 Massachusetts Avenue, N.W., Washington, D.C. 20036. The catalog was prepared for use in research for this book because, as far as we could discover, no complete inventory of ethics cases existed.

The following sources were useful in preparing both the catalog and the lists that follow. *Historical Summary of Conduct Cases in the House of Representatives*, Committee Print, House Committee on Standards of Official Conduct (GPO, April 1992); Robert L. Tienken, *House of Representatives Exclusion, Expulsion and Censure Cases from 1789 to 1973*, Committee Print, Joint Committee on Congressional Operations (GPO, 1973); Richard D. Hupman, *Senate Election, Expulsion and Censure Cases from 1793 to 1972*, Senate document 92-7 (Subcommittee on Privileges and Elections of the Committee on Rules and Administration, 1972); and *Congressional Ethics: History, Facts, and Controversy* (Washington: Congressional Quarterly, 1992), pp. 168–69.

Senate
Individual Corruption

Member	Year	Charges	Sanction
Humphrey Marshall (Kentucky)	1796	Perjury	None
Timothy Pickering (Massachusetts)	1811	Breach of confidence	Censure
John Ruggles (Maine)	1838	Improper influence/conflict of interest	None
Walter Colquitt (Georgia)	1846	Improper influence	None
Spencer Jarnagin (Tennessee)	1846	Improper influence	None
John Clayton (Delaware)	1846	Improper influence	None
Henry Rice (Minnesota)	1858	Fraud/extortion	None
James Simmons (Rhode Island)	1862	Bribery/influence peddling	None
Schuyler Colfax (Indiana)	1873	Insider trading	None
Roscoe Conkling (New York)	1873	Insider trading	None
John Logan (Illinois)	1873	Insider trading	None
James Patterson (New Hampshire)	1873	Insider trading	Recommended expulsion[1]
James Harlan (Iowa)	1873	Insider trading	None
Henry Wilson (Massachusetts)	1873	Insider trading	None
Charles Dietrich (Nebraska)	1904	Bribery/improper influence	None
Joseph Burton (Kansas)	1906	Bribery/conflict of interest	Conviction[2]
Burton Wheeler (Montana)	1924	Conflict of interest	None
Thomas Dodd (Connecticut)	1967	Misuse of campaign contributions	Censure
Edward Long (Missouri)	1967	Improper intervention/bribery	None
Mark Hatfield (Oregon)	1977	Disclosure	None

1. Recommendation for expulsion prompted member's resignation.
2. Criminal conviction prompted member's resignation.

Member	Year	Charges	Sanction
Herman Talmadge (Georgia)	1979	Misuse of campaign funds, illegitimate gifts/disclosure/ false reimbursement	Denouncement
Edward Brooke (Massachusetts)	1979	Disclosure	None
Howard Cannon (Nevada)	1980	Conflict of interest	None
Harrison Williams (New Jersey)	1981	Bribery/improper influence	Probable expulsion[3]/ conviction
Mark Hatfield (Oregon)	1984	Conflict of interest	None
David Durenberger (Minnesota)	1990	Illegitimate outside income/ illegitimate gifts/disclosure/ misuse of campaign funds	Denouncement
Phil Gramm (Texas)	1990	Conflict of interest	None
Mark Hatfield (Oregon)	1991	Disclosure/conflict of interest	Rebuke (disclosure)

Institutional Corruption

Member	Year	Charges	Sanction
Benjamin Tappan (Ohio)	1844	Breach of confidence	Censure
Powell Clayton (Arkansas)	1872	Vote buying/improper influence	None
Alexander Caldwell (Kansas)	1873	Vote buying/bribery	Recommended exclusion[4]
Hiram Bingham (Connecticut)	1929	Conflict of interest	Censure
John Overton (Louisiana)	1934	Campaign irregularities	None
Huey Long (Louisiana)	1934	Campaign irregularities	None
William Benton (Connecticut)	1953	Financial disclosure	None
Joseph McCarthy (Wisconsin)	1953	Campaign irregularities	None
Joseph McCarthy (Wisconsin)	1954	Defamation of candidate/ obstruction of legislative process/improper intervention	Censure
Hugh Scott (Pennsylvania)	1975	Illegal campaign contributions/ misuse of funds	None

3. Member resigned before vote on expulsion.
4. Recommendation to invalidate election prompted member's resignation.

Member	Year	Charges	Sanction
Robert Morgan (North Carolina)	1980	Conflict of interest/accepting improper campaign contributions	None
Birch Bayh (Indiana)	1980	Misuse of frank/misuse of campaign funds	None
Alan Cranston (Arizona)	1991	Improper intervention for campaign contributor	Reprimand
Dennis DeConcini (Arizona)	1991	Improper intervention for campaign contributor	Rebuke
Donald Riegle (Michigan)	1991	Improper intervention for campaign contributor	Rebuke
John Glenn (Ohio)	1991	Improper intervention for campaign contributor	Rebuke
John McCain (Arizona)	1991	Improper intervention for campaign contributor	Rebuke
Alfonse D'Amato (New York)	1991	Improper use of office/bribery/ improper influence	Rebuke for misuse of office; none on other charges

House
Individual Corruption

Member	Year	Charges	Sanction
William Welch (Connecticut)	1857	Bribery	None
William Gilbert (New York)	1857	Bribery	Recommended expulsion[5]
Orsamus Matteson (New York)	1857	Bribery	Reprimand[6]
Francis Edwards (New York)	1857	Bribery	Recommended expulsion[7]
Orsamus Matteson (New York)	1858	Bribery	None
Roderick Butler (Tennessee)	1870	Bribery/improper influence	Censure
John Deweese (North Carolina)	1870	Bribery	Censure
Benjamin Whittemore (South Carolina)	1870	Bribery	Censure[8]
Oakes Ames (Massachusetts)	1873	Bribery/insider trading	Censure
James Brooks (New York)	1873	Bribery/insider trading	Censure
John Langley (Kentucky)	1924	Bribery	Suspension[9]
Frederick Zihlman (Maryland)	1924	Bribery	Suspension[10]
John Coffee (Washington)	1941	Bribery/conflict of interest	None
Adam Clayton Powell (New York)	1967	Misuse of office/obstruction of legislative process	Exclusion
John Dowdy (Texas)	1972	Bribery/conspiracy/perjury	Conviction
Wayne Hays (Ohio)	1976	Improper employment practices	None
Robert Sikes (Florida)	1976	Disclosure/conflict of interest	Reprimand
Andrew Hinshaw (California)	1976	Bribery/embezzlement/misuse of public funds/misuse of office for campaign	Conviction

5. Expulsion recommended prompting member's resignation.
6. Expulsion resolution tabled upon member's resignation.
7. Expulsion recommendation tabled upon member's resignation.
8. Expulsion recommendation tabled upon member's resignation.
9. Because of criminal conviction, committee took no further action.
10. Member temporarily suspended until acquitted of criminal charges.

Member	Year	Charges	Sanction
Tom Foley (Washington)	1977	Bribery/misuse of office, improper intervention	None
Joshua Eilberg (Pennsylvania)	1978	Conflict of interest/illegal compensation	Criminal conviction
John McFall (California)	1978	Misuse of campaign contribution/disclosure	Reprimand
Edward Roybal (California)	1978	Misuse of campaign contribution/disclosure/ perjury	Reprimand
Edward Patten (New Jersey)	1978	Misuse of campaign contribution	None
Charles Wilson (California)	1978	Perjury/disclosure	Reprimand
William Boner (Tennessee)	1979	Misuse of campaign funds, misuse of office/bribery	None
Charles Diggs (Michigan)	1979	Misuse of office funds/voting misconduct	Censure/ restitution/ criminal conviction
Raymond Lederer (Pennsylvania)	1980	Bribery/influence peddling	Recommended expulsion[11]/ conviction
Michael J. Myers (Pennsylvania)	1980	Bribery/influence peddling	Expulsion/ conviction
John Jenrette (South Carolina)	1980	Bribery/influence peddling	Recommended expulsion[12]/ conviction
Frank Thompson (New Jersey)	1980	Bribery/influence peddling/ conspiracy/interstate travel to aid racketeering	Forfeiture of committee chair/ conviction
Daniel Flood (Pennsylvania)	1980	Bribery/influence peddling	Criminal conviction
Charles Wilson (California)	1980	Illegitimate gifts/conflict of interest/improper employment practices/misuse of campaign funds	Censure
John Murtha (Pennsylvania)	1981	Improper influence	None
Frederick Richmond (New York)	1982	Tax evasion/improper influence/ drug possession	Criminal conviction
Ronald Dellums (California)	1983	Drug use	None
John Burton (California)	1983	Drug use	None

11. Member resigned before vote on expulsion.
12. Member resigned before vote on expulsion.

Member	Year	Charges	Sanction
Gerry Studds (Massachusetts)	1983	Sexual misconduct	Censure
Frederick Richmond (New York)	1983	Drug use	None
Daniel Crane (Illinois)	1983	Sexual misconduct	Censure
Charles Wilson (California)	1983	Drug use	None
Barry Goldwater (California)	1983	Drug use	None
Geraldine Ferraro (New York)	1984	Disclosure	None
George Hansen (Idaho)	1984	Disclosure	Reprimand/ conviction
Dan Daniel (Virginia)	1984	Illegitimate gifts/disclosure	None
James Weaver (Oregon)	1986	Misuse of campaign funds/ disclosure	None
William Boner (Tennessee)	1987	Misuse of campaign funds/ improper intervention/ illegitimate gifts	None
Richard Stallings (Idaho)	1987	Misuse of campaign funds	Letter of rebuke
Mary Rose Oakar (Ohio)	1987	Improper employment practices	Restitution
Mario Biaggi (New York)	1987	Illegitimate gifts/improper influence/disclosure	Recommended expulsion[13]/ conviction
Robert Garcia (New York)	1988	Bribery/extortion	Forfeiture of committee chair/ conviction
James Wright (Texas)	1988	Conflict of interest/improper intervention/illegitimate outside income/illegitimate gifts	None[14]
Charles Rose (North Carolina)	1988	Misuse of campaign funds/ disclosure	Letter of reproval
Harold Ford (Tennessee)	1988	Influence peddling/bank, mail, and tax fraud	Forfeiture of committee chair/ criminal conviction[15]
Patrick Swindall (Georgia)	1989	Improper intervention/perjury	None

13. Member resigned before vote on expulsion.
14. Committee's preliminary findings prompted member's resignation.
15. On appeal to Supreme Court.

Member	Year	Charges	Sanction
Gus Savage (Illinois)	1990	Improper sexual conduct	None
Donald Lukens (Ohio)	1990	Improper sexual conduct	Criminal conviction
Barney Frank (Massachusetts)	1990	Misuse of office	Reprimand
Nicholas Mavroules (Massachusetts)	1992	Bribery/tax fraud/influence peddling/illegitimate gifts	Forfeiture of committee chair/ conviction

Institutional Corruption

Member	Year	Charges	Sanction
Joshua R. Giddings (Ohio)	1842	Offensive paper	Censure
Thomas L. Blanton (Texas)	1921	Offensive paper	Censure
Thomas P. O'Neill (Massachusetts)	1977	Extortion	None
Michael Harrington (Massachusetts)	1977	Breach of confidence	None
Tony Coelho (California)	1985	Misuse of office for campaign	None
Michael Andrews (Texas)	1985	Misuse of office for campaign	None
Edward Feighan (Ohio)	1985	Misuse of office for campaign	None
Mac Sweeney (Texas)	1987	Misuse of office for campaign	None
Fernand St. Germain (Rhode Island)	1987	Bribery/tax fraud/illegitimate gifts/disclosure/improper intervention	None
Austin Murphy (Pennsylvania)	1987	Vote fraud/misuse of office/ improper employment practices	Reprimand
Jim Bates (California)	1989	Sexual misconduct/misuse of office for campaign	Letter of reproval
Newt Gingrich (Georgia)	1990	Illegitimate outside income/ illegitimate gifts/misuse of office funds	None

Notes

Introduction

1. From 1789 through 1977 (the year before the Ethics in Government Act) Congress took official notice of charges of ethics violations involving fifty-three members, of whom twenty-one received sanctions from either a committee or the full body, eleven resigned, and two served prison terms. From 1978 through 1992 Congress considered charges involving sixty-three members; thirty-one were sanctioned or convicted and sixteen resigned or announced their intention to retire. In the Senate alone the total since 1978 has been lower than it was in the earlier period, although the annual rate of cases has been much higher (1.1 compared to 0.15). See the appendix for lists of cases and the criteria used to identify them.

2. *Congressional Ethics: History, Facts, and Controversy* (Washington: Congressional Quarterly, 1992), p. vii.

3. Gallup Organization, CNN/*U.S.A. Today* survey, national sample of 1,007 adults, October 22–25, 1994 (Roper Center for Public Opinion Research, University of Connecticut, 1995); Hart and Teeter research, NBC News/*Wall Street Journal* survey, national sample of 1,502 adults, June 10–14, 1994 (Roper Center for Public Opinion Research, University of Connecticut, 1995); and Gallup Organization, CNN/*U.S.A. Today* survey, national sample of 1,010 adults, December 28–30, 1994 (Roper Center for Public Opinion Research, University of Connecticut, 1995). In March 1995, public confidence in Congress remained at historically low levels, with only

13 percent of all Americans having a great deal or quite a lot of confidence in the institution. See *Los Angeles Times* poll, national sample of 1,285 adults, March 15–19, 1995 (Roper Center for Public Opinion Research, University of Connecticut, 1995). More generally, see Karlyn Bowman and Everett Carll Ladd, "Public Opinion toward Congress: A Historical Look," in Thomas E. Mann and Norman J. Ornstein, eds., *Congress, the Press, and the Public* (American Enterprise Institute and Brookings, 1994), pp. 48–53.

4. Newt Gingrich, "Foreword," in Gordon S. Jones and John A. Marini, eds., *The Imperial Congress* (Pharos Books, 1988), p. x. Presumably this member's post-1994 assessment of the institution will be more generous.

5. Richard Allan Baker, "The History of Congressional Ethics," in Bruce Jennings and Daniel Callahan, eds., *Representation and Responsibility: Exploring Legislative Ethics* (Plenum Press, 1985), p. 8. Although Webster's behavior was criticized at the time, "wide segments of society probably viewed [it] as tolerable." See Charles Stewart III, "Ain't Misbehavin', Or Reflections on Two Centuries of Congressional Corruption," occasional paper 94-4, Center for American Political Studies, Harvard University, April 1994, pp. 10–11.

6. *Congressional Ethics* (1992), p. 51.

7. W. Allan Wilbur, "The Crédit Mobilier Scandal, 1873," in *Congress Investigates: A Documented History, 1792-1974*, vol. 3, eds. Arthur M. Schlesinger, Jr., and Roger Bruns (Chelsea House, 1975), pp. 1849–63.

8. *Historical Summary of Conduct Cases in the House of Representatives*, Committee Print, House Committee on Standards of Official Conduct (Government Printing Office, April 1992), p. 7. The full insult, uttered on the floor in 1875 by Representative John Young Brown, is worth reproducing. He described another member as "one who is outlawed in his own home from respectable society; whose name is synonymous with falsehood; who is the champion, and has been on all occasions, of fraud; who is the apologist of thieves; who is such a prodigy of vice and meannesses that to describe him would sicken imagination and exhaust invective" and as "pussilanimous in war, inhuman in peace, forbidden in morals, and infamous in politics." Other insults that drew a vote of censure were milder: Representative William Stanberry was censured in 1832 for commenting that "the eyes of the Speaker are too frequently turned from the chair you occupy toward the White House" (*Historical Summary*, p. 1).

9. *Congressional Ethics* (1992), pp. 18–19, 168, 170–71.

10. Roger H. Davidson and Walter J. Oleszek, *Congress and Its Members*, 4th ed. (Washington: CQ Press, 1994), p. 443; and Brit Hume, "Now It Can Be Told . . . Or Can It?" *More*, vol. 5 (April 1975), p. 6ff.

11. Edmund Beard and Stephen Horn, *Congressional Ethics: The View*

from the House (Brookings, 1975), p. 77. An earlier study of congressional ethics in this century concluded that members "have not cared deeply enough for public regard to protect either the reputation of their parties or that of Congress itself. They have not demanded . . . that Congress investigate allegations of fraud and corruption . . . of individual members." H. H. Wilson, *Congress: Corruption and Compromise* (Rinehart, 1951), p. 11.

12. *Congressional Ethics* (1992), p. 3. The charges against Hinshaw referred to actions that took place before he was elected to the House.

13. Davidson and Oleszek, *Congress and Its Members*, p. 441; Norman J. Ornstein, "Less Seems More: What to Do about Contemporary Political Corruption," *Responsive Community*, vol. 4 (Winter 1993–94), p. 8; and Morris P. Fiorina, *Congress: Keystone of the Washington Establishment* (Yale University Press, 1989), p. 129. There is no systematic study comparing the competence or honesty of members in recent years with that of members in previous periods. Such a study would be difficult to conduct in a systematic way and probably would be no more convincing than the testimony of observers who follow Congress closely and are familiar with its history.

14. James J. Doyle, "Will and Ariel Durant: Two Authorities of the Past Look Ahead," *Chicago Tribune*, December 10, 1977, sec. 1, p. 11, cited in Paul Simon, *The Glass House: Politics and Morality in the Nation's Capital* (Continuum, 1984), p. 3.

15. Simon, *Glass House*, p. 5.

16. Some of the general deterioration in confidence in Congress is probably attributable to this increased openness of the institution, which is partly the result of the reforms of the 1970s. Other effects of those reforms, in particular the weakened control of the leadership in both chambers, together with divided government and increased partisanship, have probably reinforced public distrust. See Ornstein, "Less Seems More," pp. 10–17. In addition, reports of ethics violations themselves negatively affect public evaluations of Congress, even though they may not directly affect public confidence in Congress. Samuel C. Patterson and Gregory A. Caldeira, "Standing Up for Congress: Variations in Public Esteem since the 1960s," *Legislative Studies Quarterly*, vol. 15 (February 1990), pp. 25–47.

17. Between 1978 and 1982 the *New York Times* averaged seventy stories on congressional ethics each year. Between 1988 and 1992 it averaged 200 each year.

18. Neither ethics committee keeps a public record of the number or nature of all the charges they receive, even those that have sufficient standing to merit review by the staff. However, staff counsels believe that the number of charges has grown significantly in recent years. Telephone in-

terviews with Beth Ryan (staff counsel, Senate Ethics Committee) and Ellen Weintraub (counsel, House Committee on Standards of Official Conduct), March 1994.

19.   In 1976 the staff of the House committee consisted of five people and that of the Senate committee of two. By 1993–94, the House committee had eleven staff members and the Senate committee twelve. See *Congressional Directory* (GPO, 1976), pp. 280, 302; (1993–94), pp. 413, 471. The expenditures of the Senate committee rose from $195,000 in 1977–78 to $333,000 in 1992–93. See *Report of the Secretary of the Senate* (1977–78), pp. 104–05; (1992–93), pp. E381–82. The corresponding House figures are accessible for the early period only by reviewing individual vouchers, but the growth appears to be about the same as for the Senate committee.

20.   *Congressional Ethics* (Washington: Congressional Quarterly, 1977), pp. 13–24; and *Congressional Ethics* (1992), pp. 145–61.

21.   Congressional Research Service, *Legislative Ethics in Democratic Countries: Comparative Analysis of Financial Standards* (1994), p. 8.

22.   Suzanne Garment, *Scandal: The Culture of Mistrust in American Politics* (Random House, 1991), p. 7, 8, 9.

23.   Benjamin Ginsberg and Martin Shefter, *Politics by Other Means: The Declining Importance of Elections in America* (Basic Books, 1990).

24.   For a brief survey of developments at the federal level, see John P. Burke, "The Ethics of Deregulation—or the Deregulation of Ethics?" in John J. DiIulio, Jr., ed., *Deregulating the Public Service: Can Government be Improved?* (Brookings, 1994), pp. 62–66. Also see Garment, *Scandal*, pp. 4–5.

25.   Department of Justice, *Report to Congress on the Activities and Operations of the Public Integrity Section* (1988), p. 30; and *Report to Congress on the Activities and Operations of the Public Integrity Section* (1985), p. 40.

26.   Imogene Akins, ed., *State Yellow Book* (Monitor Publishing, 1993), p. 935.

27.   Telephone interview with DeEtte Spencer, Office of Government Ethics, Office of Education and Liaison, September 25, 1991. For an analysis of the office, see Burke, "Ethics of Deregulation," pp. 66–84.

28.   Cynthia B. Cohen, "Ethics Committees: Birth of a Network," *Hastings Center Report*, vol. 18 (February–March 1988), p. 11; Marc Rodwin, *Medicine, Money, and Morals: Physicians' Conflicts of Interest* (Oxford University Press, 1993), pp. 19–52; and National Institutes of Health, *NIH Guide for Grants and Contracts*, vol. 21 (November 27, 1992), p. 2.

29.   A survey of 2,000 U.S. corporations in 1987–88 found that 85 percent had an ethics code or its equivalent, and 50 percent required training as part of new employee orientation. David Perry, *Ethics Policies and Pro-*

grams in American Business: Report of a Landmark Survey of U.S. Corporations (Washington: Ethics Resource Center and the Behavior Research Center, 1990), pp. 6, 8.

30.   David B. Wilkins, "Who Should Regulate Lawyers?" *Harvard Law Review*, vol. 105 (February 1992), pp. 801–87.

31.   For an informal survey of some of these developments, see *Ethics: Easier Said than Done*, a magazine started in 1988 and published by the Josephson Institute for the Advancement of Ethics, Los Angeles, California.

32.   See Seymour Martin Lipset and William Schneider, *The Confidence Gap: Business, Labor and Government in the Public Mind*, rev. ed. (Johns Hopkins Press, 1987). Also Arthur H. Miller and Stephen A. Borrelli, "Confidence in Government during the 1980s," *American Politics Quarterly*, vol. 19 (April 1991), pp. 147–73; and Larry Hugick and Graham Hueber, "Pharmacists and Clergy Rate Highest for Honesty and Ethics," *Gallup Poll Monthly*, no. 308 (May 1991), pp. 29–31.

33.   See Davidson and Oleszek, *Congress and Its Members*, pp. 31–34; David E. Price, *The Congressional Experience: The View from the Hill* (Boulder, Colo.: Westview Press, 1992); Bruce Cain, John Ferejohn, and Morris Fiorina, *The Personal Vote: Constituency Service and Electoral Independence* (Harvard University Press, 1987); Frank J. Sorauf, *Inside Campaign Finance: Myths and Realities* (Yale University Press, 1992); and Eric M. Uslaner, *The Decline of Comity in Congress* (University of Michigan Press, 1993), esp. pp. 21–43.

34.   Suzanne Garment attributes this view to ethics reformers: "The deepening crisis of public corruption . . . is the root cause of our persisting political scandals and calls for a continuation or even an intensification of the campaign for more ethics in government. But this crisis of public corruption almost surely does not exist" (*Scandal*, p. 5). Although she argues that "this crisis of public corruption almost surely does not exist," she recognizes that some forms of corruption, such as that revealed in the case of the Keating Five, pose serious threats to the political system: in that case "years of punitive legalism had left the ethics committee incapable of making the sorts of ethical judgments on which a political system truly depends" (p. 257).

35.   *Institutional corruption* replaces what in an earlier work I called *mediated corruption*; see Dennis F. Thompson, "Mediated Corruption: The Case of the Keating Five," *American Political Science Review*, vol. 87 (June 1993), pp. 369–81. The term *mediated* there was intended to emphasize the way in which an institutional role stands between individual conduct and its effects on the political process and defines the character of the corruption. But to many readers the term implied that the public official acts as a kind of mediator between a private citizen and another public official and does

not himself directly commit the corrupt acts, which is only one of the forms this corruption can take. *Institutional* does not have this connotation. It also has the significant advantage of focusing attention on what identifies the relevant conduct (the *institutional* role, rather than only interests or actions of individuals) and on what makes it improper (the *institutional* norms and values, rather than only principles of individual morality). But like any term intended to capture a complex phenomenon, *institutional* carries its own possibilities for misunderstanding. It should not be taken to refer only to the *effects* of the corruption, since almost all corruption has effects on institutions. Neither should it be understood to imply that only the institution, not any individual, is responsible for the corruption.

36.   This concept is intended to be consistent with a wide variety of definitions in the social science literature. However, further specification of the concept beyond this level of generality remains controversial (mostly with regard to what should count as improper). For a review of various approaches, see Arnold J. Heidenheimer, Michael Johnston, and Victor T. LeVine, eds. *Political Corruption: A Handbook*, 2d ed. (New Brunswick, N.J.: Transaction, 1989), pp. 7–14; and John G. Peters and Susan Welch, "Political Corruption in America: A Search for Definitions and a Theory," *American Political Science Review*, vol. 78 (September 1978), pp. 974–84. An individualist conception of corruption tends to dominate most of the social science literature. A notable exception is Peter deLeon, *Thinking about Political Corruption* (Armonk, N.Y.: M. E. Sharpe, 1993).

37.   The element of institutional impropriety is a necessary but not sufficient condition for conduct to qualify as institutional corruption. Some substantial connection to private interests is necessary. In its absence, abuse of office (ordinary malfeasance or even constitutional transgressions) would not count as corruption at all. As chapter 2 shows, an essential characteristic of the general concept of political corruption is the idea of the pollution of the public by the private. When a legislator simply violates institutional rules, the conduct does not yet constitute corruption in this sense; the violation must be in the service of a private interest. Thus in the case of the Keating Five (whose misadventures are recounted in chapter 2), the fact that the five senators were promoting the private interests of Charles Keating is a necessary condition for bringing their conduct under the concept of corruption in the first place.

38.   Chapter 3 explains the criteria for classifying the cases as institutional, and the appendix lists the cases in each category. In a different study of historical trends in ethics cases, Charles Stewart has found a shift from charges involving the "integrity of the national union" to the "integrity of individual legislators" ("Ain't Misbehavin'," p. 17). His finding correctly captures a broad contrast between cases in the nineteenth century and those

in the twentieth, but it does not distinguish, as does the appendix here, between individual and institutional cases in this century. Stewart's "individual" category includes not only cases that are here called individual but also some that should be regarded as institutional.

Chapter One

1.   Pike conceded that Americans could stand to learn *something* more about ethics: "We are not sure whether the word [ethics] is singular or plural." *Congressional Ethics Reform*, Hearings before the House Bipartisan Task Force on Ethics, 101 Cong. 1 sess. (Government Printing Office, May 1989), pp. 34–35. "We may not be able to define it, but ethics is or are 'in' and must have their or its day" (p. 31).

2.   M. A. DeWolfe Howe, *Portrait of an Independent: Moorfield Storey, 1845–1929* (Houghton Mifflin, 1932), p. 151.

3.   *Congressional Ethics: History, Facts, and Controversy* (Washington: Congressional Quarterly, 1992), pp. 88–89. More generally on the relevance of private conduct for judging public officials, see Dennis F. Thompson, *Political Ethics and Public Office* (Harvard University Press, 1987), pp. 123–47.

4.   Charles R. Babcock and Bob Woodward, "Tower: The Consultant as Advocate," *Washington Post*, February 13, 1989, p. A1.

5.   Lamar Alexander, "Cut Their Pay and Send Them Home," Governors' Forum Lecture, Heritage Foundation, Washington, July 27, 1994, p. 7. For more nuanced and qualified arguments for term limits, see Mark P. Petracca, "Restoring 'The University in Rotation': An Essay in Defense of Term Limitation," in Edward H. Crane and Roger Pilon, eds., *The Politics and Law of Term Limits* (Washington: Cato Institute, 1994), pp. 57–82; and George F. Will, *Restoration: Congress, Term Limits and the Recovery of Deliberative Democracy* (New York: Free Press, 1992).

6.   Petracca, "Restoring 'The University in Rotation,'" p. 73.

7.   Thompson, *Political Ethics*, pp. 148–77.

8.   Will, *Restoration*, pp. 141–42.

9.   The often cited slogan "public office is a public trust" expresses in a simple form the important idea that public officials have fiduciary obligations, which in both law and morality are more demanding than most ordinary obligations. It was Grover Cleveland who popularized the idea in the 1884 campaign, though he could never manage the brevity to express it in the form in which his campaign aide W. C. Hudson proposed. According to Cleveland's biographer, "throughout the campaign, and throughout the remainder of his life . . . Cleveland continued to express this, his most cherished conviction, not in the words of Hudson's brilliant slogan, but in pon-

derous phrases of his own which he persisted in considering better because longer." Robert McElroy, *Grover Cleveland: The Man and the Statesman*, vol. 1 (Harper, 1923), p. 88. The idea, of course, has a long history; it was expressed in various ways by Edmund Burke and Thomas Jefferson, among others. By 1872 Charles Sumner could say, "The phrase, 'public office is a public trust' has of late become common property." William Safire, *Safire's New Political Dictionary* (Random House, 1993), p. 623.

10.   There are, of course, important differences between legislative politics and professions such as medicine and law (see Thompson, *Political Ethics*, pp. 96–97). Legislators do not regulate the education and licensing of would-be members of the legislature. A legislator's "clients" constitute a determinate class of individuals (constituents) who have the power to prevent the legislator from practicing his or her profession. But the legislative calling shares with that of medicine, law, and many other professions a critical characteristic that makes a professional ethics necessary: like other professionals, legislators act for the good of others who must give them some discretion but to whom they are accountable.

11.   This attitude may in part explain the epidemic of ethics violations that broke out in the mid-1980s in the executive branch. More than a hundred federal officials (mostly political appointees) were indicted or charged with ethics offenses during the early years of the Reagan administration. George Lardner, Jr., "Conduct Unbecoming an Administration," *Washington Post National Weekly Edition*, January 3, 1988, pp. 31–32. This outbreak of misconduct was partly the result of the increase in the sheer number and variety of new ethics rules and laws, but it also seemed to be the product of an underlying attitude of disrespect toward government service, a skepticism about the need for restrictions on upstanding citizens who, after all, were often accepting significant financial sacrifices to come to Washington.

12.   Richard M. Nixon, quoted in "Quotables," *Chicago Tribune*, July 21, 1989, p. C19. Some version of this complaint is repeated like an incantation in almost every debate on government ethics. See, for example, the Senate debate on the gift ban in 1994, *Congressional Record*, daily ed., May 4–5, 1994, especially the statements of Senator Phil Gramm ("I hope my mama is not watching this process when we are debating silly, trivial things . . . when there are so many fundamental issues that ought to be decided and on which we should be concentrating" [p. S5279]), and Senator Mitchell McConnell ("Do we want to devote the best efforts . . . of every member . . . to passing a crime bill, reforming health care, and changing welfare as we know it—or are we instead going to force each of us to waste endless time determining whether a particular meal or trinket fits under the . . . ban . . . ? [p. S5162]). Also see the statement of Senator Jay Rockefeller (p. S5235). Similar comments can be found in *Congressional Ethics Reform*,

p. 2; and *Recommending Revisions to the Procedures of the Senate Select Committee on Ethics* (Hearings), Committee Print, Senate Ethics Study Commission, 103 Cong. 1 sess. (GPO, May 1993), p. 71.

13.   Senate rule XXXV, as amended May 11, 1994. See *Congressional Record*, vol. 140 (May 11, 1994), p. S5532.

14.   Among recent scholars, Joseph M. Bessette presents the most sustained discussion of the role of deliberation in Congress; see *The Mild Voice of Reason: Deliberative Democracy and American National Government* (University of Chicago Press, 1994). His conception of deliberation—"reasoning on the merits of public policy" (p. 46)—is in many respects consistent with the view of legislative ethics developed here. However, in at least three ways his conception goes beyond what legislative ethics needs to accept. First, he gives greater emphasis to the value of deliberation as a filter on passionate and spontaneous expressions of mass opinion; one implication is that he favors more secrecy than would be permitted by the principle of accountability. Second, his conception is more restrictive: it excludes most forms of political bargaining and any political discussion that fails to produce a change of mind. Third, he argues that deliberation substantially influences actual policymaking in the contemporary Congress, and to a much greater extent than most political scientists believe. Legislative ethics makes no such explanatory claim because it emphasizes the normative aspects of the conception of deliberation.

15.   *The Debates and Proceedings in the Congress of the United States*, 4 Cong. 1 sess. (Washington: Gales and Seaton, 1849), p. 494. Alexander Hamilton observed that, compared to the executive, the legislature is characterized by "differences of opinion and the jarring of parties . . . though they may sometimes obstruct salutary plans, yet often promote deliberation." *The Federalist Papers*, Clinton Rossiter, ed. (New American Library, 1961), no. 70, pp. 426–27. A principal responsibility of representatives in Madison's view is "to refine and enlarge the public views" and to ensure that "the true interest of their country" is not sacrificed to "temporary or partial consideration" (*Federalist Papers*, no. 10, p. 82). He also believed that one of the two principal considerations in determining the size of the legislature should be "the benefits of free consultation and discussion" (*Federalist Papers*, no. 55, p. 342). In the constitutional convention Madison argued in favor of political discussion, in which "minds of the Members [are] changing . . . much [is] gained by a yielding and accommodating spirit," and in which no citizen is "obliged to retain his opinions any longer than he [is] satisfied of their propriety and truth." See "Jared Sparks: Journal," [summarizing some of James Madison's comments] in Max Farrand, ed., *The Records of the Federal Convention of 1787* (Yale University Press, 1966), vol. 3, p. 479.

16.   These principles express in a political mode the formal requirements of moral discourse, the conditions that philosophers of many persua-
sions have set for the possibility of making any kind of moral judgment. For
a general discussion of these conditions as applied to legislative ethics, see
Thompson, *Political Ethics*, pp. 96–122 (which are there referred to as
autonomy, generality, and publicity). The conditions are simplified and pol-
iticized versions of what John Rawls calls the "formal constraints of the
concept of right" and what some other philosophers call the conditions for
"the moral point of view." See Rawls, *A Theory of Justice* (Harvard University Press, 1971), pp. 130–36; and Kurt Baier, *The Moral Point of View*
(Cornell University Press, 1958), pp. 187–213.

17.   Although the ideal seems closer to the trustee theory of representation, even Edmund Burke, the most celebrated proponent of that view,
believed that representatives should take into account local interests, the
feelings of their constituents, and party loyalty. See *Burke's Politics*, Ross
J. S. Hoffman and Paul Levack, eds. (Knopf, 1959), pp. 42, 114–20, 397–98.
On the limitations of the trustee-delegate dichotomy, see Thompson, *Political Ethics*, pp. 99–102.

18.   For condemnations of personal gain see *Federal Register*, vol. 56,
July 23, 1991, p. 33788.

19.   Thomas E. Mann and Norman J. Ornstein, *Renewing Congress: A
First Report* (American Enterprise Institute and Brookings, 1992), p. 4.

20.   *Congressional Ethics Reform*, p. 18. Also see David E. Price, *The
Congressional Experience: A View from the Hill* (Boulder, Colo.: Westview
Press, 1992), esp. pp. 137–53.

21.   The value of accountability of course goes beyond the duty to sustain confidence in government. For the broader concept (presented as a form
of responsibility), see Dennis F. Thompson, "Representatives in the Welfare
State," in Amy Gutmann, ed., *Democracy and the Welfare State* (Princeton
University Press, 1988), pp. 131–55. For a theory of congressional accountability that focuses on how legislators anticipate *potential* preferences of
constituents, see R. Douglas Arnold, *The Logic of Congressional Action* (Yale
University Press, 1990).

22.   *Preliminary Inquiry into Allegations Regarding Senators Cran-
ston, DeConcini, Glenn, McCain, and Riegle, and Lincoln Savings and Loan*,
Hearings before the Senate Select Committee on Ethics, 101 Cong. 2 sess.
(GPO, 1991), pt. 1, pp. 121–22.

23.   See Stacey Joyce, "Westerners Win Grazing-Fee Fight," *Billings
Gazette*, November 10, 1993, p. A1; Timothy Egan, "Wingtip 'Cowboys' in
Last Stand to Hold on to Low Grazing Fees," *New York Times*, October 29,
1993, p. A1; and Keith Schneider, "Clinton the Conservationist Thinks
Twice," *New York Times*, April 4, 1993, section 4, p. 1.

Chapter Two

1.   William L. Riordan, *Plunkitt of Tammany Hall* (E. P. Dutton, 1963), p. 3.

2.   William Safire, *Safire's New Political Dictionary* (Random House, 1993), p. 334. The author of an informative journalistic account of campaign finance acknowledges his debt to William Riordan's chronicle of Plunkitt's "political philosophy": Brooks Jackson, *Honest Graft: Big Money and the American Political Process* (Knopf, 1988), p. 322. In his modernization of Plunkitt, James Q. Wilson takes a more tolerant view of honest graft, which in his view includes some personal as well as political gain. See "Corruption Is Not Always Scandalous," in John A. Gardiner and David J. Olson, eds., *Theft of the City: Readings on Corruption in Urban America* (Indiana University Press, 1974), pp. 29–32.

3.   Joseph R. Weeks, "The Institutionalized Corruption of the Political Process, the Impotence of Criminal Law to Reach It, and a Proposal for Change," *Journal of Legislation*, vol. 13 (1986), pp. 123–48; Amitai Etzioni, *Capital Corruption: The New Attack on American Democracy* (Harcourt Brace Jovanovich, 1984); and John T. Noonan, Jr., *Bribes* (University of California Press, 1984), pp. 621–51, 687–90, 696–97. Daniel Hays Lowenstein agrees that contributions are a form of corruption, but thinks they should be regarded as illegal: "Political Bribery and the Intermediate Theory of Politics," *UCLA Law Review*, vol. 32 (April 1985), pp. 826–28; and "On Campaign Finance Reform: The Root of All Evil Is Deeply Rooted," *Hofstra Law Review*, vol. 18 (Fall 1989), pp. 301–35.

4.   See especially Baron de Montesquieu, *De l'Esprit des Lois*, in *Montesquieu: Oeuvres Complètes*, ed. Roger Caillois (Paris: Gallimard, 1949–51), vol. 2, book 11, chap. 6, and more generally, vol. 2, book 8, ("The Corruption of Principle in the Three Governments"), pp. 349–66. For the discussions of Montesquieu and other traditional political theorists' views of corruption, see J. Patrick Dobel, "The Corruption of a State," *American Political Science Review*, vol. 72 (September 1978), pp. 958–73; and J. Peter Euben, "Corruption," in Terrence Ball, James Farr and Russell L. Hanson, eds., *Political Innovation and Conceptual Change* (Cambridge University Press, 1989), pp. 220–45.

5.   It is therefore a mistake, though one with a long tradition, to try to determine in advance whether interests are private or public and create rules that block private interests. See Beth Nolan, "Public Interest, Private Income: Conflicts and Control Limits on the Outside Income of Government Officials," *Northwestern University Law Review*, vol. 87 (Fall 1992), pp. 73–77. Nolan recognizes that interests can be mixed, but she does not suffi-

ciently emphasize that their public significance is legitimated only through the political process.

6. *Investigation of Senator David F. Durenberger*, Committee Print, Senate Select Committee on Ethics, 101 Cong. 2 sess. (Government Printing Office, July 1990), p. 14.

7. The barrier between personal and campaign funds is of course not absolute. Any campaign contribution, at least in theory, replaces funds that a candidate might have to supply from personal resources and in this way confers an indirect economic benefit (a personal gain). But for most candidates, the amount that they could provide themselves is a very small part of the cost of the campaign. Furthermore, the traditional ways of converting campaign funds to personal use are now prohibited. For example, members are no longer permitted to use campaign funds for personal use even when they retire. *Congressional Ethics: History, Facts, and Controversy* (Washington: Congressional Quarterly, 1992), pp. 155–57. Nearly all the members who retired from the House in 1992 who could convert campaign contributions to personal use instead gave the funds to charity, nonprofit foundations, or political parties or returned them to contributors. See Richard L. Hall and Robert P. Van Houweling, "Avarice and Ambition in Congress: Representatives' Decisions to Run or Retire from the U.S. House," *American Political Science Review*, vol. 89 (March 1995), pp. 121–36.

8. In cases of extortion the member denies or threatens to deny a citizen a service that the citizen does deserve. But even here a primary consideration is whether the citizen's cause satisfies general standards of justice. For an analysis showing how the offenses of bribery and extortion overlap, see James Lindgren, "The Elusive Distinction between Bribery and Extortion: From the Common Law to the Hobbs Act," *UCLA Law Review*, vol. 35 (June 1988), pp. 815–909.

9. Even in instances of individual corruption the service may still be institutional in the sense that it is provided to constituents or others to whom members are related only by virtue of their institutional role (as when a constituent bribes a member). Therefore it could be said the purer form of individual corruption is that which occurs when the official provides the service to someone whose relationship to the official is primarily personal (a family member or friend) rather than official.

10. Wright's case could therefore be regarded as mixed. But the sense in which it is mixed should not be confused with the sense in which most instances of corruption (including this one) are impure. Impure cases are those in which one instance of corruption contains elements of more than one type. Mixed cases are those that include more than one instance of corruption, of which at least one is (relatively) individual and one (relatively) institutional.

11.   *Investigation of Durenberger*, p. 11.

12.   Durenberger failed to report expense reimbursements on his financial disclosure forms (rule 34), converted campaign contributions to his personal use (rule 38), used Senate space for commercial purposes (40 UJSC 193d and Senate regulations), and accepted the gift of transportation for personal travel (rule 35).

13.   *Investigation of Durenberger*, p. 60.

14.   Ibid., p. 54.

15.   Ibid., p. 9.

16.   Ibid., p. 5.

17.   *Congressional Ethics* (1992), p. 35.

18.   See chapter 6.

19.   *Investigation of Durenberger*, p. 13.

20.   Norman Ornstein quoted in Steve Berg, "The Rise and Fall of Dave Durenberger," *Minneapolis Star Tribune*, April 4, 1993, p. 1A.

21.   This campaign for openness resulted in an earlier brush with the ethics committee. Just after leaving the chairmanship of the Senate Intelligence Committee, he revealed some classified information to two fundraising events in Florida in 1987, which led the ethics committee to "reprove" him.

22.   *Investigation of Durenberger*, p. 105.

23.   Ibid., p. 96.

24.   This account of the affair relies largely on the evidence presented during the hearings and in the reports of the special counsel and the ethics committee. See *Preliminary Inquiry into Allegations Regarding Senators Cranston, DeConcini, Glenn, McCain, and Riegle, and Lincoln Savings and Loan*, Hearings before the Senate Select Committee on Ethics, 101 Cong. 2 sess., November 15, 1990–January 16, 1991, six parts (GPO, 1991); and *Investigation of Senator Alan Cranston together with Additional Views*, Committee Print, Senate Select Committee on Ethics, 102 Cong. 1 sess. (GPO, November 1991). Two readable accounts of the affair, which include some valuable background material, are Stephen Pizzo and others, *Inside Job: The Looting of America's Savings and Loan* (McGraw Hill, 1989), pp. 263–97; and James Ring Adams, *The Big Fix: Inside the S&L Scandal* (John Wiley, 1990), pt. 4.

25.   *Investigation of Cranston*, p. 18.

26.   Frank J. Sorauf, *Inside Campaign Finance* (Yale University Press, 1992), p. 54.

27.   Jill Abramson and David Rogers, "The Keating 535: Five Are on the Grill but Other Lawmakers Help Big Donors Too," *Wall Street Journal*, January 10, 1991, pp. A1, A6; and Amitai Etzioni, "Keating Six?" *Responsive Community*, vol. 1 (Winter 1990–91), pp. 6–9.

28.   *Preliminary Inquiry*, pt. 4, December 14, 1990, p. 178.

29.   The McCain family took some vacation trips to Keating's Bahamas home in the early 1980s, for which McCain eventually paid when notified by Keating's company in 1989. *Investigation of Cranston*, pp. 18–19.

30.   *Investigation of Cranston*, pp. 17, 19.

31.   *Congressional Record*, daily ed., May 31, 1989, p. H2248.

32.   *In the Matter of Representative James C. Wright, Jr.*, Committee Print, House Committee on Standards of Official Conduct, 101 Cong. 2 sess. (GPO, April 1989), pp. 90–91.

33.   The first charge seems less serious than the counsel or the committee implied, as is argued later. The second charge was a new accusation that had arisen in the course of the investigation, and even the committee acknowledged that the evidence for it was weak.

34.   According to one account, the committee "did not discuss the decision to cite Wright sixty-nine times, but [John] Myers [the ranking minority member] later said, 'It was discussed by the chairman, myself, and Phelan. We were aware of the impact it would have.'" John M. Barry, *The Ambition and the Power* (Viking, 1989), p. 715.

35.   *In the Matter of Wright*, p. 35.

36.   About the royalty, Calvin Trillin made the point well: "My publishers couldn't seem to understand that what I wanted for my new book was simply the same publishing arrangement Jim Wright had. 'I'll just take the straight fifty-five percent royalty deal,' I told them. 'I loathe quibbling.'" *Enough's Enough (And Other Rules of Life)* (Ticknor and Fields, 1990), p. 162.

37.   *Congressional Record*, daily ed., May 31, 1989, p. H2245.

38.   Barry, *Ambition*, p. 761. As Wright said in his farewell speech: "Now maybe book royalties should not have been exempt. But the rules clearly say that they are." *Congressional Record*, daily ed., May 31, 1989, p. H2245.

39.   Barry, *Ambition*, p. 761.

40.   *Report of the Special Outside Counsel in the Matter of Speaker James C. Wright, Jr.*, House Committee on Standards of Official Conduct, 101 Cong. 2 sess. (GPO, February 1989), pp. 192–93.

41.   Ibid., pp. 18–25, 192–278.

42.   *In the Matter of Wright*, pp. 83–84.

43.   Ibid., p. 84. Both special counsel and the committee dismissed with even less discussion another charge of improper intervention: Wright's letter to the Interior Department on behalf of Texas Oil & Gas Company. Their focus was on whether Wright himself had a financial interest in the company at the time; they paid little attention to the intervention itself, and none to the question of whether the company was a potential source of

campaign contributions. See *In the Matter of Wright*, pp. 18–19; and *Report of the Special Outside Counsel*, pp. 48–52.

44.   *In the Matter of Wright*, p. 63.

45.   *Congressional Ethics* (1992), pp. 58–59.

46.   The House ethics committee in that case had held members to a higher standard than corrupt motive: "even if a Member did not . . . actually know of any corrupt motivation underlying the gift offered, the Member should still be subjected to at least some sanction if the circumstances *placed him on notice* that the gift was tendered in an attempt by a foreign government to influence his present or future official actions and he *took no action (or insufficient action)* to attempt to discover the true nature and purpose of the gift." *In the Matter of Wright*, p. 52.

47.   See the defense by Barry, *Ambition*, pp. 690–96, 760–61. Although Barry is clearly sympathetic to Wright and the arguments he makes are not conclusive, they raise sufficient doubts about the charge that one cannot assume it would have been sustained during the next phase of the committee's proceedings, the formal investigation in which Wright's attorneys would have had more scope. Also see Wright's own defense: *Congressional Record*, daily ed., May 31, 1989, pp. H2239–H2244.

48.   *In the Matter of Wright*, p. 58.

49.   Newt Gingrich, "Foreword," in Gordon S. Jones and John A. Marini, eds., *The Imperial Congress: Crisis in the Separation of Powers* (Washington: Pharos Books, 1988), p. x.

50.   Barry, *Ambition*, pp. 630–31, quoting Representative Robert Livingston, who also suggested that Common Cause's complaint was a necessary factor, a point many other observers also make. In the few pages he devotes to the affair in his memoir, Wright himself blames his ethics difficulties on the "vengeance" of Gingrich and "a right wing . . . out for blood." *Worth It All: My War for Peace* (Washington: Brassey's, 1993), pp. 182–85.

51.   Barry, *Ambition*, p. 641.

Chapter Three

1.   House Committee on Standards of Official Conduct, *Ethics Manual for Members, Officers, and Employees of the U.S. House of Representatives*, 102 Cong. 2 sess. (Government Printing Office, April 1992), p. 1. (Hereafter *House Ethics Manual.*)

2.   John T. Noonan, Jr., *Bribes* (Macmillan, 1984), p. 704.

3.   Of the 116 Senate and House ethics violations between 1789 and 1992 that prompted official action by Congress or its committees, 86 in-

volved some kind of illegitimate personal gain for the member or a constituent. See the appendix.

4.   For an analysis showing that the decisions of House members to retire are more influenced by legitimate financial considerations (pension benefits) than "ethically questionable" gains (honoraria and campaign contributions converted to personal use), see Richard L. Hall and Robert P. Van Houweling, "Avarice and Ambition in Congress: Representatives' Decisions to Run or Retire from the U.S. House," *American Political Science Review*, vol. 89 (March 1995), pp. 121–36.

5.   William Safire, *Safire's New Political Dictionary* (Random House, 1993), p. 294.

6.   *The Records of the Federal Convention of 1787*, Max Farrand, ed. (Yale University Press, 1966), vol. 1, p. 219.

7.   James Madison in ibid., vol. 3, p. 315.

8.   Ibid., vol. 3, p. 314.

9.   Steven Kelman argues that current revolving-door restrictions must be justified partly on the basis of an "argument from profiting out of public service, which expresses an ideal of public spirit in public service"; "What is Wrong with the Revolving Door?" in *Public Management: The State of the Art*, Barry Bozeman, ed. (San Francisco: Jossey-Bass, 1993), p. 239. Worries about "opulence and acquisitiveness," he believes, may warrant restrictions to "provide a visible example of public-spirited behavior that may encourage citizens outside government to choose to live their private lives in ways that emphasize things that life has to offer other than material acquisition" (p. 243). The "very visibility of government makes it an apt candidate" to promote this ideal (p. 244). However, Kelman's interpretation of the aim of these restrictions is too broad. It would imply many more restrictions on public officials than seem necessary or desirable. Also, it would imply that profiting from public office is morally no different from profiting in general. If (as his argument suggests) acquisitiveness is what is suspect, then there is no moral reason to restrict (or criticize) public officials any more than to restrict (or criticize) ordinary citizens for seeking personal gain. Contrary to Kelman's view, the problem is not gain as such but excessive or improper gain. To determine what is excessive or improper, one has to consider the distinctive features of public office rather than the general evils of opulence.

10.   In face of public criticism—some from members of his own party— House Speaker-elect Newt Gingrich decided in late 1994 to forgo a $4.5 million advance from the publisher of two books he planned to write. Some of the criticisms seemed to reflect the mistaken view that one should not profit at all from public office, but many other objections focused on the source, magnitude, and timing of the profit, which raised legitimate ques-

tions of independence and fairness. The publishing company was owned by Rupert Murdoch, who had a substantial interest in pending changes in federal regulations and legislation that were to come before the next Congress. The sheer size and timing of the advance also caused many to believe that Gingrich was taking unfair advantage of the Republicans' recent electoral successes. Peter Applebome, "Gingrich Gives Up $4 Million Advance on His Book Deal," *New York Times*, December 31, 1994, pp. 1, 6; and "Group Backs 'Ethics Adviser' to Review Gingrich Book Deal," *Washington Post*, February 3, 1995, p. A14.

11.   *Post-Employment Restrictions Act of 1989*, P.L. 101-194, 103 Stat 1716, 18 USCA § 207e (Supp. 1990). The provision that allows former officials who have "special knowledge" to make statements to government agencies for which they worked "if no compensation is received" is an unusual exception to the restrictions; 18 USCS § 207 (1993) (j)(4).

12.   John Harwood, "Politics and Policy: Former Lawmaker Says Lucrative Job as Lobbyist Offered Way Out of Congress," *Wall Street Journal*, January 24, 1994, p. B14.

13.   The cases usually cited to show that personal gain is wrong per se often appeal implicitly to a standard of fairness (the gain has come to the official unfairly or gives him or her an unfair advantage). A standard work on executive ethics offers this hypothetical example: "it is possible to imagine the case of an official who acts impartially, does not play favorites, and is a model of public decorum, but who, for example, speculates on the grain market on the basis of inside government information. The universal condemnation of such action indicates that the prevention of the use of public office for private gain is an independent and separate objective." Association of the Bar of the City of New York, Special Committee on the Federal Conflict of Interest Laws, *Conflict of Interest and Federal Service* (Harvard University Press, 1960), p. 7. But surely it is possible to condemn the use of inside information on grounds that it is unfair without assuming that the use of public office for personal gain is an independent wrong.

14.   Recent cases in which Congress or its committees imposed sanctions for these offenses include fraudulent reimbursement (David Durenberger, 1990, Herman Talmadge, 1979, and Thomas Dodd, 1967); sexual misconduct (Donald Lukens, 1990, Gerry Studds, 1983, and Daniel Crane, 1983); use of staff for personal services (Austin Murphy, 1987, Charles Wilson, 1980); illegal drugs (five cases in 1983 that were dropped); personal use of campaign or office funds (David Durenberger, 1990, William Boner, 1987, Richard Stallings, 1987, Charles Wilson, 1980, Herman Talmadge, 1979, Charles Diggs, 1979, John McFall, 1978, Edward Roybal, 1978, Thomas Dodd, 1967, Adam Clayton Powell, 1967); perjury (Daniel Flood,

1980, Edward Roybal, 1978, Charles Wilson, 1978, John Dowdy, 1972); fraud (Harold Ford, 1988); embezzlement or theft (Andrew Hinshaw, 1976); tax evasion (Nick Mavroules, 1992). See the appendix.

15.   Senate Committee on Rules and Administration, *Senate Manual*, 97 Cong. (GPO, 1981), S. res. 338 (as amended, 88 Cong. 2 sess., 1964); and William Holmes Brown, *Rules of the House of Representatives*, 103 Cong. (GPO, 1993), H. rule XLIII.

16.   *Congressional Ethics: History, Facts, and Controversy* (Washington: Congressional Quarterly, 1992), p. 40.

17.   Of the fifty-nine cases on which the committees took action from 1978 to 1992, thirty-one also were subject to criminal investigation. See the appendix.

18.   This analysis of the concept of conflict of interest draws on Dennis F. Thompson, "Understanding Financial Conflicts of Interest," *New England Journal of Medicine*, vol. 329 (August 19, 1993), pp. 573–76.

19.   "Senator Kerr Talks about Conflict of Interest," *US News and World Report*, September 3, 1962, p. 86.

20.   Robert S. Getz, *Congressional Ethics: The Conflict of Interest Issue* (Princeton, N.J.: Van Nostrand, 1966), pp. 57–58.

21.   *House Ethics Manual*, pp. 120–23. Faced with an especially egregious conflict in 1976 in which a member sponsored legislation that directly benefited commercial development of land that he owned, the House ethics committee invoked the rules against using improper influence to secure personal gain. See *In the Matter of a Complaint against Representative Robert L. F. Sikes*, House Committee on Standards of Official Conduct, 94 Cong. 2 sess. (GPO, 1976), p. 21.

22.   Edmund Beard and Stephen Horn, *Congressional Ethics: The View from the House* (Brookings, 1975), pp. 42–45.

23.   *Senate Manual*, S. rule XXXVII; and Brown, *Rules of the House*, H. rule 47.

24.   This approach also neglects the other purpose of prohibitions on outside income, the so-called supplementation offenses of 18 U.S.C. § 209 (1992), which do not require an intent to influence or for that matter any relationship between the supplementation and an official act. Their purpose is to prevent divided loyalties ("serving two masters"). See Beth Nolan, "Public Interest, Private Income: Conflicts and Control Limits on the Outside Income of Government Officials, *Northwestern University Law Review*, vol. 87 (Fall 1992), pp. 88–93.

25.   *Senate Manual*, S. rule XXXVII, sec. 7.

26.   Consider Senator David Boren's comment on the effects of revolving-door practices: "It plants in the minds of the American people the suspicion that those people were thinking ahead to the next job, already think-

ing ahead to pleasing the interests of those outside our country when they were supposed to be representing our own national interests." *Congressional Record*, daily ed., May 5, 1994, p. S 5242.

27.   Report prepared by the staff of Senator Boren, cited in *Congressional Record*, daily ed., May 5, 1994, p. S 5242.

28.   Commissioners in the Federal Communications Commission who went to work for the broadcasting industry after leaving public office were more likely than commissioners who did not take industry jobs to cast proindustry votes during the last year of their term, but not earlier in their terms. Jeffrey E. Cohen, "The Dynamics of the 'Revolving Door' on the FCC," *American Journal of Political Science*, vol. 30 (November 1986), pp. 689–708. Correlations between votes and jobs do not rule out the possibility that proindustry commissioners got their jobs because of their votes rather than that they voted the way they did because they wanted the jobs. In general, however, the problem is not on which side officials vote but whether they are or appear to be influenced. It would be no less improper for officials to vote against the industry to impress their prospective employers with their toughness and independence.

29.   18 USCS § 207(a)(1) (1994).

30.   There are reasons to doubt a strong net harm from postemployment regulations. Some of the most talented citizens may be more attracted to government when it maintains high standards and greater respectability. The decision to seek and hold public office is also affected by so many important personal and political factors that the burden of ethics rules is likely to be a minor consideration. Finally, studies of the executive branch, where restrictions have been more stringent for a long time, generally find no effect on recruitment. The General Accounting Office, for example, concluded that it is "extremely difficult, if not impossible, to attribute any specific degree of federal recruiting difficulty to the Ethics Act or to any of its provisions." *Information on Selected Aspects of the Ethics in Government Act of 1978* (GPO, 1983), appendix 1, p. 1.

31.   The Senate adopted an amendment to the gift ban bill in May 1994 that would have extended the ban on lobbying from one to two years after members leave office. The House bill on gifts did not address this issue, and the provision was dropped in conference. The final bill was still pending in 1995.

32.   Lamar Alexander, "Cut Their Pay and Send Them Home," a Governors' Forum lecture, Washington: Heritage Foundation, 1994, p. 7.

33.   In his eloquent plea for term limits, George F. Will, *Restoration: Congress, Term Limits and the Recovery of Deliberative Democracy* (Free Press, 1992), p. 211, acknowledges this problem. It is "possible" that legislators with limited terms will "be corrupted by the temptation to use their

last years in power to ingratiate themselves with potential employers." He then asks: "would such corruption be worse . . . than legislative careerism has proved to be?" But that is not exactly the right question. Term limits would not entirely eliminate the corrupting effects of careerism (within the limits, legislators may still worry at least as much as they do now about their reelection). The question should be whether the probable decrease in corruption from careerism will outweigh the probable increase in corruption resulting from term limits. But whatever the answer, Will's acknowledgement is consistent with my claim that under a regime of term limits more restrictive postemployment rules would be necessary.

34. *Investigation of Senator David F. Durenberger*, Committee Print, Senate Select Committee on Ethics, 101 Cong. 2 sess. (GPO, 1990), pp. 92–95.

35. *Inquiry into the Operation of the Bank of the Sergeant-at-Arms of the House of Representatives*, Report, House Committee on Standards of Official Conduct, 102 Cong. 2 sess. (GPO, March 1992), p. 2.

36. Ibid., p. 29.

37. *Preliminary Inquiry of the Special Counsel to the Attorney General Concerning the House Banking Facility* (Department of Justice, December 16, 1992). Wilkey left four cases unresolved, but they also later received clearance letters from the Justice Department.

38. *Los Angeles Times*, national telephone interview of 1,521 adults, March 27–29, 1992 (Roper Center for Public Opinion Research, University of Connecticut).

39. Peter Hart and Breglio Research Companies, national telephone interview of 1,001 registered voters, March 11–14, 1992 (Roper Center for Public Opinion Research, University of Connecticut). Only the "handling of problems with the savings and loan industry" ranked higher: it was the greatest concern for 30 percent of respondents; 22 percent were most bothered by "members of Congress bouncing checks at the House Bank."

40. CBS News/*New York Times* interview of 1,280 adults, October 5–7, 1991 (Roper Center for Public Opinion Research).

41. Gallup Organization, telephone interview of 1,000 adults, October 10–13, 1991 (Roper Center for Public Opinion Research).

42. Glenn R. Simpson, "One Year after Bank Revelations," *Roll Call*, September 21, 1992, p. 1. See also Gary C. Jacobson and Michael A. Dimrock, "Checking Out: The Effects of Bank Overdrafts on the 1992 Elections," *American Journal of Political Science*, vol. 38 (August 1994), pp. 601–24; and the discussion in chapter 6.

43. About half the respondents believed that taxpayers' money was used to pay for the overdrawn checks; a quarter thought that it was the money of other congressmen. Sixty-six percent believed that members had

broken the law. CBS/*New York Times* telephone interview of 1,638 adults, March 26–29, 1992 (Roper Center for Public Opinion Research).

44.   Technically, as the special counsel noted, the deposits were public funds because they were held in treasury accounts under the legal control of the government until actually withdrawn by members. But all the funds were due to members and any losses would have been suffered only by members. *Inquiry into the Operation of the Bank*, pp. 11–13.

45.   American Viewpoint, telephone interview of 1,000 adults, March 28–April 1, 1992 (Roper Center for Public Opinion Research).

46.   Former representative Tom Downey, commenting on the Senate action on gift rules, said, "the perks that members enjoy—and they do enjoy some—are probably the same level as those of mid-level managers in business. They are not nearly as lavish as those at the top of the corporate world or university presidents." National Public Radio, *Morning Edition*, May 12, 1994.

47.   For discussion and recommendations concerning the support system, see Thomas E. Mann and Norman J. Ornstein, *Renewing Congress: A First Report* (American Enterprise Institute and Brookings, 1992), pp. 69–74. For a survey of the privileges and exemptions of Congress, see *Congressional Pay and Perquisites: History, Facts, and Controversy* (Washington: Congressional Quarterly, 1992).

48.   On the recent discussions concerning personal use of campaign contributions, see Beth Donovan, "Election Commission Hearing Revisits Personal Spending," *Congressional Quarterly*, January 15, 1994, pp. 58–59; and "Defining 'Personal Use,'" *Roll Call*, January 17, 1994, p. 4.

49.   *Congressional Record*, January 17, 1995, pp. H252–86.

50.   "Lawmakers Rush to Admit Check Problems," *New York Times*, March 13, 1992, p. A19.

51.   Mark Z. Barabak, "Cranston Son's Group Assailed," *San Francisco Chronicle*, August 11, 1989, p. A1, A6.

52.   This qualification about what he believed is necessary because voter registration efforts that increase turnout do not always have the effects commonly expected. For example, the conventional wisdom that higher turnout helps the Democrats has been challenged: see James DeNardo, "Turnout and the Vote: The Joke's on the Democrats," *American Political Science Review*, vol. 74 (June 1980), pp. 406–20; Harvey J. Tucker and Arnold Vedlitz; and James DeNardo, "Does Heavy Turnout Help Democrats in Presidential Elections?" *American Political Science Review*, vol. 80 (December 1986), pp. 1292–1304.

53.   A pioneering work that exemplifies both the strengths and weaknesses of this approach is Susan Rose-Ackerman, *Corruption: A Study in Political Economy* (Academic Press, 1978), esp. pp. 6–10.

54.   A variation on this example actually took place. According to the

testimony of James Grogan, a Keating aide, Senator DeConcini's wife at times solicited contributions from Keating for her favorite charities in the community (*Preliminary Inquiry into Allegations Regarding Senators Cranston, DeConcini, Glenn, McCain, and Riegle, and Lincoln Savings and Loan*, Hearings before the Senate Select Committee on Ethics, 101 Cong. 2 sess. (GPO, December 1990), pt. 4, pp. 248–49).

55.   The incident is described in James Q. Wilson, "Corruption is Not Always Scandalous," in John A. Gardiner and David J. Olson, eds., *Theft of the City: Readings on Corruption in Urban America* (Indiana University Press, 1974), p. 37. The story, unfortunately, may be apocryphal; the incident is not mentioned in any of the standard biographical sources on Yerkes.

56.   The discussion of any political gain that is improper as a result of its *connection* to a favor or service that the politician provides is deferred until chapter 5. The implications for the principle of accountability are examined in chapter 6.

57.   Roger H. Davidson and Walter J. Oleszek, *Congress and Its Members*, 4th ed. (Washington: CQ Press, 1994), pp. 1, 4–5.

58.   *Revising the U.S. Senate Code of Ethics*, *Hastings Center Report*, special supplement (February 1981), p. 20.

59.   *Congressional Ethics Reform*, House Bipartisan Task Force on Ethics, 101 Cong. 1 sess. (GPO, May 1989), p. 18.

60.   *Congressional Pay and Perquisites*, pp. 27–35.

61.   Some modest changes, such as extending the limit to 120 days before a general election, and 90 days before a primary, would be useful. See Mann and Ornstein, *Renewing Congress*, p. 72.

62.   David Twenhafel, ed., *Setting Course: A Congressional Management Guide* (Washington: Congressional Management Foundation and American University, 1992), p. 120.

63.   Congressional Management Foundation and House Administration Assistants Association, "Balancing on a Congressional/Campaign Tightrope: How to Manage Ethics in a Campaign Year," April 8, 1994.

64.   *Common Cause* v. *Bolger*, 574 F. Supp. 672 (D.D.C. 1982), aff'd, 461 U.S. 911 (1983) at 683. Also see Advisory Opinion 2, House Committee on Standards of Official Conduct (July 11, 1973), reprinted in *Congressional Record*, July 12, 1973, pp. 23691–92.

65.   *People* v. *Ohrenstein*, 77 N.Y. 2d at 38; 565 N.E. 2d at 493; 563 N.Y.S. 2d at 744 (1990). See James A. Gardner, "The Uses and Abuses of Incumbency: *People* v. *Ohrenstein* and the Limits of Inherent Legislative Power," *Fordham Law Review*, vol. 60 (November 1991), pp. 217–54.

66.   *House Ethics Manual*, p. 280.

67.   Gardner, "Uses and Abuses," p. 219.

68.   But see *Common Cause* v. *Bolger*: "It is clear from the record that

Congress has recognized the basic principle that government funds should not be spent to help incumbents gain reelection" (574 F. Supp. at 683).

69.   Charges were brought against four other members during this period, but the ethics committees took no action. In addition, House Minority Whip Newt Gingrich was charged in 1989–90 with improperly using his congressional payroll for political purposes. He gave what appeared to be large bonuses (one-time, year-end salary increases) to staff members when they returned from a leave during which they worked on his campaign. Gingrich argued that the charges were politically motivated (retaliation for his attack on Speaker Jim Wright), and besides, many other members engaged in the same practice. The ethics committee concluded the investigation without taking action against him (*Congressional Ethics* [1992], pp. 73, 106–07).

70.   Richard F. Fenno, Jr., *Home Style: House Members in their Districts* (Little, Brown, 1978), pp. 167–68. For a broader description of the institutional effects of similar individualism (for instance, the tendency of "the officeholder to go his own way, even when that conflicts with the goals of the caucus or faction or political party to which he nominally belongs" and the attitude that "I answer to no one, only the electorate"), see Alan Ehrenhalt, *The United States of Ambition: Politicians, Power, and the Pursuit of Office* (Times Books, 1992), p. 274 and throughout.

71.   For this and other proposals that could have similar effects, see Thomas E. Mann and Norman J. Ornstein, *Renewing Congress: A Second Report* (American Enterprise Institute and Brookings, 1993), pp. 48–58.

Chapter Four

1.   *Preliminary Inquiry into Allegations Regarding Senators Cranston, DeConcini, Glenn, McCain, and Riegle, and Lincoln Savings and Loan,* Hearings before the Senate Select Committee on Ethics, 101 Cong. 2 sess., November 19, 1990 (Government Printing Office, 1991), pt. 1, pp. 10, 13.

2.   Richard F. Fenno, Jr., *Home Style: House Members in their Districts* (Little, Brown, 1978), p. 101.

3.   *Investigation of Senator Alan Cranston together with Additional Views,* Committee Print, Senate Select Committee on Ethics, 102 Cong. 1 sess. (GPO, November 1991), pp. 14–16; and *Preliminary Inquiry,* November 16, 1990, pt. 1, pp. 126–32; November 19, 1990, pt. 1, pp. 91–92.

4.   This is the most striking substantive difference between the confidential report prepared by the special counsel and the final report issued by the committee. The two reports can be compared because Senator Helms, to the dismay of his colleagues, issued the confidential report with only

minor changes as "Additional Views," appended to the committee report (*Investigation of Senator Alan Cranston together with Additional Views*). Because for many pages the two reports are identical, deletions and additions stand out. For example: the committee omits a significant portion of the discussion of various legal limits on intervention ("Report," pp. 9–10, and "Additional Views," p. 96); adds a section saying that only the voters should judge whether a member has mistakenly intervened for a constituent ("Report," p. 10, and "Additional Views," p. 97), omits the statement "even in the absence of threats . . . the intervention may be improper" ("Report," p. 11, and "Additional Views," p. 97), and deletes a list of questions intended to test whether an intervention is proper ("Report," p. 11, and "Additional Views," p. 98).

5.   The most celebrated, and controversial, of such cases were those growing out of the FBI's undercover operation (ABSCAM) in 1980, in which six House members and one senator were convicted for promising, in return for cash and other gifts, to help Arab sheiks (actually FBI agents in disguise) obtain approval to emigrate to the United States. One was expelled by the House, three resigned to avoid certain expulsion, and three were defeated in the next election. *Congressional Ethics: History, Facts, and Controversy* (Washington: Congressional Quarterly, 1992), pp. 63–68.

6.   *U.S.* v. *John Dowdy*, 479 F.2d 213 at 218.

7.   Ibid. at 218–19.

8.   The senators and representatives shall "be privileged from Arrest during their attendance at the Session of their respective Houses . . . and for any Speech or Debate in either House, they shall not be questioned in any other Place" (U.S. Constitution, Article I, sec. 6).

9.   *Congressional Ethics* (1992), p. 49.

10.   The special counsel in the case of Speaker Jim Wright made a similar distinction and suggested that it is implicit in the House rules and practices. See *Report of the Special Outside Counsel in the Matter of Speaker James C. Wright, Jr.*, House Committee on Standards of Official Conduct, 101 Cong. 2 sess. (GPO, February 1989), p. 193. More generally, the distinction between procedure and substance is familiar in all branches of the law, and in this respect the legal process can provide appropriate guidance for ethics standards here.

11.   *In the Matter of Representative James C. Wright, Jr.*, Committee Print, House Committee on Standards of Official Conduct, 101 Cong. 2 sess. (GPO, April 1989), p. 12; and *Report of the Special Outside Counsel*, pp. 28–33.

12.   *Report of the Special Outside Counsel*, pp. 31–32.

13.   Ibid., p. 33.

14. Senate Select Committee on Ethics, "Statement of the Committee Regarding D'Amato," August 2, 1991.

15. Ibid.; and "Senator Sensitive," *New York Times*, August 21, 1991, p. A24.

16. Senate Select Committee on Ethics, "Statement of the Committee Regarding D'Amato," p. 8.

17. Jonathan Rabinovitz, "Armand D'Amato Found Guilty of Fraud in a Lobbying Scheme," *New York Times*, May 8, 1993, p. A1; and "Ruling Backs D'Amato Kin in Fraud Case," *New York Times*, November 1, 1994, p. A1. In an editorial, "Legal Maybe, But Wrong," November 2, 1994, p. 22, the *Times* saw the reversal as a reminder that "not all ethics breaches constitute a crime."

18. "Legal Maybe, But Wrong."

19. Joe Canason, "Exclusive: '91 Ethics Testimony Reveals D'Amato Flubbed His Lines," *New York Observer*, April 25, 1994, pp. 1, 11. After the committee and D'Amato repeatedly declined to release the record of the hearings, the *Observer* obtained excerpts of D'Amato's testimony from sources it did not name.

20. The 10 percent estimate comes from Bruce Cain, John Ferejohn, and Morris Fiorina, *The Personal Vote: Constituency Service and Electoral Independence* (Harvard University Press, 1987), p. 53.

21. *Preliminary Inquiry*, November 19, 1990, pt. 1, p. 11.

22. Ibid., November 16, 1990, pt. 1, p. 111; and November 19, 1990, pt. 1, p. 23.

23. Ibid., December 10, 1990, pt. 4, pp. 58–94.

24. Ibid., November 19, 1990, pt. 1, pp. 14–17; December 10, 1990, pt. 4, pp. 9–12; and January 10, 1991, pt. 6, pp. 137–40.

25. Cain, Ferejohn, and Fiorina, pp. 174–82, 189–94, 213–14; and Morris Fiorina, *Congress: Keystone of the Washington Establishment*, 2d ed. (Yale University Press, 1989), pp. 39–43, 55–56, 86–93, 98–99. The electoral effect of constituency service is still a subject of some controversy among political scientists. See Diana Evans Yiannakis, "The Grateful Electorate: Casework and Congressional Elections," *American Journal of Political Science*, vol. 25 (August 1981), pp. 568–80; Morris Fiorina, "Some Problems in Studying the Effects of Resource Allocation in Congressional Elections," *American Journal of Political Science*, vol. 25 (August 1981), pp. 543–67; John C. McAdams and John R. Johannes, "Does Casework Matter? A Reply to Professor Fiorina," *American Journal of Political Science*, vol. 25 (August 1981), pp. 581–604; John R. Johannes, *To Serve the People: Congress and Constituency Service* (University of Nebraska Press, 1984); John R. Johannes and John C. McAdams, "En-

trepreneur or Agent; Congressmen and the Distribution of Casework, 1977–78," *Western Political Quarterly*, vol. 40 (September 1987), pp. 535–53; John R. Johannes, "Congress, The Bureaucracy and Casework," *Administration and Society*, vol. 16 (May 1984), pp. 41–69; and Gary C. Jacobson, *The Politics of Congressional Elections*, 3d ed. (HarperCollins, 1992), pp. 41–43.

26.   Morris Fiorina, "The Case of the Vanishing Marginals: The Bureaucracy Did It," *American Political Science Review*, vol. 71 (March 1977), p. 180.

27.   Mathew D. McCubbins and Thomas Schwartz, "Congressional Oversight Overlooked: Police Patrols versus Fire Alarms," *American Journal of Political Science*, vol. 28 (February 1984), pp. 165–79. But on the limitations of this and other forms of retrospective monitoring, see Mathew D. McCubbins, Roger Noll, and Barry R. Weingast, "Administrative Procedures as Instruments of Political Control," *Journal of Law, Economics and Organization*, vol. 3 (Fall 1987), pp. 243–77.

28.   Irwin Ross, "Congressmen as Local Ombudsmen," *New York Times*, February 2, 1992, "Long Island Weekly Desk," p. 1. Also see the examples cited in Jay P. Urwitz, "After Keating, Must I Never Call My Congressman?" *Wall Street Journal*, December 31, 1991, p. A6.

29.   Michael Winerip, "Overhauling School Grants: Much Debate but Little Gain," *New York Times*, February 4, 1994, pp. A1, A16.

30.   Norman J. Ornstein, Thomas E. Mann, and Michael J. Malbin, *Vital Statistics on Congress, 1993-94* (Washington: Congressional Quarterly, 1994), tables 5-3, 5-4.

31.   Fiorina, *Congress*, pp. 91–92.

32.   H.R. 8017, 91 Cong. 1 sess. (1969). The bill had been introduced in more or less the same form in many earlier sessions: H.R. 388, 90 Cong. 1 sess. (1967); H.R. 4273, 89 Cong. 1 sess. (1965); and H.R. 7593, 88 Cong. 1 sess. (1963). For an analysis of the proposal and discussion of similar reforms, see Robert Klonoff, "The Congressman as Mediator between Citizens and Government Agencies: Problems and Prospects," *Harvard Journal on Legislation*, vol. 16 (Summer 1979), pp. 701–34.

33.   Fiorina, *Congress*, pp. 48–66; and Jacobson, *Politics of Congressional Elections*, pp. 41–43.

34.   In one of the most balanced assessments of constituent service by a sitting member, Representative Lee H. Hamilton has written "we need to amend congressional rules to clear up members' confusion over the proper limits of constituent representation . . . vague standards may even lead to overly cautious members cutting back too much in legitimate constituent service." "Constituent Service and Representation," *Public Manager*, vol. 21 (Summer 1992), p. 15. He recommends public disclosure of interventions,

more preventive efforts by the ethics committees, and greater emphasis on broader standards rather than "legalistic nuances of a specific rule."

35. For example, Urwitz, "After Keating," p. A6.

36. *The Pillsbury Co.* v. *Federal Trade Commission,* 354 F.2d 952 at 964. The most helpful guide to this line of decisions as well as to the other restrictions on congressional intervention is Morton Rosenberg and Jack Maskell, *Congressional Intervention in the Administrative Process: Legal and Ethical Considerations* (Congressional Research Service, September 1990). Also see Richard Lewis Gelfond, "Judicial Limitations of Congressional Influence on Administrative Agencies," *Northwestern University Law Review,* vol. 73 (December 1979), pp. 931–56.

37. *D.C. Federation of Civic Associations* v. *Volpe,* 459 F.2d 1231 (D.C. Cir. 1971) at 1246–48.

38. A recent commentator criticizes what he sees as an erosion of the *Pillsbury* standard in subsequent cases and argues that courts should apply it to informal agency proceedings as well as quasi-judicial ones. See Brett G. Kappel, "Judicial Restrictions on Improper Congressional Influence in Administrative Decision-making: A Defense of the *Pillsbury* Doctrine," *Journal of Law and Politics,* vol. 6 (Fall 1989), pp. 135–71.

39. To invalidate a quasi-legislative administrative decision, it must be shown not only that the congressional intervention actually influenced the agency but also that it was directed at and affected the individual in the agency who actually made the decision. *Koniag* v. *Kleppe,* 405 F. Supp. 1360 (D.D.C. 1975), modified *sub nom. Koniag* v. *Andrus,* 580 F.2d 601 (D.C. Cir. 1978) at 610, *cert. denied* 439 U.S. 1052 (1978); and *Peter Kiewit Sons' Co.* v. *U.S. Army Corps of Engineers,* 714 F.2d (D.C. Cir. 1983) at 169–70.

40. *Power Authority of the State of New York* v. *Federal Energy Regulatory Commission,* 743 F.2d 93 (2d Cir. 1984) at 110. Also see *Texas Oil and Gas Corp* v. *Watt,* 683 F.2d 427 (D.C. Cir. 1982) at 434, where pressure on an agency by several senators is called "regrettable."

41. 5 U.S.C.S. § 557 (1994). See also the discussion in the House Committee on Standards of Official Conduct, *Ethics Manual for Members, Officers, and Employees of the U.S. House of Representatives,* 102 Cong. 2 sess. (GPO, April 1992), pp. 242–44 (hereafter *House Ethics Manual*).

42. *D.C. Federation of Civic Associations* v. *Volpe* at 1246.

43. *Texas Medical Association* v. *Matthews,* 408 F. Supp. 303 (W.D. Tex 1976) at 313.

44. *Gulf Oil Corp.* v. *Federal Power Commission,* 563 F.2d 588 (3d Cir. 1977) at 611.

45. *Pillsbury* v. *Federal Trade Commission,* 354 F.2d at 964.

46. *Investigation of Senator Alan Cranston,* p. 50; and *Additional Views,* pp. 97–100.

47.   S. Res. 273, 102 Cong. 2 sess., approved July 2, 1992. See *Congressional Record*, daily ed., July 2, 1992, pp. S9762–S9764.

48.   S. Res. 273, sec. 3.

49.   *Congressional Record*, daily ed., July 2, 1992, pp. S9762–S9764. In the Senate the criticism was attributed to Common Cause. However, its source is a statement of the obligations of members as presented in a report by a Senate subcommittee chaired by Paul Douglas in the early 1950s. See *Ethical Standards in Government*, Committee Print, Senate Committee on Labor and the Public Welfare, Special Subcommittee on the Establishment of a Commission on Ethics in Government, 82 Cong. 1 sess. (GPO, 1951), pp. 29–30.

50.   *House Ethics Manual*, pp. 241–66. Instead of permitting members to challenge an administrative response on grounds that it is not consistent with "statutes, regulations or consideration of equity and public policy" (the language of the Senate rule), the House rule allows challenges only on the basis that the response is not consistent with "established law, Federal Regulation or legislative intent" (p. 264). The House formulation is preferable if one assumes that legislators who disagree with current law should try to change it through action in the legislative process rather than through intervention in the administrative process. Even if one believes that citizens (including judges and lawyers) may sometimes challenge law on grounds of equity and public policy, one might still hold that legislators have a more exacting duty than others to observe the law to the extent that they fail to change it.

51.   Ibid., p. 249.

52.   Specifically, special counsel charged a violation of House rule 63, clause 1 ("A Member . . . shall conduct himself at all times in a manner which shall reflect creditably on the House"), and invoked the standard of "undue influence" as interpreted under the committee's "Advisory Opinion no. 1." See *Report of the Special Outside Counsel,* pp. 193–94.

53.   Ibid., pp. 218–37.

54.   Ibid., pp. 240–55.

55.   Ibid., p. 23.

56.   Ibid., pp. 256–57.

57.   *In the Matter of Wright*, p. 84.

58.   *Investigation of Cranston*, p. 84.

59.   Paul H. Douglas, *Ethics in Government* (Harvard University Press, 1952), p. 88. Also see *Ethical Standards in Government*, pp. 29–30.

60.   "Statement of the Committee Regarding D'Amato," pp. 5–6.

61.   In interviews, members who were lawyers were more likely than nonlawyers to adopt this adversary view of their role as legislators. Although certainly not systematic, this evidence suggests that further empir-

ical investigation of the relation between role conceptions and previous professional experience would be illuminating.

62. *House Ethics Manual*, p. 252.

63.   James M. Falvey addresses this and other problems of a similar legal standard, but his proposal would prohibit representational services for out-of-state interests as a matter of law and seems to permit an unwarranted intrusion of the criminal trial process into the responsibilities of the legislature. See "The Congressional Ethics Dilemma: Constituent Service or Conflict of Interest?" *American Criminal Law Review*, vol. 28 (Fall 1991), pp. 372–73.

64.   5 U.S.C.S. § 552a (b) (1994).

65.   "Testimony of Gwendolyn van Paasschen," *Preliminary Inquiry*, pt. 1, November 20, 1990, pp. 97–98.

66.   In a panel discussion on the ethics of congressional intervention, an administrator in the Food and Drug Administration described some of the ways that she and her colleagues could tell when a member is making an inappropriate request. See John C. Stennis Center for Public Service Training and Development, and Congressional Management Foundation, producers, *Constituent Services: The Ethics of Congressional Intervention*, video (Washington: Congressional Management Foundation, 1993).

67.   During the hearings, Senator Howell Heflin questioned whether the standards of the Administrative Procedure Act applied to the Bank Board in the Lincoln case. The legal issue was never resolved by the committee, but most witnesses seemed to take it for granted that the case was more adjudicatory than not. *Preliminary Inquiry*, pt. 3, December 4, 1990, pp. 156–58.

68.   Compare Rosenberg and Maskell, *Congressional Intervention*, pp. 5–9; and Kappel, "Judicial Restrictions," pp. 135–71.

69.   *Preliminary Inquiry*, pt. 1, November 16, 1990, pp. 99–100.

70.   See the closing rebuttal of the special counsel, *Preliminary Inquiry*, pt. 6, January 16, 1991, pp. 180–83.

71.   Many of the opinions in the line of cases interpreting the Administrative Procedures Act *(Pillsbury* v. *Federal Trade Commission* and its progeny) are especially critical of secret congressional interventions, even when the courts do not invalidate the agency results. See Kappel, "Judicial Restrictions," pp. 144–47.

72.   See 21 C.F.R. §§ 10.65, 10.70, 10.80 (1988), "FDA Code of Regulations" (April 1994), pp. 94–103; and 47 C.F.R. §§ 1.1200-1.1216 (1988), "FCC Code of Regulations" (October 1993), pp. 226–35. Also see Susan Low Bloch, "Orphaned Rules in the Administrative State: The Fairness Doctrine and Other Orphaned Progeny of Interactive Deregulation," *Georgetown Law Journal*, vol. 76 (October 1987), pp. 126–28.

Chapter Five

1.   Senator Malcolm Wallop, *Congressional Record*, daily ed., May 5, 1994, p. S5224. The legislation that finally passed banned most gifts of any value, which in Wallop's view implied that members could not be trusted even for one penny. See also Norman J. Ornstein, "Lobbying Reform: Gift Horse Looks Back at Members," *Roll Call*, May 12, 1994, pp. 5, 51.

2.   Some members who otherwise agreed with Wallop still thought the ban was necessary to restore public confidence and voted for it for that reason. See, for example, Senator Frank Lautenberg's remarks, *Congressional Record*, daily edition, May 4, 1994, pp. S5156–57.

3.   In *attempted* bribery the connection is through only the mind of one party, the citizen proposing the bribe: "so long as a bribe is 'offered or promised' with the requisite intent 'to influence *any* official act,' the crime is committed." *U.S.* v. *Jacobs*, 431 F.2d 760 (2d Cir. 1970).

4.   A related criminal offense, acceptance of an illegal gratuity, requires a somewhat lesser standard of criminal intent. See, for example, *U.S.* v. *Strand*, 574 F.2d 993, 995 (9th Cir. 1978), which states that bribery requires "heightened criminal intent" (no quid pro quo), whereas illegal gratuity needs only "simple *mens rea.*" Some commentators distinguish a bribe and an illegal gratuity this way: a bribe motivates a future act; a gratuity is a reward for a past act. A bribe says "please" and a gratuity says "thank you." See Department of Justice, "Appendix: Bribery and Gratuities," *Prosecution of Public Corruption Cases* (1988), p. 300.

5.   As was noted in chapter 2, even if the gain is political and the service deserved, the connection can still be of the type that characterizes individual corruption. When the gain is personal, the service undeserved, and the connection motivational, the corruption is purely individual. Similarly, a personal gain and undeserved service can be connected institutionally.

6.   *Investigation of Senator Harrison A. Williams, Jr., Report*, Committee Print, Senate Select Committee on Ethics, 97 Cong. 1 sess. (Government Printing Office, September 1981).

7.   *Congressional Ethics: History, Facts, and Controversy* (Washington: Congressional Quarterly, 1992) p. 65. Also see *In the Matter of Representative John W. Jenrette, Jr.*, Committee Print, House Committee on Standards of Official Conduct, 96 Cong. 2 sess. (GPO, December 1980).

8.   *Investigation of Williams, Report*, pp. 4–5.

9.   Ibid., pp. 5, 7 (italics added). The main section of Williams's own defense to the committee is entitled "Senator Williams's Innocent Intentions." *Investigation of Senator Harrison A. Williams, Jr., Response of Senator Williams*, Committee Print, Senate Select Committee on Ethics, 97 Cong. 1 sess. (GPO, September 1981), p. 5.

10.   Floor Statement of Senator Howell Heflin, "consideration of S. Res. 204, March 3, 1982," photocopy provided by committee counsel, pp. 28, 6, 19.

11.   See for example, Senator Alan Cranston's comment: "If the F.B.I. is allowed to do what it did, that presents a dire danger to the separation of powers." Steven V. Roberts, "Senators and the Senate on Trial with Williams," *New York Times*, March 10, 1982, p. B2.

12.   Williams's statement continued: "In Abscam, it is the Senate that stands accused and intimidated by another branch of Government to whom we may be forever subordinated and subjugated unless we are successful in our resistance." *New York Times*, March 12, 1982, p. B2. Also see *Investigation of Williams, Response*, pp. 20–26.

13.   Joseph F. Sullivan, "Williams Backers in Senate Urge Censure Rather Than Expulsion," *New York Times*, March 3, 1982, p. A1.

14.   *Congressional Ethics* (1992), p. 168. The House's first expulsion for corruption and only the fourth expulsion in its history took place some two years earlier: the offender, Michael J. "Ozzie" Myers, had also been caught in the ABSCAM sting (pp. 18–19). See *In the Matter of Representative Michael O. Myers*, Committee Print, House Committee on Standards of Official Conduct, 96 Cong. 2 sess. (GPO, September 1980).

15.   Senator Dale Bumpers, quoted in Roberts, "Senators and the Senate on Trial," p. B2.

16.   *Investigation of Senator David F. Durenberger*, Committee Print, Senate Select Committee on Ethics, 101 Cong. 2 sess. (GPO, July 1990), p. 105 [italics added].

17.   On the difficulty of distinguishing bribery and extortion, see James Lindgren, "The Elusive Distinction between Bribery and Extortion: From the Common Law to the Hobbs Act," *UCLA Law Review*, vol. 35 (June 1988), pp. 815–909.

18.   *In the Matter of Representative James C. Wright, Jr.*, Committee Print, House Committee on Standards of Official Conduct, 101 Cong. 2 sess. (GPO, April 1989) pp. 12–14; and *Report of the Special Outside Counsel in the Matter of Speaker James C. Wright, Jr.*, House Committee on Standards of Official Conduct, 101 Cong. 2 sess. (GPO, February 1989), p. 45.

19.   *Report of the Special Outside Counsel*, pp. 40–41. The counsel also charged that Wright violated the disclosure rule.

20.   *Congressional Record*, daily edition, May 5, 1994, pp. S5231–33. The House bill allowed privately paid travel for various charitable, speaking, and fact-finding activities. For a comparison of the two versions of the bill, see Alice A. Love, "Senate Passes Significantly Tougher Gift Bill than House; Measure Headed to Conference," *Roll Call*, May 12, 1994, pp. 10, 46.

21. *Congressional Record*, daily ed., May 4, 1994, p. S5153.

22. *Congressional Record*, daily ed., May 5, 1994, pp. S5229, S5281. The amendment carried, 66–29, but (as senators no doubt foresaw) the prohibition did not survive in the conference committee.

23. Ibid., p. S5283.

24. The objection to relying exclusively on motives as the test of corruption also applies to some kinds of personal gain, especially those that are otherwise legitimate and are also closely related to motives that could be seen as part of the duty of a legislator. For example, Wright's interest in oil wells, though a personal gain, is hard to separate from his interest in representing his constituents whose livelihood depends on the oil industry.

25. Paul H. Douglas, *Ethics in Government* (Harvard University Press, 1952), pp. 44, 85–92.

26. House Committee on Standards of Official Conduct, *Ethics Manual for Members, Officers, and Employees of the U.S. House of Representatives*, 102 Cong. 2 sess. (GPO, April 1992), pp. 250–51, 257–58 (hereafter *House Ethics Manual*); and Senate rule XLIII. The Senate rule, adopted in response to the Keating Five case, merely prohibits providing assistance on the basis of contributions or services to a member's political campaigns or other organizations in which a member has an interest (S. Res. 273, 102 Cong. 2 sess., July 2, 1992). The section of the *House Ethics Manual* on assisting supporters repeats the ethics committee's conclusion from the Gingrich case of 1990: "As long as there is no quid pro quo, a Member is free to assist all persons equally" (p. 250). The longest discussion in the *House Ethics Manual* is a quotation from the Senate ethics committee's report on the Keating Five case (pp. 250–51; also see more generally, pp. 257–58.) However, the *Manual*, as well as the committee report, does warn members to "be aware of the appearance of impropriety" in assisting contributors.

27. See also James Q. Wilson, "Corruption Is Not Always Scandalous," in John A. Gardiner and David J. Olson, eds., *Theft of the City: Readings on Corruption in Urban America* (Indiana University Press, 1974): "Money, for reasons I do not fully understand, converts a compromise or exchange of favors into a corrupt act" (p. 31).

28. *Preliminary Inquiry into Allegations Regarding Senators Cranston, DeConcini, Glenn, McCain, and Riegle, and Lincoln Savings and Loan*, Hearings before the Senate Select Committee on Ethics, 101 Cong. 2 sess., pt. 4, December 14, 1990 (GPO 1991), p. 178.

29. *Investigation of Senator Alan Cranston, Together with Additional Views*, Committee Print, Senate Select Committee on Ethics, 102 Cong. 1 sess. (GPO, November 1991), p. 36.

30. Russell Long, "Statement," *Financing Political Campaigns*, Hear-

ings before the Senate Committee on Finance, 89 Cong. 2 sess. (GPO, 1966), cited in John T. Noonan, *Bribes* (University of California Press, 1984), p. 650. More generally, see Noonan, pp. 621–51, 687–90, 696–97.

31.   Daniel H. Lowenstein, "Political Bribery and the Intermediate Theory of Politics," *UCLA Law Review*, vol. 32 (April 1985), pp. 808–09, esp. notes 86, 87. Also, see the opinions of Justices William Brennan and Byron White in *U.S. v. Brewster*, 408 U.S. 521, 558 (1977).

32.   Noonan, *Bribes*, p. 645.

33.   *McCormick* v. *U.S.*, 500 U.S. 257 at 272 (1991).

34.   See, for example, Amitai Etzioni, *Capital Corruption: The New Attack on American Democracy* (Harcourt Brace Jovanovich, 1984), and "Keating Six?" *Responsive Community*, vol. 1 (Winter 1990–91), pp. 6–9; Francis Wilkinson, "Rules of the Game: The Senate's Money Politics," *Rolling Stone*, August 8, 1991, pp. 31 ff.; and Noonan, *Bribes*, pp. 621–51. Also see the affidavit of Senator Ernest Hollings, *Preliminary Inquiry*, exhibits of Sen. Dennis DeConcini, pp. 493–95. Daniel H. Lowenstein concludes: "The legislative process is not corrupt, but it is tainted with corruption. Legislators, by and large, are not corrupt . . . though sometimes they are corrupted. The campaign finance system is corrupt." "On Campaign Finance Reform: The Root of All Evil is Deeply Rooted," *Hofstra Law Review*, vol. 18 (Fall 1989), p. 335.

35.   Some further specification of what should count as a general political orientation or an important issue may be necessary in some circumstances, but it should be clear that agreement on the value of constituent service itself (the principle on which Keating and the Keating Five evidently most strongly agreed) is not sufficient. Constituent service may itself undermine the democratic process. Furthermore, Keating's actions suggest he was less interested in constituent service as a general practice that could be justified for all citizens than in the specific services provided for one constituent.

36.   Daniel Lowenstein proposes a similar distinction between contributions that are "intended to influence official conduct and accepted with the knowledge that they are so intended" and those "intended solely to help the candidate get elected" ("Political Bribery," p. 847). The distinction drawn in the text differs in at least two respects: it takes the function rather than actual intentions as the criterion; and it treats elections as only one of the relevant parts of the political process. John Noonan also distinguishes contributions from bribes (*Bribes*, pp. 696–97), but the two characteristics he regards as critical—size and secrecy—are better interpreted as indicators of the more basic distinction made in the text. If a contribution is small relative to other contributions a candidate receives (not relative to the total

contributions), and if it is public (or if the pattern of which it is a part is made public), the contribution could be more plausibly seen as support for the candidate rather than an attempt to influence official conduct.

37.   This may be part of the rationale underlying the Supreme Court decision upholding a law that places limits on the ability of corporations to make independent expenditures on behalf of political candidates; *Austin* v. *Michigan Chamber of Commerce*, 494 U.S. 652 (1990). Wealth accumulated by a corporation has "little or no correlation to the public's support for the corporation's political ideas," and therefore has "corrosive and distorting" effects on the political process (p. 1397). The idea presumably is that although the corporation is using the money to express substantive political views, the corporation's ability to do so does not derive from any substantive political support. Its economic success ought not be translated so directly into political influence. See Samuel M. Taylor, "*Austin* v. *Michigan Chamber of Commerce*: Addressing a 'New Corruption' in Campaign Financing," *North Carolina Law Review*, vol. 69 (April 1991), pp. 1060–79; and more generally, Andrew Stark, "Corporate Electoral Activity, Constitutional Discourse, and Conceptions of the Individual," *American Political Science Review*, vol. 86 (September 1992), pp. 626–37.

38.   For a brief discussion of what principles of legislative ethics imply for campaign finance reform, see Dennis F. Thompson, *Political Ethics and Public Office* (Harvard University Press, 1987), pp. 114–16. Other analyses that relate theory to practice include Charles R. Beitz, *Political Equality: An Essay in Democratic Theory* (Princeton University Press, 1989), pp. 192–213; and Lowenstein, "On Campaign Finance Reform," pp. 301–67. Among the most helpful recent work by political scientists are Gary C. Jacobson, *The Politics of Congressional Elections*, 3d ed. (HarperCollins, 1992), pp. 63–79; David B. Magleby and Candice J. Nelson, *The Money Chase: Congressional Campaign Finance Reform* (Brookings, 1990), pp. 48–71; and Frank J. Sorauf, *Inside Campaign Finance: Myths and Realities* (Yale University Press, 1992).

39.   Michael Walzer, *Spheres of Justice: A Defense of Pluralism and Equality* (Basic Books, 1983), pp. 95–128. On the claim that money is a "unique political resource because it can be converted into many other political resources," see Lowenstein, "On Campaign Finance Reform," pp. 301–02, and the citations there.

40.   See Baron de Montesquieu, *De l'Esprit des Lois*, in *Montesquieu: Oeuvres Complètes*, ed. Roger Caillois (Paris: Gallimard, 1949–51), vol. 1, book 5, chap. 19; and Jeremy Bentham, "The Rationale of Reward," *The Works of Jeremy Bentham*, ed. John Bowring (Edinburgh: William Tait, 1843), vol. 5, pp. 246–48. More generally, see Albert O. Hirschman, *The*

Passions and the Interests: Political Arguments for Capitalism before Its Triumph (Princeton University Press, 1977).

41.   Sorauf, *Inside Campaign Finance*, p. 187.

42.   Magleby and Nelson, *Money Chase*, also conclude that more should be spent on campaigns "only if the spending is done by challengers and heightens competition" (p. 47).

43.   Most studies find little or no relationship or suggest that other factors are more significant. See Henry Chappell, "Campaign Contributions and Voting on the Cargo Preference Bill," *Public Choice*, vol. 36 (1981), pp. 310–12; Benjamin Ginsberg, *The Consequences of Consent: Elections, Citizen Control and Popular Acquiescence* (Addison-Wesley, 1978); Janet M. Grenzke, "PACs and the Congressional Supermarket: The Currency is Complex," *American Journal of Political Science*, vol. 33 (February 1989), pp. 1–24; W. P. Welch, "Campaign Contributions and Legislative Voting: Milk Money and Dairy Price Supports," *Western Political Quarterly*, vol. 35 (December 1982), pp. 478–95; and John R. Wright, "PACs, Contributions, and Roll Calls: An Organizational Perspective," *American Political Science Review*, vol. 79 (June 1985), pp. 400–14. For a study that finds a stronger relationship see James B. Kau and Paul H. Rubin, *Congressmen, Constituents and Contributors: Determinants of Roll Call Voting in the House of Representatives* (Boston: Martinus Nijhoff, 1982).

For a critical review of the literature finding a strong influence of personal ideology on voting decisions, see John E. Jackson and John W. Kingdon, "Ideology, Interest Group Scores, and Legislative Votes," *American Journal of Political Science*, vol. 36 (August 1992), pp. 805–23.

44.   "Whether money follows votes or vice versa is one of those chicken-and-egg problems that as yet has no clear answer. . . . None of the studies on the question of whether money buys or follows votes can be considered definitive." Morris P. Fiorina, *Congress: Keystone of the Washington Establishment*, 2d ed. (Yale University Press, 1989), p. 129.

45.   For a critical review contending that contributors exercise more influence than much of the social science literature implies, see Lowenstein, "On Campaign Finance Reform," pp. 313–35.

46.   Author's interviews with members of Congress and staff, March–June, 1994. Also see Magleby and Nelson, *Money Chase*, pp. 77–80.

47.   Richard L. Hall and Frank W. Wayman, "Buying Time: Moneyed Interests and the Mobilization of Bias in Congressional Committees," *American Political Science Review*, vol. 84 (September 1990), esp. p. 814. This study also reveals patterns that may violate the fairness principle: the distribution of mobilization evidently favors wealthier groups.

48.   "The allegation need not be that the legislators are for sale, but

that they routinely act within a position of conflict of interest. Perhaps it is likely that legislators would have acted in the same manner if the conflict of interest had not been present. That likelihood does not change the fact that, when they did act, the conflict existed." Lowenstein, "On Campaign Finance Reforms," p. 335.

49.   The phrase "veil of ignorance" comes from John Rawls, *A Theory of Justice* (Harvard University Press, 1971), pp. 136–42, where it is used in a much more systematic way to establish the foundations of principles of justice.

50.   Joseph R. Weeks, "Bribes, Gratuities and the Congress: The Institutionalized Corruption of the Political Process, the Impotence of the Criminal Law to Reach It, and a Proposal for Change," *Journal of Legislation*, vol. 13 (1986), p. 146.

51.   *Investigation of Cranston*, p. 102.

52.   *Preliminary Inquiry*, pt. 5, January 4, 1991, p. 177.

53.   In newspapers, universities, and other institutions the separation of financial from core functions is generally assumed to better protect the latter from the influence of the former. Advertising and fundraising are kept distinct, respectively, from editorial and admissions functions. But the existence of different professional cultures and a common commitment to keeping the core functions free of financial influence is probably just as important as the organizational separation of personnel and operations.

54.   *Investigation of Cranston*, p. 27.

55.   Glenn R. Simpson, "Second Memo Links Official Act, Support," *Roll Call*, April 11, 1994, p. 20.

56.   Glenn R. Simpson, "Cash and Aid Linked in Lautenberg Memo," *Roll Call*, March 31, 1994, pp. 1, 47.

57.   Ibid., p. 46.

58.   Glenn R. Simpson, "Lautenberg Tells Ethics, Aide Violated No Rule," *Roll Call*, April 4, 1994, pp. 1, 11.

59.   Simpson, "Cash and Aid," p. 47.

60.   "The Lautenberg Memo," *Roll Call*, April 4, 1994, p. 4. It was a *Roll Call* reporter who first broke the story.

61.   Author's interviews, May–June 1994.

62.   Simpson, "Lautenberg Tells Ethics," p. 11.

63.   Simpson, "Second Memo," p. 20.

64.   *Congressional Record*, daily ed., May 4, 1994, p. S5157.

65.   See the survey in *Investigation of Cranston*, pp. 14–16.

66.   In the small body of academic literature on the standard, most writers have opposed its use against public officials, just as commentators on legal ethics have objected to its use in the discipline of lawyers). See Peter W. Morgan, "The Appearance of Propriety: Ethics Reform and the

Blifil Paradoxes," *Stanford Law Review*, vol. 44 (February 1992), pp. 593–621; and Robert N. Roberts, "'Lord, Protect Me from the Appearance of Wrongdoing,'" in David H. Rosenbloom, ed., *Public Personnel Policy: The Politics of Civil Service* (Port Washington, N.Y.: Associated Faculty Press, 1985), pp. 177–89. A more balanced view is Andrew Stark, "The Appearance of Official Impropriety and the Concept of Political Crime," *Ethics*, vol. 105 (January 1995), pp. 326–51. More favorable is Brett G. Kappel, "Judicial Restrictions on Improper Congressional Influence in Administrative Decision-making: A Defense of the *Pillsbury* Doctrine," *Journal of Law and Politics*, vol. 6 (Fall 1989), pp. 154–71. A helpful (and rare) discussion of the appearance standard by a philosopher is Julia Driver, "Caesar's Wife: On the Moral Significance of Appearing Good," *Journal of Philosophy*, vol. 89 (July 1992), pp. 331–43.

67.   *Investigation of Cranston*, pp. 17, 19.

68.   Robert N. Roberts, *White House Ethics: The History of the Politics of Conflict of Interest Regulation* (Greenwood Press, 1988), pp. 181–82.

69.   House rule XLIII, clause 1; and *Investigation of Cranston*, p. 15.

70.   See Frederick Schauer, *Playing by the Rules: A Philosophical Examination of Rule-Based Decision-Making in Law and in Life* (Oxford University Press, 1991), esp. pp. 47–52. The appearance standard is not, however, overinclusive with respect to *its own purpose*, understood as prohibiting appearances of corruption.

71.   The justification for this kind of standard thus should not be confused with the type of argument (common in discussions of rule utilitarianism) that justifies particular acts by appeals to general rules or policies. In the rule utilitarian argument, an overly broad rule is justified by showing that the costs of deciding each case are greater than the costs of wrongly deciding some cases. The argument for the appearance standard differs in two respects. First, it counts as a cost not simply the risk that a case might be wrongly decided, but also the likelihood that the public will perceive the case to have been wrongly decided. Public confidence could be undermined and misconduct by others encouraged, even if a case were rightly decided but not so perceived. Second, the rationale for the appearance standard rests on the accountability principle, which implies that the reasons on which public officials may be assumed to act should be accessible to citizens. Appearances in these ways, then, are valuable beyond their role as evidence for corrupt motives or even institutional patterns.

72.   In Thomist ethics, "giving scandal" is defined as providing the "occasion for another's fall." The potential effect on the conduct of others is the principal reason that many Thomists traditionally treat appearing to do wrong under certain conditions as a distinct wrong. Giving scandal is considered a sin if one's otherwise permissible action is of the kind that is

in itself conducive to sin, and it remains sinful whether or not one intends it to have any effect on others. St. Thomas Aquinas, *Summa Theologiae* (London and New York: Blackfriars with McGraw-Hill, and Eyre and Spottiswoode, 1972), vol. 35, question 43, "Scandal," pp. 109–37.

73. *Investigation of Cranston*, p. 79.

74. *Preliminary Inquiry*, pt. 1, November 16, 1990, pp. 121–22.

75. R. W. Apple, "A Sununu 'Appearance Problem' Is Conceded by a Still-Loyal Bush," *New York Times*, June 20, 1991, p. A1.

76. House rule 8, *House Ethics Manual*, p. 119.

77. *Investigation of Cranston*, pp. 14–16; *House Ethics Manual*, pp. 24–25, 85–88; *Congressional Ethics* (1992), p. 46; and *Federal Register*, vol. 56, no. 141 (July 23, 1991), p. 33785, pt. VI. The Office of Government Ethics uses a more specific formulation: "the perspective of a reasonable person with knowledge of the relevant facts." Notice, however, that if the phrase "with knowledge of the relevant facts" is interpreted too strongly, the appearance standard is in danger of collapsing into an actual conduct standard. The OGE regulations also establish a procedure by which an agency ethics officer may authorize officials who have an appearance problem in particular cases not to disqualify themselves. This procedure is a "means to ensure that their conduct will not be found, as a matter of hindsight, to have been improper," and thus provides a further objective basis for the appearance standard. *Federal Register* § 2536.502 (d), p. 33786.

78. *Congressional Record*, daily ed., May 4, 1994, p. 5170. But see Senator Mitch McConnell's objections at p. 5164. More generally, it should be noted that it is preferable to formulate the criterion in a way that refers to grounds of judgments (conclusions that citizens can reasonably reach) rather than to attributes of persons (conclusions that reasonable citizens reach). The latter taken literally is too demanding, and in any case the former more precisely focuses on the point of the appearance standard.

Chapter Six

1. *Ethics Process: Testimony of Hon. Louis Stokes, Hon. James Hansen, and a Panel of Academic Experts*, Hearing before the Joint Committee on the Organization of Congress, 103 Cong. 1 sess. (Government Printing Office, February 1993), pp. 7–8. See also the comments of the majority and minority leaders announcing the establishment of the Senate Ethics Study Commission: "there is an inherent difficulty in the current system of Senators judging their colleagues." "Senate Leaders Announce Ethics Study Commission," press release, U. S. Senate, Office of the Majority Leader, March 4, 1993.

2.   Article I, section 5 of the Constitution states, "Each House may determine the Rules of its Proceedings, punish its members for disorderly Behavior, and, with the concurrence of two thirds, expel a Member."

3.   "Nemo esse judex in sua causa potest" is usually attributed to Publilius Syrus (sometimes called Publius). See *Sentences de Publilius Syrus*, translated by Jules Chenu (Paris: C.L.F. Pancoucke, 1835), p. 555. Also see the similar saying in Blaise Pascal, *Pascal's Pensées*, trans. with an introduction by Martin Turnell (Harper, 1962), p. 130: "It is not permissible for the most equitable man to be judge in his own cause."

4.   *The Federalist Papers*, Clinton Rossiter, ed. (New American Library, 1961), no. 10, p. 179. Also see Alexander Hamilton, no. 80, pp. 475–81.

5.   See *Congressional Record*, daily ed., November 1, 1993, pp. S14725–S14738, and November 2, 1993, pp. S14778–S14832.

6.   Richard Bryan, chair of the ethics committee, said in the debate, Packwood's claim implied that there should be "two standards in America, one for 250 million ordinary citizens minus 100, and that separate standards be established for the 100 of us who are privileged to serve as members of this institution." Ibid., p. S14789.

7.   *Recommending Revisions to the Procedures of the Senate Select Committee on Ethics*, Hearings, Committee Print, Senate Ethics Study Commission, 103 Cong. 1 sess. (GPO, June 1993), p. 61.

8.   Author's interviews with two members of the committee, April 1994.

9.   See, for example, the editorial comment in *Roll Call*: "questions linger about the Senator's conduct and the quality of the Ethics probe" ("The D'Amato Files," *Roll Call*, May 12, 1994, p. 4). There may have been justification for withholding the transcript while the criminal investigation of D'Amato was continuing, but the committee resisted appeals to make it public long after the investigation had concluded.

10.   House rule XLIII in William Holmes Brown, *Rules of the House of Representatives*, 103 Cong. (GPO, 1993); and Senate resolution 338 as amended, 88 Cong. 2 sess. (1964), in Senate Committee on Rules and Administration, *Senate Manual* (GPO, 1981).

11.   David B. Wilkins, "Who Should Regulate Lawyers?" *Harvard Law Review*, vol. 105 (February 1992), pp. 801–87.

12.   Troyen Brennan, *Just Doctoring: Medical Ethics in the Liberal State* (University of California Press, 1991), pp. 121–46.

13.   Marc A. Rodwin, *Medicine, Money, and Morals: Physicians' Conflicts of Interest* (Oxford University Press, 1993), chaps. 2, 7.

14.   The most prominent example of the prohibition of self-referral is the *Ethics in Patient Referrals Act of 1989* (the so-called Stark Bill), H.R. 939, 101 Cong. 1 sess. (1989). Generally, see Theodore N. McDowell, Jr., "Physician Self-Referral Arrangements: Legitimate Business or Unethical

'Entrepreneurialism,'" *American Journal of Law and Medicine*, vol. 89 (1989), pp. 61–109.

15.   On the regulation of universities, see Derek Bok, *Beyond the Ivory Tower: Social Responsibilities of the Modern University* (Harvard University Press, 1982), pp. 37–60.

16.   See Margaret P. Battin, *Ethics in the Sanctuary: Examining the Practices of Organized Religion* (Yale University Press, 1990); and James P. Wind and others, eds., *Clergy Ethics in a Changing Society: Mapping the Terrain* (Louisville: Westminster/John Knox Press, 1991).

17.   Alicia C. Shepard, "Talk Is Expensive," *American Journalism Review* (May 1994), pp. 20–27, 42.

18.   *Recommending Revisions*, Hearings, p. 59.

19.   Edmund Beard and Stephen Horn, *Congressional Ethics: The View from the House* (Brookings, 1975), p. 66. See also *Investigation of Senator Alan Cranston together with Additional Views*, Committee Print, Senate Select Committee on Ethics, 102 Cong. 1 sess. (GPO, November 1991), p. 10.

20.   *Congressional Record*, daily ed., May 4, 1994, p. S5153.

21.   One of the earliest such proposals was offered by Senator Lowell Weicker: S. resolution 109, cited in *Congressional Ethics: History, Facts, and Controversy*, 2d ed. (Washington: Congressional Quarterly, 1980), p. 57.

22.   *Burke's Politics: Selected Writings and Speeches of Edmund Burke on Reform, Revolution, and War*, Ross J. S. Hoffman and Paul Levack, eds. (Knopf, 1959), p. 116.

23.   One of the most balanced brief discussions is Joel L. Fleishman, "The Disclosure Model and its Limitations," in *Revising the United States Senate Code of Ethics, Hastings Center Report*, special supplement (February 1981), pp. 15–17.

24.   *Ethics in Government Act of 1978*, as amended, 5 USC appendix 6, §§ 101–11, incorporated into House and Senate rules. These provisions are among the most impenetrable of any ethics rules. The House Committee on Standards of Official Conduct, *Ethics Manual for Members, Officers, and Employees of the U.S. House of Representatives*, 102 Cong. 2 sess. (GPO, April 1992), pp. 153–80 (hereafter *House Ethics Manual*), provides a helpful guide to their rationale and scope.

25.   Senator Edward Brooke (1979) and Representatives George Hansen (1984) and Geraldine Ferraro (1984).

26.   The seven were John McFall (1978), Edward Royball (1978), Charles Wilson (1978), Herman Talmadge (1979), George Hansen (1984) (disclosure only), David Durenberger (1990), and Mark Hatfield (1991). Although Hatfield was ultimately rebuked for disclosure violations only, the

original charges included acceptance of gifts and favors from individuals with an interest in legislation. Talmadge and Hansen were defeated for reelection.

27. *Congressional Ethics* (1992), p. 42. See *In the Matter of Representative George V. Hansen*, Committee Print, House Committee on Standards of Official Conduct, 98 Cong. 2 sess. (GPO, July 1984).

28. *Congressional Ethics* (1992), pp. 76–77. Also see *Investigation of Financial Transactions Participated In and Gifts of Transportation Accepted by Representative Fernand J. St. Germain*, Committee Print, House Committee on Standards of Official Conduct, 100 Cong. 1 sess. (GPO, April 1987). St. Germain also survived a House vote to oust him from the chairmanship of the Banking Committee from which he had led the movement to deregulate the savings and loan industry, one of the causes of the collapse of institutions such as Lincoln Savings and Loan, the preoccupation of the Keating Five. He was defeated in 1988 in an upset that evidently resulted more from local political factors than his ethics troubles.

29. See, for example, Helen Dewar and Eric Pianin, "Senators Heed Constituents on Lifestyle," *Washington Post*, June 15, 1994, p. A8.

30. Only one member, Michael J. "Ozzie " Meyers, has been expelled in this century; Harrison Williams, John Jenrette, Raymond Lederer, and Mario Biaggi resigned under the threat of expulsion. All had been convicted of criminal charges before the ethics committees were willing to act; the charges against all except Biaggi resulted from the ABSCAM operation.

31. See the appendix; and Mary Ann Noyer, "Catalog of Congressional Ethics Cases," Brookings, 1993.

32. Calculated from tables in Norman J. Ornstein, Thomas E. Mann, and Michael J. Malbin, *Vital Statistics on Congress, 1993–1994* (Washington: Congressional Quarterly, 1994), pp. 58–59.

33. The rate of defeat for members whose cases reached the ethics committee but received no sanction was actually higher (28 percent) than that of those who were sanctioned. In the thirty-two cases of which committees took official notice, nine members were defeated in the next election and four (13 percent) retired. The single most important cause of departures from the House in the past half century have been voluntary retirements, not electoral defeats. See citations in the appendix.

34. John G. Peters and Susan Welch, "The Effects of Charges of Corruption on Voting Behavior in Congressional Elections," *American Political Science Review*, vol. 74 (September 1980), pp. 703, 706. This study covered eighty-one candidates in five House elections from 1968 to 1978 and controlled for election effect, prior partisan vote, terms served, and incumbency. The authors used the *Congressional Quarterly's Special Reports* to identify the races in which corruption was an important issue.

35.   Peters and Welch, "Effects of Charges of Corruption," p. 702.

36.   Ibid., p. 706. The authors emphasize that this suggestion is speculative and must "await the results of individual-level studies."

37.   Ibid., p. 705.

38.   The essential studies are by Gary C. Jacobson and Michael A. Dimock, "Checking Out: The Effects of Bank Overdrafts on the 1992 House Elections," *American Journal of Political Science*, vol. 38 (August 1994), pp. 601–24; and Michael A. Dimock and Gary C. Jacobson, "Checks and Choices: The Impact of the House Bank Scandal on Voting Behavior in the 1992 Elections," paper prepared for the 1994 annual meeting of the Midwest Political Science Association. Also see John Alford and others, "Overdraft: The Political Cost of Congressional Malfeasance," *Journal of Politics*, vol. 56 (August 1994), pp. 788–801; Susan A. Banducci and Jeffrey A. Karp, "Electoral Consequences of Scandal and Reapportionment in the 1992 House Elections," *American Politics Quarterly*, vol. 22 (January 1994), pp. 3–26; and Timothy Groseclose and Keith Krehbiel, "Golden Parachutes, Rubber Checks, and Strategic Retirements from the 102d House," *American Journal of Political Science*, vol. 38 (February 1994), pp. 75–99. Postretirement pension benefits were a more important factor in decisions to retire from the House than was the ability to convert campaign contributions to personal use or the loss of honoraria income. See Richard L. Hall and Robert P. Van Houweling, "Avarice and Ambition in Congress: Representatives' Decisions to Run or Retire from the U.S. House," *American Political Science Review*, vol. 89 (March 1995), table 3.

39.   Jacobson and Dimock, "Checking Out," p. 602.

40.   Ibid., pp. 607–08. The study controlled for the effects of redistricting, member's age and electoral security, and the fact that this was members' last chance to use leftover campaign funds.

41.   Dimock and Jacobson, "Checks and Choices," p. 9.

42.   Ibid., pp. 3–9.

43.   Jacobson and Dimock, "Checking Out," p. 622.

44.   Craig Wolff, "D'Amato's Hometown Disdains Inquiry," *New York Times*, August 3, 1991, p. 22.

45.   Compare Peters and Welch, "Effects of Charges of Corruption," p. 698: "If . . . a voter likes a particular candidate's political party or stand on important issues, the voter may discount any corruption charge leveled against the candidate and vote for him (or her) anyway. This discounting is particularly easy to do when the charges of corruption have not been proven."

46.   *Ethics Process*, p. 15.

47.   See chapter 3, pp. 53–54.

48.   J. Herbert Burke (1978), Frank M. Clark (1978), Otto E. Passman

(1979), Nick Galifianakis (1979), Claude Leach (1980), Richard Kelly (1980), Jon Hinson (1981), James Traficant (1983), Nick Joe Rahall (1984), Bobbi Fiedler (1984), Mario Biaggi (1988), Floyd Flake (1991), Joseph McDade (1992), Kay Bailey Hutchison (1993). Because some of these members were acquitted, the failure to take any action should not be taken to imply any laxity on the part of the committees.

49. *Ethics Process*, p. 16.

50. Lee Hamilton and H. Richardson Preyer, "Additional Views" in *Korean Influence Investigation, Report*, Committee Print, Committee on Standards of Official Conduct, 95 Cong. 2 sess. (GPO, December 1978), p. 124. This joint statement remains one of the most thoughtful brief discussions of the difference between the legal and ethical process by any member.

51. See, for example, the criminal statues that apply to members: 18 USC 415, 417, 420.

52. *Ethics Process*, p. 16.

53. Senate Select Committee on Ethics, *Rules of Procedure*, February 1993 (GPO, 1993), p. 20.

54. *U.S.* v. *Durenberger*, 1993 WL 738477 (D. Minn.). Also see Glenn R. Simpson, "Durenberger Ruling Boosts Ethics Process," *Roll Call*, December 9, 1993, pp. 1, 15. For the objections to the practice raised by members and especially the attorneys who defend accused members, see Susan B. Glasser, "Three Legal Cases, Including Packwood, Threaten to 'Chill' Cooperation with Ethics Committees," *Roll Call*, December 2, 1993, pp. 1, 15.

55. *U.S.* v. *Durenberger*, 1995 WL 72446 (D.C. Cir.).

56. *U.S.* v. *Rose*, 28 F.3d at 181, 189.

57. *U.S.* v. *Rose*, 28 F.3d at 190.

58. During the long reign of Louis Stokes (chair) and James Hansen (ranking member for part of the time) on the House committee, it was generally agreed, as these two members later testified, that they "never had a case that was decided on a partisan basis" (*Ethics Process*, p. 8). According to a recent study, one of the trends that stands out in the history of congressional ethics is that the proceedings have become less partisan; see Charles Stewart III, "Ain't Misbehavin' or, Reflections on Two Centuries of Congressional Corruption," occasional paper 94-4, Center for American Political Studies, Harvard University, April 1994, pp. 21–22.

59. From 1978 to 1992 in the House, 4 Democrats of 260 and 1 Republican of 174 on the average received sanctions every two years. In the Senate 1.75 Democrats of 51.5 and 1.25 Republicans of 48.5 on the average received sanctions every four years. Based on data in the appendix; and Noyer, "Catalog of Congressional Ethics Cases."

60. Peters and Welch, "Effects of Charges of Corruption," p. 703.

61. Author's interviews, April–May 1994.

62. Eric M. Uslaner, *The Decline of Comity in Congress* (University of Michigan Press, 1993), esp. pp. 21–43.

63. Senator Warren Rudman citing Senator Howell Heflin and Representative Robert Livingston, *Recommending Revisions*, Hearings, pp. 48–49, 235–36.

64. Brown, *Rules of the House*, 103 Cong. (GPO, March 1993), pp. 12–13.

65. *Recommending Revisions*, Hearings, pp. 228–37.

66. *Recommending Revisions*, Report, Committee Print, Senate Ethics Study Commission, 103 Cong. 2 sess. (GPO, March 1994), pp. 7–12.

67. The term *bifurcate* is commonly used to describe the change to a two-step process (see *Recommending Revisions*, Hearings, pp. 47, 220; and *Recommending Revisions*, Report, pp. 21–22). Although the future of the republic may not hang on this point, the term is misleading and should not be used to describe this process. Bifurcation denotes a process that divides into two tracks that go in different directions. All the proposals for so-called bifurcation actually recommend a process in which one step or phase *follows* the other. This would be more accurately described as a process of separated powers or functions, or more simply as a two-step process.

68. Senate Select Committee on Ethics, *Rules of Procedure*, rev. ed. (GPO, February 1993), rule 16(b) (3).

69. See Chair Richard Bryan's comment on Bob Packwood's claim quoted in note 6 from *Congressional Record*, daily ed., November 2, 1993, p. S14789.

70. Senate *Rules of Procedure*, pp. 22–23; and Brown, *Rules of the House*, pp. 42–43.

71. Steven V. Roberts, "Ethics Panel Says 2 Congressmen Had Sexual Relations with Pages," *New York Times*, July 15, 1983, p. A1.

72. Also see the comment of James Hansen, ranking member of the ethics committee at the time, *Ethics Process*, pp. 23–24.

73. Special Counsel Joseph A. Califano and the committee recommended that the two members, Daniel B. Crane and Gerry E. Studds, be reprimanded, but the House decided after debate to impose the more severe sanction, *Congressional Ethics* (1992), pp. 39–41. See also *Report of the Committee on Standards of Official Conduct on the Inquiry under House Resolution 12*, Committee Print, House Committee on Standards of Official Conduct, 98 Cong. 1 sess. (GPO, July 1983).

74. Brown, *Rules of the House*, pp. 20–21; and Senate *Rules of Procedure*, pp. 16–17.

75. Author's interview, February 1994.

76. After considering proposals to limit further the steps necessary to

trigger an investigation, the Senate Ethics Study Commission decided that the committee should continue to "evaluate information from all sources about possible improper conduct" (*Recommending Revisions*, Report, p. 5).

77. *Congressional Ethics*, (1992), p. 76. One of the two complaints that the House committee officially cited as the reason for initiating the investigation of Speaker Wright came from press reports. See *Report of the Special Outside Counsel in the Matter of Speaker James C. Wright Jr.*, House Committee on Standards of Official Conduct, 101 Cong. 2 sess. (GPO, February 1989), p. 1.

78. House rule 43, clause 1, *House Ethics Manual,* p. 12; S. Res. 338 sec. 2(a) (1), 88 Cong. 2 sess. (1964); *Congressional Record*, vol. 110 (1964), p. 16939; and S. Rep no. 1125, 88 Cong. 2 sess. (1963).

79. For a thoughtful discussion of collegial responsibility from the perspective of a political scientist who had served in Congress since 1987, see David E. Price, *The Congressional Experience: A View from the Hill* (Boulder, Colo.: Westview Press, 1992), esp. pp. 137–53.

80. *Korean Influence Investigation*, Committee Print, p. 7.

81. Jeremy Bentham, *The Rationale of Reward* (London: Robert Heward, 1830), pp. 21, 43. Jean-Jacques Rousseau identified another consequence of a system based on reward: citizens give "more consideration to persons than to isolated deeds [and can therefore honor] sustained and regular conduct . . . the faithful discharge of the duties of one's station . . . in sum deeds that flow from a man's character and principle." "Gouvernement de Pologne," *The Political Writings of Jean-Jacques Rousseau*, ed. C. E. Vaughan (Oxford: Blackwell, 1962), vol. 2, p. 498n (my translation of the passage).

82. Because of confidentiality, it is difficult to describe let alone evaluate certain parts of the process with any confidence. In interviews with the author, members and staff spoke freely about some of the discussions committees have had in private, even about some specific cases, but always on the condition that they not be identified by name. Since this anonymity prevents any independent verification, the account in the text is limited to general conclusions that could be inferred from the public record or would be readily confirmed by most members in public.

83. Public hearings in the Senate were held on the cases of the Keating Five (1990–91), David Durenberger (1990), Harrison Williams (1981), Herman Talmadge (1979), and the Korean Influence affair (1978). In the House public hearings were held for the cases of Austin Murphy (1987), James Weaver (1986), and the Korean Influence affair (1977). The House issued more extensive public reports on more cases during this period than the Senate did.

84. Author's interviews, February 1994.

85.   Brown, *Rules of the House*, pp. 26–27; and Senate *Rules of Procedure*, p. 21.

86.   Senate Select Committee on Ethics, "Statement of the Committee Regarding Senator D'Amato," August 2, 1991.

87.   The *New York Observer* obtained excerpts of D'Amato's testimony from sources it declined to name. See Joe Conason, "Exclusive: '91 Ethics Testimony Reveals D'Amato Flubbed His Lines," *New York Observer*, April 25, 1994, pp. 1, 11.

88.   *Recommending Revisions*, Report, pp. 14–15; and Brown, *Rules of the House*, p. 23.

89.   *Recommending Revisions*, Report, pp. 15–19.

90.   Ibid., p. 17.

91.   For a critical comment, see "Selective Ethics," *New York Times*, August 4, 1993, p. A18.

92.   The Senate Ethics Study Commission took a step in this direction by recommending that the Senate rather than only the party conference have the authority to remove chairs of committees. The commission stopped short of proposing that any authority to rescind ranking minority status or seniority be removed from the party conferences. See *Recommending Revisions*, Report, pp. 17–18.

93.   Ibid., p. 2.

94.   H. Res. 43, 103 Cong. (1993) and H. Res. 465, 102 Cong. (1992); S. Res. 190, 102 Cong. (1991); S. Res. 221, 102 Cong. (1991); S. Res. 327, 102 Cong. (1992); and H. Res 526, 100 Cong. (1988). For one of the earliest versions of such a proposal see *Revising the Senate Code of Official Conduct*, Hearings before the Senate Select Committee on Ethics, 96 Cong. 2 sess. (GPO, 1981), pp. 75ff; and Dennis F. Thompson, "The Ethics of Representation," in *Hastings Center Report*, pp. 13–14.

95.   Imogene Akins, ed., *State Yellow Book* (Monitor Publishing, 1993) p. 935.

96.   For another version, which gives former members a greater role, see Norman Ornstein's statement to the Senate Ethics Study Commission in *Recommending Revisions*, Hearings, pp. 69–74, 257.

97.   For example, *Recommending Revisions*, Report, p. 12; and *Recommending Revisions*, Hearings, p. 59.

98.   *Vander Jagt* v. *O'Neill*, 524 F. Supp. 519 (D.D.C. 1981), *aff'd*. 699 F.2d 1166 (D.C. Cir. 1982), *cert. denied* 464 U.S. 823 (1983).

99.   *Recommending Revisions*, Report, p. 12.

100.   Author's interview with former members of an ethics committee, February and March 1994.

101.   "A number of possible outsiders, like former Members, would have their own potential conflicts of interest, without the public accountability

that results from presently holding government office." *Recommending Revisions*, Report, p. 12.

102.   Lee H. Hamilton in *Ethics Process*, pp. 7–8.

Conclusion

1.   The initials refer, respectively, to the Department of Housing and Urban Development (under Secretary Samuel Pierce), the Bank of Credit and Commerce International, and the Atlanta branch of Banca Nazionale del Lavoro. For a discussion that emphasizes the institutional aspect of some of these scandals, see Peter deLeon, *Thinking about Political Corruption* (Armonk, N.Y.: M. E. Sharpe, 1993).

2.   Mark J. Rozell, "Press Coverage of Congress, 1946–92," in Thomas E. Mann and Norman J. Ornstein, eds., *Congress, the Press, and the Public* (Washington: American Enterprise Institute and Brookings, 1994), p. 71. Also see Stephen Hess, "The Decline and Fall of Congressional News," in the same volume, pp. 141–42.

3.   *Time*/CNN/Yankelovich Partners survey, national sample of 600 adults, June 2, 1994 (Roper Center for Public Opinion Research, University of Connecticut, 1995).

4.   The demand is consistent with a "consensus mode of decision" that John W. Kingdon has found best describes the way members decide how to vote; *Congressmen's Voting Decisions*, 2d ed. (Harper and Row, 1981), pp. 242–61. Also see John E. Jackson and John W. Kingdon, "Ideology, Interest Group Scores, and Legislative Votes," *American Journal of Political Science*, vol. 36 (August 1992), pp. 805–23.

5.   Senator Pete Domenici has expressed doubts that an outside commission will cause "constituents or the media [to] change their view of the effectiveness of ethics against members" and argued that if ethics reform "is motivated principally by changing the perception of the public, I truly believe that's very little gain when we want a Senate and a House to continue on for decades and centuries to do something for a little tiny bit of press." *Ethics Process: Testimony of Hon. Louis Stokes, Hon. James Hansen, and a Panel of Academic Experts*, Hearing before the Joint Committee on the Organization of Congress, 103 Cong. 1 sess. (GPO, 1993), pp. 39, 41. Also see the remarks of Senator J. Bennett Johnston on the gift ban bill: "The assumption is . . . if we pass this bill, somehow it will satisfy the American public . . . it will only bring more and more incidents to the Ethics Committee to make the headlines . . . the appetite [of "Congress-bashing groups"] is insatiable." *Congressional Record*, daily ed., May 5, 1994, pp. S5232–S5233.

6.   *Ethics Process*, p. 47.

7.   *Preliminary Inquiry into Allegations Regarding Senators Cranston, DeConcini, Glenn, McCain, and Riegle, and Lincoln Savings and Loan*, Hearings before the Senate Select Committee on Ethics, 101 Cong. 2 sess. (GPO, 1991), p. 86.

8.   Some recent proposals to help Congress present itself more effectively to the public could also help the press and public better understand its institutional ethics. See Thomas E. Mann and Norman J. Ornstein, "Introduction," in *Congress, the Press, and the Public*, pp. 10–13.

9.   Baron de Montesquieu, *De l'Esprit des Lois*, in *Montesquieu: Oeuvres Complètes*, ed. Roger Caillois (Paris: Gallimard, 1949–51), vol. 2, book 9, chap. 6, p. 407.

Index